D0786658

MASSIVE ENTANGLEMENT, MARGINAL INFLUENCE

MASSIVE ENTANGLEMENT, MARGINAL INFLUENCE

Carter and Korea in Crisis

WILLIAM H. GLEYSTEEN JR.

BROOKINGS INSTITUTION PRESS
Washington, D.C.

ABOUT BROOKINGS

The Brookings Institution is a private nonprofit organization devoted to research, edu-. cation, and publication on important issues of domestic and foreign policy. Its principal purpose is to bring knowledge to bear on current and emerging policy problems. The Institution maintains a position of neutrality on issues of public policy. Interpretations or conclusions in Brookings publications should be understood to be solely those of the authors.

The paper used in this publication meets minimum requirements of the American National Standard for Information Sciences—Permanence of Paper for Printed Library Materials: ANSI Z39.48-1984.

Typeset in Minion

Composition by Cynthia Stock
Silver Spring, Maryland

Printed by R. R. Donnelley and Sons
Harrisonburg, Virginia

Contents

Acknowledgments and a Note about Documents

I THANK MY GOOD friends and former government colleagues William Clark Jr., Evelyn S. Colbert, Richard C. Holbrooke, John C. Monjo, Robert G. Rich Jr., Thomas Stern, and John A. Wickham Jr., not only for the part they played in the events of this book, but also for encouraging me to write it. All of them reviewed the manuscript at various stages and made constructive suggestions. Beyond this, Bob Rich generously devoted much time to editorial improvements and expediting government clearance for publication. Evelyn Colbert applied her sharp intelligence and editorial skill to enhance the organization and coherence of my narrative. I regret that Robert G. Brewster's untimely death deprived me of his advice about how I should recount events in which he played such an admirable role.

I am most grateful that another of my colleagues, Michael H. Armacost, president of the Brookings Institution, suggested that Brookings sponsor my work and publish the book. I thank Richard Haass and the Brookings reviewers for their excellent advice.

My family, including my four-footed walking companion, made it possible for me to complete this project. They pushed me to begin, and they paid the price of living with me during the strains of the book writing. My wife, Marilyn, and youngest daughter, Anna, were on the front line; my oldest daughter, Thea Clarke, who contributed her professional services as an editor, was only a few steps away.

After Park Chung Hee's assassination, I knew I was going to be a participant in and witness to historic events that I would need to record accurately. Thus, I began to record in considerable detail what I observed and what I thought, resulting in a very expansive file for the years 1978 through 1981. The papers kept in my office were almost a diary of my official life. Given my ambassadorial status, my copies of these papers were considered personal, and on retirement from the foreign service, I chose to have them preserved in the Department of State so that they would be available when I found time to write this account. Disastrously, this did not happen.

Without notifying me, officers in the Department of State retrieved my files twice, once in the early 1980s and again in 1988 while the department was preparing the white paper on Kwangju released in June 1989. The files were innocently but improperly transferred to drafting officers of the white paper who used them and then put them aside, not knowing their origin. A few years later an office of the department that should have known better destroyed most of the papers, considering them redundant to records contained in the department's central computer.

I discovered this situation in 1995 when I began to assemble files for writing this book. The "accident" cost me nine miserable months while I used my memory and every conceivable device to identify missing documents. An embarrassed Department of State helped me do this by giving me priority in retrieval of messages, and I was finally able to reconstruct 95 percent of my old files, except, of course, the marginalia on my personal copies. The department also was very cooperative in clearing my manuscript for publication, including all the material quoted or paraphrased from my files.

Another event complicated my effort to clarify the historical record. Shortly after I began preparations for the book I discovered to my surprise that the Department of State had chosen to release a large number of telegrams exchanged during these years between the department and the U.S. embassy in Seoul, including many drafted by me, to a critic of our policy who was convinced we had been in collusion with the Korean authorities during the Kwangju crisis. The department had hoped that this exposure would help dissipate controversy over the U.S. role. Unfortunately, some of the recipients of these documents used them selectively, distorting their meaning and sometimes conveying the reverse of the truth.

To help cope with this problem, I asked the Department of State for permission to reproduce all the communications mentioned in the book. Some were approved for release and have been reproduced in the appendix, but most were not, even twenty years after the events. I believe, nevertheless, that this book fulfills my historical responsibility and perhaps answers those with half knowledge of the events described here.

Chronology of Events

1960

In April, President Syngman Rhee is forced to resign and is replaced by Interim President Huh Chung.

In July, an election is held, resulting in a new government headed by President Yun Po-sun and Prime Minister Chang Myon.

1961

On May 16, a military coup d'état is led by Major General Park Chung Hee and Lieutenant Colonel Kim Jong Pil.

1963

A new constitution is approved by popular referendum. Park Chung Hee is elected president of the Republic of Korea.

1965

The first contingent of South Korean military forces is sent to South Vietnam.

1967

Park Chung Hee is reelected president.

1968

The United States begins peace talks with North Vietnam.

1969

In Guam, President Nixon declares that U.S. allies must bear prime responsibility for manpower in defending against attack.

1970

United States announces plans to withdraw the Seventh Infantry Division from Korea, leaving the Second Infantry Division as the only ground combat force.

1971

Kim Dae Jung almost defeats Park Chung Hee in presidential election. United States begins rapprochement with China.

1972

On February 28, the United States and the People's Republic of China issue the Shanghai Communiqué.

On July 4, North and South Korea issue a joint declaration on unification.

On October 17, President Park imposes tough new *Yushin* Constitution under conditions of martial law.

1973

On August 8, Kim Dae Jung is abducted by Koreans from a Tokyo hotel. Korea withdraws the last elements of its military deployments in Vietnam.

1975

The South Vietnamese government collapses.

United States pressures President Park to halt South Korea's nuclear weapons program.

Presidential candidate Jimmy Carter announces his intention, if elected, to withdraw U.S. ground forces from Korea.

Efforts within the U.S. Congress to require a phased withdrawal of U.S. forces from Korea are unsuccessful.

1976

In August, North Korea attacks a U.S. work party in Panmunjom (the ax murder incident).

In October, the press in Washington leaks a story about a grand jury investigation of a massive South Korean effort to bribe U.S. officials and members of Congress (Koreagate).

In November, Jimmy Carter is elected president of the United States.

1977

On January 26, President Carter announces his plan to withdraw all U.S. ground combat forces from Korea in four to five years (Presidential Review Memorandum 13).

In April, Presidential Review Memorandum 13 study on troop withdrawals is completed.

In April and May, Carter rejects conservative recommendation from the secretaries of state and defense and orders the complete withdrawal of all U.S. ground forces from Korea by 1981–82.

In May and June, U.S. negotiations with President Park result in a backloaded schedule of troop withdrawal and a generous military aid program.

1978

U.S. government orders comprehensive army and Central Intelligence Agency appraisal of North Korean forces.

On April 21, Carter cuts back troop withdrawal schedule, limiting withdrawals in 1978 to one battalion rather than one brigade of combat forces.

On October 25, with authorization from Secretary of State Vance, Ambassador Gleysteen talks to President Park about the possibility of holding a summit meeting with President Carter.

In November, the United States withdraws one combat battalion (800 men) plus 2,600 noncombat personnel from Korea.

In November, the United States and Korea form the Combined Forces Command.

In December, President Park loses a majority of elected members of the National Assembly but retains control through appointed members.

In December, anticipating the summit meetings, Park releases many prominent political prisoners.

1979

In January, the conclusions of the army and Central Intelligence Agency study on North Korean forces are leaked to the *Army Times*.

On January 20, President Carter authorizes a new policy review of withdrawal plans (Presidential Review Memorandum 45).

On February 9, Carter suspends further troop withdrawals pending conclusions of a policy review.

In April, summit meetings are set for June 30–July 2.

On June 30, President Carter visits U.S. troops at Camp Casey near the demilitarized zone.

On July 1–2, summit meetings are held between President Carter and President Park.

On July 1, the United States and Republic of Korea submit a joint proposal to the Democratic People's Republic of Korea for a trilateral summit meeting with President Kim Il Sung.

On July 5, responding to President Carter, President Park agrees to release 180 political prisoners over a six-month period.

On July 20, President Carter suspends all further troop withdrawals from Korea pending a review of the military balance on the peninsula in 1981.

In August, anti-Park tension builds in Korea as a result of a textile workers' strike supported by opposition politicians. Ambassador Gleysteen complains to the foreign minister about Park's heavy-handed police tactics.

In September, Ambassador Gleysteen meets with Blue House Secretary Choi and Korean CIA Director Kim to urge political moderation.

In October, President Park has his supporters in the National Assembly expel the leader of the opposition for his involvement with the textile strike.

In September and October, Secretary Vance admonishes the Korean foreign minister regarding Kim Young Sam; the United States publicly criticizes Park's action against Kim Young Sam and recalls the ambassador for consultations.

October sees widespread student and labor demonstrations and rioting in the cities of Masan and Pusan. President Park cracks down forcefully, using local martial law.

On October 18, Secretary of Defense Brown and Ambassador Gleysteen call on President Park during the security consultative meeting. They caution him on the costs of political repression.

On October 26, Korean CIA Director Kim Chae Kyu assassinates President Park and Presidential Security Chief Cha Chi Chol.

Prime Minister Choi Kyu Ha becomes acting president.

On October 27, Korean authorities declare martial law with Army Chief of Staff Chong Seung Hua as the administrator of martial law.

United States reaffirms its security commitment to South Korea and dispatches a carrier group to Korea.

In November, the United States publicly states the hope that political developments in Korea will advance commensurately with economic and social progress.

On November 3, Secretary of State Vance heads a delegation to President Park's funeral and urges Acting President Choi to move toward political liberalization.

On November 10, Acting President Choi publicly commits himself to progress in the political field.

On December 7, Acting President Choi is elected president by the *Yushin* Constitution's electoral college.

On December 12, Defense Security Commander Chun Doo Hwan arrests the martial law administrator and seizes control of the Korean army in a swift military coup.

On December 12, the United States publicly warns forces within South Korea against disrupting political progress and reiterates its commitment to defense.

On December 13, 14, and 18, Ambassador Gleysteen meets successively with President Choi, Defense Security Commander Chun Doo Hwan, and the prime minister to protest Chun's actions and urge resumption of the political program.

1980
On January 9, President Carter writes President Choi to protest the violation of command arrangements on December 12 and to caution against their recurrence.

In late January, a Korean military official, speaking for thirty disaffected general officers, seeks American support for a counter-coup.

In early February, the United States declines to support the counter-coup, telling disgruntled officers not to risk strife within the Korean army and Defense Security Commander Chun Doo Hwan not to expand powers over the civilian sector.

In January and March, modest political relaxation, the so-called Seoul Spring, occurs, including government consultation with the opposition, easing of censorship, reopening of universities, freeing of Kim Dae Jung from all restraints, and cancellation of Emergency Measure 9.

In March and April, tension builds in Seoul, including student protests, labor strife, hardening of political opposition, and warnings by martial law authorities.

On April 14, President Choi appoints Major General Chun Doo Hwan acting director of the Korean CIA.

In April, the United States protests Chun's appointment in a meeting with President Choi, postpones the security consultative meeting, and seeks an appointment for the ambassador to make points directly to Chun Doo Hwan.

In April and May, the protest movement ratchets upward.

In May, political leaders ride rather than oppose the wave of student protests that begins to move off campus and into city streets.

On May 9, Kim Young Sam issues militant public demands to the government. Also on May 9, after a long delay, Chun agrees to see Ambassador Gleysteen. Gleysteen registers U.S. unhappiness over Korean CIA appointment. Most of the discussion focuses on the burgeoning protest. Gleysteen cautions Chun to exercise moderation and care in dealing with students and political leaders and underscores the dangers of using soldiers to reinforce the police. He makes the same points to the Blue House secretary general.

On May 13, General Wickham sees Chun, chairman of the Joint Chiefs of Staff, and the defense minister to makes the same points, explicitly warning of the dangers if soldiers kill civilians.

On May 12 and 13, Gleysteen meets with political leaders to urge restraint.

On May 14 and 15, student protests mushroom and turn violent.

On May 17, yielding to hard-line recommendations of the military, President Choi declares emergency martial law and orders a harsh political crackdown. Kim Dae Jung, Kim Young Sam, and Kim Jong Pil are arrested.

May 18 is quiet throughout the country except Kwangju, where students ignore martial law warnings and demonstrate against the arrest of Kim Dae Jung. The Korean Special Warfare Forces employ brutal tactics against Kwangju students, antagonizing the citizenry of Kwangju.

On May 19 and 20, irate Kwangju citizens rise up against Korean army forces, seize weapons and ammunition, burn vehicles and buildings, and take control of the city. U.S. authorities receive the first relatively objective accounts of army behavior in Kwangju and citizen response.

On May 20, Secretary of State Muskie publicly expresses concern about the unrest in Korea.

On May 21, violence in Kwangju peaks. The Korean army withdraws to the city's perimeter.

Ambassador Gleysteen holds a backgrounder for foreign press, stressing that the United States is appalled by Korean government actions in Seoul on May 17 and the subsequent brutality in Kwangju. He says that the United States is urging both sides to negotiate a peaceful resolution.

On May 22, Korean authorities begin talks with the Kwangju citizens committee for an agreement allowing restoration of government control in return for an apology, indemnification, and amnesty to protesters.

Martial law authorities accuse Kim Dae Jung of masterminding the Kwangju insurrection.

The Policy Review Committee of the National Security Council meets in Washington. Members recognize the priority of restoring order using the minimum force necessary followed by pressure toward political evolution.

The United States issues a public statement calling for maximum restraint and dialogue toward a negotiated settlement and warns external forces against seeking to exploit the situation in South Korea.

Korean authorities agree (but then fail) to broadcast and airdrop the U.S. statement in Kwangju.

On May 23 and 24, as a result of Korean army disinformation, Kwangju citizens hear broadcasts alleging that the United States encouraged the use of troops in Kwangju. General Wickham and Ambassador Gleysteen protest vehemently to military and civilian authorities.

On May 25, Kwangju negotiations are deadlocked by hard-liners on both sides.

On May 26, the Korean army prepares to reenter Kwangju using forces of the Twentieth Infantry Division (trained in martial law supervision), reinforced by the Special Warfare Forces. The United States does not oppose the plan if necessary as a last resort but stresses the need for care and restraint.

On May 27, the Korean army successfully reenters the city with few casualties except among militant holdouts at provincial headquarters.

The foreign minister informs the ambassador, and the chairman of the Joint Chiefs of Staff informs General Wickham, that President Choi will establish a new civilian-military Committee for National Security Affairs and that Chun will head the Steering Group.

On May 31, in a CNN-Television interview, President Carter stresses that security interests must sometimes override human rights concerns in allied countries.

In May and June, the U.S. government conducts an extensive policy review in Washington and Seoul. No radical sanctions are approved, but agreement is reached on the need to maintain a "cool and reserved" stance toward Chun's emerging regime.

In June, a new committee structure under Chun effectively replaces the Choi government.

On June 4, Gleysteen meets with Chun to review U.S. distress over emergency martial law, events in Kwangju, the new committee structure, and accusations against Kim Dae Jung.

On June 26, Gleysteen meets again with Chun to warn that both internal stability and American support will be jeopardized unless political progress is made, that manipulation of anti-American sentiment could be highly dangerous, and that execution of Kim Dae Jung would have a grave and crippling impact on U.S.-Korean relations.

On July 8, as the result of a long meeting with Secretary Muskie, Gleysteen sees Chun again to accuse him of "abusing" the American security commitment. He also raises the subject of the trial of Kim Dae Jung and gets Chun's agreement to allow foreign observers.

On July 15, Ambassador Gleysteen returns to United States for leave. Monjo becomes chargé.

In July and August, Chargé Monjo meets several times with Chun and others, urging fair treatment of Kim Dae Jung and international coverage of the trial.

On August 7, General Wickham talks on a not-for-attribution basis with American journalists who report a "highly placed U.S. military official" as saying that the United States could support Chun's presidency under certain conditions.

On August 8, Wickham meets with Chun to review various U.S. policies and express hope that President Choi will remain in office.

In August, Chun and cohorts distort Wickham's remarks as U.S. support for Chun's presidency.

When asked, U.S. State Department spokesman comments that Wickham's reported remarks do not reflect U.S. policy.

The United States publicly and privately emphasizes that it has not endorsed Chun for president and expects him to seek validation from the Korean people through the political reforms promised by President Choi.

On August 16, Choi Kyu Ha resigns as president of the Republic of Korea.

In August, after being promoted to four-star general, Chun Doo Hwan retires from the Korean army.

On August 27, Chun Doo Hwan is elected president of the Republic of Korea by the electoral college of the *Yushin* Constitution.

In August, the U.S. government decides to give overriding importance to saving the life of Kim Dae Jung.

On August 28, Gleysteen returns from Washington to Seoul.

On September 1, Chun Doo Hwan is inaugurated president.

On September 3, Gleysteen calls on Chun to present a letter from President Carter about Kim Dae Jung, to review recent events, and to provide a blunt assessment of American attitudes toward his regime.

On September 5, Gleysteen urges Washington to minimize public comment when the Kim Dae Jung verdict is announced.

On September 16, Gleysteen meets privately with President Chun to stress the gravity with which President Carter would view Kim's execution or even his receipt of a death sentence. Chun takes note but refuses to promise commutation of the sentence and requests U.S. public restraint and noninterference in Korea's judicial process.

On September 17, Kim Dae Jung is sentenced to death. The United States issues a restrained statement, the Carter administration's last public comment on Kim's fate.

On October 17, emergency martial law is lowered to partial martial law.

On October 22, a popular referendum is passed to approve a new constitution.

In October and December, noncommittal, hypothetical discussions are held between Gleysteen and the Blue House secretary general about how the United States might react to the commutation of Kim's sentence.

In November, Ronald Reagan defeats President Carter in the U.S. presidential election.

On November 13, Korea's foreign minister discusses the impact of the election with Gleysteen, urges Secretary Brown to visit Korea, and reports Gleysteen's comments to President Chun.

On November 20, in an assessment to the U.S. State Department, Gleysteen for the first time drops his optimism and concludes that Chun will not commute Kim's sentence.

On November 21, both Roh Tae-Woo and President Chun ask Gleysteen to call on them before returning to Washington. Their comments leave Gleysteen less pessimistic.

In November, in Washington, Gleysteen urges Reagan advisers to reinforce the Carter administration's efforts, warns the administration against a public attack on Chun, and suggests making one last pitch to Chun, preferably by Secretary Brown.

On December 13, Secretary Brown is in Seoul and delivers Carter's message to Chun regarding Kim Dae Jung.

In December, with authority of President-elect Reagan, Richard Allen warns Chun's emissaries against killing Kim Dae Jung and reaches an agreement for Chun to visit the White House after he commutes Kim's sentence.

1981

On January 21, the White House announces that President Chun is invited to visit President Reagan.

On January 23, the Korean Supreme Court upholds Kim Dae Jung's death sentence.

On January 24, President Chun commutes Kim Dae Jung's death sentence to life in prison and lifts martial law.

On February 2, a Reagan-Chun summit meeting is held in the White House.

On February 25, Chun Doo Hwan is elected president of the Republic of Korea by an expanded electoral college under the new constitution.

1982

In December, Kim Dae Jung is allowed to leave Korea for medical exile in the United States.

1987

On June 29, Roh Tae-Woo declares that he favors popular election of Chun's successor.

On December 16, Roh Tae-Woo is elected president of the Republic of Korea.

1988–89

The National Assembly holds an investigation and hearings on Kwangju.

1989

On June 19, the U.S. government issues a white paper in response to the Korean National Assembly's questions about the U.S. role in the December 12 incident and Kwangju.

1992

In December, Kim Young Sam is elected president of the Republic of Korea.

1996

Former presidents Chun Doo Hwan and Roh Tae-Woo are detained (for investigation of political corruption as well as their roles during the December 12 incident and Kwangju) and are tried, sentenced, and jailed.

1997

In December, Kim Dae Jung is elected president of the Republic of Korea.

1998

President Kim commutes the sentences of Chun Doo Hwan and Roh Tae-Woo.

1

Introduction

I WAS BOTH PLEASED and challenged by my selection in 1978 to be ambassador to the Republic of Korea. Although I was considered a China specialist for most of my foreign service career, I had been exposed at an early stage to Korean events and dealt extensively with Korea as part of my East Asian responsibilities in several Washington assignments. For a person with my background, the embassy in Seoul was a prized post. South Korea was in the midst of a fascinating transformation, and since so much was at stake for the United States, special care was required in the management of our relationship. Quite frankly, I also was relieved to be leaving Washington. By this time, Korea had lost its image among Americans as one of East Asia's economic miracles and had become something of a political pariah. The basic problem was the surge of political oppression, but many Americans went beyond this disturbing turn of events to bash Korea quite indiscriminately. As an official dealing with Korea, I was weary of being treated as a surrogate for the offending Koreans. Far more disturbing to me, I was deeply dismayed by President Carter's stubborn effort to withdraw U.S. ground combat forces from Korea, doing so in the face of almost universal hope in East Asia that the United States would strengthen, not weaken, its presence in the region after the demoralizing end of the war in Vietnam.

Before leaving for Korea in mid-1978, I felt that the worst was over on the troop withdrawal issue, and I was mildly hopeful that I could contribute

The opinions and views expressed in this book are solely those of the author and do not necessarily represent the views of the Department of State or the United States Government.

usefully to a normalization of our relations with Korea. Nevertheless, I went to Seoul with my eyes open. I knew that President Park Chung Hee, kingpin of the Korean political scene and architect of its remarkable economic progress, was in serious trouble. As a taxi driver once put it to me, Park had been "too much of a dictator for too long." I was also aware of the animus pervading many of the groups opposing him. Within our official American community, I had thought and talked about the possibility that his regime might not survive. Yet, along with everyone else, I was stunned when President Park was assassinated on the night of October 26, 1979, by one of his most trusted aides, thus beginning an extraordinary period in the Republic of Korea and in its relations with the United States.

Korea's Circumstances in 1979

During the eighteen years of President Park's rule, the Republic of Korea flourished, changing rapidly from a weak, essentially agrarian society highly dependent on foreign aid to a militarily strong, industrial nation with per capita gross domestic product (GDP) and foreign trade approaching the levels of some developed countries. The formula for this extraordinary transformation combined many elements: stability from relatively enlightened rule, massive educational efforts, social mobility, hard work, strong entrepreneurial spirit, and an export-driven development scheme that blended the government's nurturing role with market forces.

Almost all South Koreans, including critics, credited Park for the vision and drive that brought about this leap of progress, but by 1979 much of the glitter had worn off. Economic growth was faltering, and people were suffering from inflation caused by escalating import costs and misguided investment decisions. Workers were restive, and many others were also grumbling about deteriorating economic conditions. More important, Park's resort in the early 1970s to heavy-handed authoritarian rule embittered a wide variety of people and generated strong opposition in political, labor, educational, and religious circles.

External events compounded South Korea's anxieties. The failure of America's engagement in Vietnam obviously worried Korea, Asia's only other evenly split nation facing a massive military threat from its northern half. Concern about the outcome was intensified for Koreans, especially the military, because two Korean divisions fought in Vietnam as part of the American-led effort. Some people also feared that the new U.S. relationship with China might somehow disadvantage South Korea. In a far more tangible way, President Carter's abortive effort to withdraw U.S. ground forces from Korea during his first years in office cast a shadow on the U.S. commitment to security, deeply disturbing almost all South Koreans, including Park's opponents. Although this threat had been lifted by the time of Park's assassination, the scars remained, made even more sensitive by the Korea bashing in America over human rights issues and a bribery scandal.

The most pervasive and constant anxiety was still the perceived threat from North Korea. South Koreans had by this time largely overcome their postwar psychological inferiority complex vis-à-vis North Korea, but memories of invasion and fear of a North Korean attack were still visceral reactions for most people. Home to a quarter of the nation's population, the city of Seoul was singularly vulnerable to artillery attack from North Korean forces massed only thirty to forty miles to the north. With rare complaint, Koreans accepted universal conscription of males for thirty months of military service, spent 5 to 6 percent of GDP on defense, put up with a toughly enforced midnight curfew, and half-accepted Park's dubious argument that his intolerant rule was necessitated by North Korean behavior. Through aggressive actions, North Korea periodically reminded South Koreans that the threat was real.

The United States was thoroughly engaged in Korea. Tracing back to the Korean War and reflecting the current reality of a hostile regime in North Korea, the United States in 1979 still maintained a major military presence in South Korea (39,000 soldiers and airmen) and retained operational command of all forces—Korean as well as U.S.—deployed for defense against an attack from the north. Although all American economic aid had been terminated, the United States provided modest amounts of concessional credit for military purchases, American banks satisfied a large portion of Korea's foreign capital needs, and the American market was critically important to the growth of Korea's export economy. These factors, together with extensive educational, religious, and cultural interaction between the two countries, constituted a complex web of relationships that entangled the United States with Korea and, at least potentially, constituted a powerful American influence on the peninsula. This did not, however, signify power to change the course of domestic developments in Korea.

U.S. relations with Korea, while basically friendly and cooperative, were marked by periodic strain and feistiness. Americans were generally responsive to Korea's concerns, and Koreans were demonstratively grateful for America's protection and other assistance. Yet there were also tensions and resentments. Many Americans, including those of us in the U.S. government, assumed that we had the right to provide a wide range of advice to improve the process of governance in Korea. Koreans sometimes reacted nationalistically to this, rarely yielding to American pressure on domestic political matters. When Koreans spoke of Korea and the United States as two brothers, they were often insinuating that the United States, the elder brother, was domineering. This was, of course, far more characteristic of government supporters than of opposition elements, who tended to welcome—even seek—U.S. intervention.

Park Chung Hee's assassination in 1979 by one of his trusted insiders exposed the U.S. government to new tensions and difficult choices. At the early stages we could not predict the nature of the regime that would ultimately replace Park. We knew that the assassination was not caused by a revolution from below; the existing establishment, dominated by individuals with military and security experience, remained in place. The violent disruption at the top, however, triggered contention over the country's leadership and political agenda. The struggle lasted about a year, marked by abrupt and unexpected turns, by excesses and violence on both sides of the political fence, by unrealistic hopes (including mine), and finally by crude repression.

From the beginning we realized we were in for a period of confusion and uncertainty. We also suspected that the Korean army might intervene at some point, although we (or at least I) assumed incorrectly that the intervention would most likely occur in response to a mass protest movement. In the first months following Park's death, the United States adopted a relatively interventionist posture, actively encouraging—even pushing—Korea's interim leaders toward a more liberal political regime. Major General Chun Doo Hwan's sudden seizure of power within the army on December 12, 1979, did not immediately blight all prospects of democratic reform, but it radically altered expectations about who would dominate the political scene. Chun's progressive assumption of political power, very pronounced by April 1980, profoundly depressed political moderates and fueled radical protest among students and workers, culminating in the May 17, 1980, declaration of emergency martial law throughout the country and an exercise in brutality in Kwangju that provoked citizens to rebel in a massive uprising. Along with many Koreans, the United States was deeply discouraged by these events, which resulted in a new regime no less harsh than the one Park had imposed on Koreans during his final years.

If only because of command relationships, Koreans often held the United States complicitous in developments, such as the Kwangju tragedy, in which we were not involved. In fact, we were often handicapped severely by lack of information and effective means of control. Our eagerness to push Korea in the direction of political liberalization, along with our propensity to publicize these efforts, left many Koreans frustrated and critical of us when liberal reform failed to occur and authoritarian control was reestablished with General Chun's assumption of the presidency.

Even though we did it grudgingly, the United States gradually accommodated itself during this tumultuous period to what amounted to a phased coup d'état by an ambitious military leader. Our responses were generally to take conservative measures to control damage rather than to impose radical sanctions on the new authorities. We judged sanctions as too dangerous to use. In particular, we feared that major military sanctions would risk North Korean exploitation, while economic ones would injure the entire Korean populace. We were also constrained by the innate conservatism of President Choi Kyu Ha, the interim constitutional leader, as well as by the unwillingness of any major group within Korean society (except perhaps some of the students) to risk a direct challenge to the newly emerging center of power.

Misperceptions of the U.S. role during this period, especially in the Kwangju crisis, were fed by mischievous distortion of facts on the part of the ruling authorities as well as by ill-informed folklore in some sectors of Korean society. Combined with our eventual acceptance of the reality of Chun's rule, these misperceptions generated substantial controversy in Korea, persisting for many years in the region around Kwangju. In the newly free atmosphere after the first democratic presidential election in 1987, the Korean National Assembly held hearings on the December 12 incident and the Kwangju crisis. The U.S. government provided the assembly with an authoritative statement summarizing U.S. actions, which was received with more objectivity than previous efforts to defend America's actions.[1] Although General John A. Wickham Jr., commander in chief, U.S. Forces, Korea, in 1979–82, and I contributed to preparation of this report, I continued to feel that, as one of the principal Americans entangled in these events, I needed to write a more personal, more thorough account of American perceptions, actions, and motives. This book represents my effort to fulfill that historical obligation.

1. On November 21, 1988, the investigating committee of the Korean National Assembly requested that General Wickham and I appear before them. Although we had to decline because of the diplomatic precedent involved, the State Department agreed to compile an authoritative statement, including answers to questions posed by the committee. The resulting report, "United States Government Statement on the Events in Kwangju, Republic of Korea, in May 1980," was transmitted to the Koreans and released to the press on June 19, 1989.

The book begins with a review of strained U.S.-Korean relations in the mid-1970s, discusses the severe aggravation of this strain by President Carter's troop withdrawal and human rights policies during the first two years of his administration, and then turns to the tumultuous events following President Park's assassination. For chapters 2 and 3, I have drawn on my experience as a deputy assistant secretary of state for East Asia and the Pacific and senior staff member of the National Security Council for East Asia (1974–78). For chapters 4–11, I have reinforced vivid memories with the extensive records I kept throughout my assignment to Seoul (June 1978–July 1981). As the senior U.S. official in Korea, I was directly involved in almost all the major events of this period, sometimes as the only American present.

Internal Struggle Followed by Coherence in American Policy

From the beginning of the Carter administration in 1977 until mid-1979, the conduct of American policy toward Korea was encumbered by fundamental opposition within the bureaucracy (both civilian and military) and the Congress (both Republicans and Democrats) to the president's effort to withdraw all U.S. ground forces from Korea. Despite this enormous handicap, the policymaking community in Washington and Seoul functioned rather impressively. The secretaries of state and defense as well as the national security adviser kept themselves well informed about Korea, and their formal machinery for making decisions was usefully supplemented—sometimes obviated—by the East Asia Informal Group, created by assistant secretary of state for East Asian and Pacific affairs, Richard C. Holbrooke, to develop consensus on both policy and operating problems in East Asia. Members of this weekly gathering at the level of assistant secretary and deputy assistant secretary were chosen for their influence as key aides to the leaders of the State Department, Defense Department (both Secretary Brown's staff and the Joint Chiefs of Staff), National Security Council, Central Intelligence Agency (CIA), and occasionally other organizations. The group normally met every Monday afternoon in Holbrooke's office to address a very fluid agenda. Since members had ready access to the top, they often were able to short-circuit bureaucratic obstructions. This efficiency and the group's easygoing working style made it an ideal forum in which to monitor a drawn-out crisis such as the one in Korea. The relationships that I, for example, developed in Washington while a member of this remarkable group served me well in Seoul. Equally important, in Seoul our country team of senior

Americans was both effective and exceptionally cooperative. Although luck played a part in the personal qualities of those around me, the cooperative spirit was not simply a matter of good fortune. All of us were aware that, in the past, U.S. policy had sometimes been disadvantaged by rivalry within the American ranks, particularly between proud ambassadors and powerful U.S. commanders in chief of the military. We worked hard to keep such distractions to a minimum.

By the time of Park's assassination in October 1979, the issue of troop withdrawals was no longer an impediment in the conduct of our policy. Events elsewhere also eased some of the other constraints complicating our dealings with Korea. Preoccupied by the crisis in Iran, President Carter now was concerned with preserving stability among allies as well as more cautious in his pursuit of human rights objectives. From my vantage point in Seoul, I credited this shift in the global strategic environment with responsibility for bringing a new coherence to our management of the Korean crisis of 1979–80. In any event, the degree of cooperation and coordination that took place in the later phases of the Carter administration was remarkable. Despite my earlier friction with President Carter over the troop question and human rights problems, during this later period I counted on Washington's support for what I felt we needed to do. I felt free to register dissent, and I knew my opinions were carefully considered at high levels, if need be by the president himself. In short, we had gone from an extremely contentious environment in Washington to one that facilitated the making of intelligent decisions.

Lessons for Korea and Perhaps Other Countries

The following chapters of this book examine what the United States did, and did not do, at each juncture of the Korean crisis and explain why. While the account confirms the good intentions of the United States, it also demonstrates how our troop withdrawal policy, our human rights efforts, and our other actions sometimes had unintended effects that worked against our basic interests in Korea. It also highlights the severe problems of operating with incomplete intelligence, the dilemmas associated with efforts to use military and economic power, the frustration of dealing with foreign authorities who virtually monopolize the power to communicate with the local populace, and the way such authorities can manipulate information to distort reality and, in this particular instance, to damage the American image.

Granting that I am not a disinterested observer, I would give the U.S. government a much higher grade for policy toward Korea after President Park's death than during the period of strain preceding it. In the period following his assassination, I believe we coped sensibly with a difficult situation. Even with the advantage of hindsight, I would not significantly revise the decisions we made twenty years ago. Although the crisis occurred during unusual circumstances in a somewhat exceptional country, I am convinced that the lessons learned still have relevance for American behavior toward Korea and perhaps toward other countries important to the United States.

2

U.S.-Korean Relations before the Carter Administration

AS I REFLECT BACK now, two decades later, I am convinced that even though President Park Chung Hee was killed in the vortex of the tensions of 1979, his regime's fate was sealed a number of years earlier, during the late 1960s and early 1970s, when he reacted so excessively to developments taking place in Korea and abroad.

Although tension between the U.S. and Korean governments was high in late 1979, the relationship had survived many periods of equal or greater strain. Despite having been America's favorite to become president of the Republic of Korea in 1948, Syngman Rhee, with his rascally mixture of democratic jargon, dictatorial methods, and corrupt practice, was an almost constant source of serious anxiety for the United States before, during, and after the Korean War. He infuriated the U.S. government by refusing (foolishly) to sign the Korean War armistice in 1953. The most heated confrontation in the postwar years occurred in April 1960, when, in a crude attempt to cling to power, he rigged the election and resorted to violence against opposition forces. His behavior provoked widespread riots, which were met with police brutality. Thousands of students marched on his residence, seeking to present their grievances. Some 200 of them were killed as Rhee's guards opened fire. Koreans were appalled. Americans vented their exasperation with Rhee in an extraordinary public statement that recognized the "legitimate grievances" of the Korean people. Influenced to some extent by American views, Korean

army leaders allowed their troops to side with the protesters, effectively ending Rhee's regime.

For a brief period the U.S. government and the Korean army had the
satisfaction of believing that their actions had been effective and that they
had identified themselves with an overwhelming majority of the Korean
people. The sense of satisfaction was short-lived, however. The new government under Prime Minister Chang Myon, while democratically elected, was
rapidly overwhelmed by problems, including severe economic conditions,
the constant North Korean challenge, the postwar role of the army, and relations with Japan. The government's authority was weakened by its own
naïveté and inexperience, while disparate elements pursued their agendas,
more or less oblivious to the effect on the nation. In the resulting atmosphere, policy toward North Korea became a highly contentious issue. Some
South Koreans responded favorably to a North Korean invitation to conduct unification talks; in particular, sizable numbers of students, lacking the
wartime experience of their elders, demonstrated in favor of discussions at
Panmunjom with North Korean students. Many other Koreans, fearing subversion of their society and North Korean manipulation of any talks, strongly
opposed them. The government appeared helpless in the face of incipient
anarchy, an impression exaggerated by Korea's first experiment with a free
press. American unhappiness was evident, but muffled.

These were the circumstances in May 1961 when Major General Park
Chung Hee seized power through a coup d'état. Although shocking to politicians and many others in Seoul, the general Korean reaction to the coup
was not particularly negative, and it became relatively tolerant as Park demonstrated that he was both determined and able to stabilize Korea as well as
move the country toward rapid economic development. The initial response
of the United States, however, was decidedly negative, because self-appointed
soldiers had boldly violated the United Nations chain of command to topple
a civilian government, in the process undermining Korea's democratic response to the arbitrary authoritarianism of the Rhee years. Americans also
worried about intelligence reports—never substantiated—alleging that General Park was actively involved with communists before the Korean War. In
any event, Park and his colleagues proceeded with their careful plans, unde-
terred by a very public, and completely unsuccessful, effort of the senior
American civilian and military leaders in Korea to resuscitate Prime Minister Chang's government.

I observed this tumult from the distance of Tokyo, where I was a young
embassy officer engaged in a high-priority American program to encourage
normalization of relations between Korea and Japan. Like American offi-

cials in Seoul, I too was disturbed by the military overthrow of a democratically elected civilian government. I was concerned that North Korea might
do something dangerous to exploit the situation, and although it seemed
utterly illogical, I could not flatly rule out the possibility that General Park
was a covert leftist. At the same time, I questioned why the United Nations
commander and the U.S. chargé in Seoul had issued sweeping orders to the
perpetrators of the coup without first making a careful estimate of their
likely reactions. The highly public failure of these orders (to return to barracks and support constitutional authority) appeared to denigrate American authority. As the weeks passed, moreover, I became more and more
convinced that the United States was damaging itself by holding the new
regime at arm's length when the Korean people were not demonstrating
much objection. These were, of course, armchair ruminations in Tokyo rather
than firm convictions of a person with responsibility in Seoul, but these
early thoughts left a lasting imprint on my mind, and they influenced my
behavior eighteen years later when I had to make difficult judgments about
how the United States should react to the renewed turmoil in Korea.

More or less coinciding with the assignment of a new ambassador to
Korea in the summer of 1961, the United States backed down and accepted
the reality of the Park regime.[1] The shift took place, correctly I believe, despite the air of independence that the new Korean authorities were exhibit-
ing in economic planning and the authoritarian threat posed by the
establishment of the Korean CIA, a powerful new institution designed for
political as well as economic control. General Park's knowledge of what he
wanted to do, combined with his firm control, allowed him to move quickly
to stabilize the economy, begin serious efforts to normalize relations with
Japan, and prepare Korea for the rapid, export-driven, Japanese model of
development later associated with his rule. Under American pressure, he
also agreed to civilianize his administration. With the advantage of incum-

---

1. I first met Park Chung Hee on a cold fall morning in late 1961 when his plane made a fuel
stop in Tokyo en route to Washington for his meeting with President Kennedy. The stop presented
a problem for the Japanese. Although it was a "nonvisit" in terms of protocol, they wanted to extend
courtesies to a man who was decisively important in negotiations to normalize Japan's relations
with Korea. Thus they selected the highly regarded director general of the Foreign Ministry's Asian
Affairs Bureau to represent them. Ambassador Reischauer designated me, an embassy second secretary, for the same purpose. Apparently for domestic political considerations, Park decided impul-
sively on arrival to boycott contact with Japanese officials, refusing to disembark and asking if there
was an American in the crowd. I was invited into Park's DC-4 aircraft, where we chatted for a few
minutes prior to his departure. I rather enjoyed my unexpected encounter, but I was embarrassed
for my Japanese colleagues, particularly Director General Iseki, who had befriended and helped me
and who was more pro-Korean than his fellow countrymen. I suspect that, in later contacts, President Park repaired the damage with Iseki.

bency, he became the constitutional leader of Korea in a relatively free presidential election in 1963 and again in 1967. By the mid-1960s, Korea's stunning economic turnaround permitted the phasing out of American economic assistance, which had been so crucial in earlier years.

While Korea's growing strength was gradually eroding American influence, U.S. relations with Korea during this rather benign phase of President Park Chung Hee's rule were far more harmonious than in President Rhee's time. A kind of tacit bargain governed the process. Park was expected to exercise political moderation and economic success at home, maintain a firm but not provocative stance toward North Korea, and cooperate with American interests elsewhere in Asia, particularly Japan and Vietnam. In return, the United States would maintain its security commitment and military presence in Korea, extend considerable but diminishing amounts of economic and military assistance, and refrain from heavy intervention in Korean affairs to achieve American political and human rights objectives. The most pronounced act of cooperation was Park's positive response to an American call for support in Vietnam. Under highly beneficial economic terms, two Korean divisions served in Vietnam from 1965 to 1973.

In the late 1960s and early 1970s, however, strain reappeared. After almost a decade of dominating the Korean scene and enjoying accolades for the country's amazing economic success, Park's sense of security was shaken by events at home and abroad. Internally, and most important to him personally, he came close to losing the 1971 presidential election to Kim Dae Jung, his charismatic rival from South Cholla Province, a region that had long suffered discrimination as a kind of outcast from the governing system. About the same time, the United States, the key to Korea's external security, adopted new strategies reflecting the American predicament over Vietnam and cold war concerns about the Soviet Union. President Johnson authorized the beginning of the Paris peace talks with North Vietnam in 1968, and not long after taking office in 1969 President Nixon announced his Guam Doctrine calling on American allies to assume primary responsibility for providing the manpower for their own defense. Shortly thereafter, the United States withdrew one of its two remaining combat divisions in Korea, with talk of possible further cuts. In a stunning change, moreover, Nixon reversed U.S. policy toward China, seeking normalization of relations with a Korean War enemy. These policy shifts took place in the context of growing public pressure to extract American forces from Vietnam and, to a lesser extent, to remove all of its forces from the Asian mainland, Korea as well as Vietnam. The new strategies were engineered in great secrecy and implemented abruptly, without much prior thought about how they would affect allies such as Korea.

At least with hindsight, it is quite clear why President Park viewed these developments as a fundamental challenge to Korea's national security and to his own political future. Thus, while trying to maintain cordial relations with American leaders, he made significant changes in policy. He virtually abandoned democratic pretense, ramming through a new constitution that severely crimped the space for any political opposition. He began a major effort to strengthen the Korean armed forces and to develop defense industries, including a clandestine nuclear weapons program. Experimenting within the new circumstances of Sino-American rapprochement, for the first time he authorized negotiations with North Korea, a process more notable for having finally occurred in 1972 than for producing enforceable agreements. Most ill-advisedly, in an attempt to influence America's Korean policy, he ordered, or allowed, Korean officials and wheeler-dealers to dispense substantial amounts of money to members of the U.S. Congress, behavior that later boomeranged into a damaging scandal, known as Koreagate.

However understandable his motives, Park's shift in course did not bring him the desired security, instead generating new sources of friction both at home and abroad. Many Koreans refused to buckle under to the regime's intimidation of critics and hobbling of oppositionists through arbitrary harassment, threats, and frequent arrests, all made easy under the *Yushin* Constitution, which was adopted under conditions of martial law in October 1972, and Emergency Measure 9 (EM-9), a sweeping regulation issued by presidential decree. The most notorious effort to silence opposition set off alarms when it was publicly exposed mid-course. Koreans brazenly abducted Kim Dae Jung from a Tokyo hotel in 1973 with the apparent purpose of killing him. Although Kim was saved from death by U.S. Ambassador Phillip C. Habib's swift intervention and the resulting loud international clamor, Park effectively kept Kim off the political scene for six years. Few other single events did as much damage to Park's reputation. Nor did it stop Kim Dae Jung many years later from becoming president of the Republic of Korea.

Although the Korean people generally resigned themselves to this new round of authoritarianism, church groups, labor activists, students, disgruntled politicians, and journalists continued to challenge the regime. They transmitted their resentment to foreign counterparts, who in turn brought it to the attention of foreign governments, which began to criticize and, in some cases, pressure Park to ease his rule. Domestic resentment and foreign criticism did not completely erase the credit Park enjoyed for Korea's rapid economic transformation, but more and more people began to view him as a leader who had overstayed his time. Making matters worse, he became increasingly isolated and dependent on certain thuggish members of his apparatus of control.

Such was the political mood in the fall of 1974 when I returned to Washington as a deputy to Ambassador Habib, who had returned from his ambassadorship in Seoul to become assistant secretary of state for East Asian and Pacific affairs. And the mood had not improved by 1976 when I served briefly as the senior staff member for East Asia in the National Security Council.

The Ford administration was preoccupied in East Asia with managing a demanding new relationship with China as well as with the consequences of America's failure in Indochina. Key figures, including Secretary of State Henry Kissinger, were determined not to let South Vietnam's defeat be interpreted as a general American retreat from the area. They wished to demonstrate steadfastness in Korea, and they made it quite clear to those of us working for them that they wanted to minimize problems with Korea. Thus we were alert to Korea's security concerns during this period and were reasonably responsive to most of its economic needs. As much as possible, the administration avoided confrontation over political and human rights issues, desisting from public criticism and generally relying on diplomatic and other traditional means to convey its views to Park's government.

The relationship was difficult, nevertheless. The United States could not remain silent when Kim Dae Jung was abducted in 1973. While limiting public comment, it made no secret of its tough reaction. President Park's secret nuclear weapons program posed a more far-reaching problem of national security. I was especially sensitive to this issue and impatient to act, having just returned from Taiwan, where we faced a similar clandestine effort by an allied government. After several months of deliberation and efforts to discourage the supply of nuclear-reprocessing equipment and technology from France as well as plutonium-producing heavy water reactors from Canada, the Ford administration concluded in early 1975 that it had to take direct action to prevent South Korea from implementing a program that not only constituted a major challenge to the nonproliferation regime but also had dangerous implications for Japan and North Korea. Frustrated by our delays, I was, nevertheless, impressed by the effectiveness with which we finally deflected President Park from his hazardous adventure. Once he understood that Korea's basic security relationship was in jeopardy,

Park tacitly agreed to desist from the nuclear effort. The United States, in turn, kept the matter secret and agreed to face-saving compensatory measures.

Critical of the administration's "complacency," journalists and congressional members helped to disseminate the stark picture of Korea prevalent among many church and labor groups. Using Kim Dae Jung and other somewhat less prominent cases, they depicted Korea under Park as a country where the government circumscribed, imprisoned, and often tortured its critics. A well-placed minority of members in the House of Representatives and a few important senators steadily berated the administration for being "soft" in dealing with the human rights transgressions of a dictatorial regime dependent on American protection. Insinuating security considerations into the argument, they also sought, unsuccessfully, to set a timetable for withdrawing our forces from Korea. Along with others, I spent many frustrating days on Capitol Hill trying to explain our policy, to acknowledge the validity of much criticism, and to rebut ignorant or extremist attacks. Koreagate also boiled into a major scandal when the U.S. media gave heavy play during the 1976 presidential and congressional election campaigns to "leaked" news about a grand jury reviewing evidence, acquired through eavesdropping, that South Korean agents had tried to bribe as many as ninety members of Congress. Although the scandal did not peak until after President Carter took office in 1977, it poisoned Korea's reputation among Americans.

A whiff of realpolitik from North Korea in August 1976 punctured this ugly mood regarding South Korea. In a brazenly provocative act (conceivably taken without explicit orders from Pyongyang), North Korean soldiers armed with axes killed two U.S. officers who were supervising a tree-cutting detail in the demilitarized zone at Panmunjom. The United States reacted swiftly, moving major air and naval reinforcements toward Korea and then successfully conducting the tree-cutting exercise under protection of a large airborne assault force, highly visible to the North Koreans. A few senior officials in Washington favored stronger measures to punish North Korea, and President Park told us that he would have preferred that we bloody North Korea's nose. President Ford, however, agreed with his military advisers that we should not risk war. An unprecedented statement of regret from President Kim Il Sung delivered shortly after completion of the counteraction in Panmunjom appeared to confirm the wisdom of Ford's decision.

During an election year—in fact, during the Republican convention in Kansas City—Americans were at least briefly reminded of Korea's critical position. Few of them complained seriously about the administration's tough but restrained response to the north, and South Koreans were relieved to see a demonstration of U.S. firmness. This firmness was not enough, however, to offset continuing anxiety in Korea, and in most of noncommunist East Asia, that the United States would overcompensate for its experience in Indochina by an excessive retraction of its military presence in the area. I remember the chorus of warnings against this when I met with Asian ambassadors and military officers during our election campaign. I tried to reassure them that the Ford administration understood their point, and, foolishly perhaps, I stuck my neck out in suggesting that if the Democrats won the election, the Carter administration would also.

3

The Carter Administration: Salt for Korean Wounds

DURING THE PRESIDENTIAL primary campaign in 1975–76, Governor Jimmy Carter appealed to populist and reformist tendencies among Democratic party supporters, and he apparently assumed that there was a moderate, if not large, groundswell in America against the kind of military commitment that had entangled the United States in Indochina. Clearly, this was the context in which he promised to withdraw all U.S. military forces (later limited to ground combat forces) from Korea as well as to intensify human rights considerations in the conduct of American foreign policy. Nevertheless, a year later, during his election campaign against President Ford, the troop issue did not receive much attention, partly because there was no great clamor among Americans in 1976 for further military retrenchment from the Asia-Pacific region. Carter's firmness in maintaining America's commitment to the North Atlantic Treaty Organization (NATO) suggested, moreover, that he was basically an internationalist who might reconsider his primary campaign remarks about Korea. At least this was my hope.

While I was at the National Security Council in the latter half of 1976, Korean security was a lively topic. Occasionally, I heard arguments within and outside the government for reducing the level of American forces, usually from people overreacting to our experience in Vietnam, often from those who found the Park regime politically repugnant, and sometimes from "Europe-firsters" who myopically wanted to move soldiers from Korea to bolster U.S. forces under NATO. These ideas struck me as naive or foolhardy. Yet I was also somewhat skeptical of the prevailing view among our military officers that North Korea was far stronger than South Korea, and I would have welcomed an objective review of the facts as well as of our policy.

Despite some differences between us about the appropriate number of U.S. forces to deploy in Korea, the clear consensus among American officials dealing with East Asia was that implementation of Carter's election promise not only would be dangerous but also would send Asia precisely the wrong signal, feeding anxieties rather than reassuring people about the firmness of America's commitment. From my vantage point at the National Security Council, I could not have reached any other conclusion. I had been deeply involved when North Korea's bullying behavior at Panmunjom created serious alarm; I was aware of new intelligence studies suggesting that North Korea's military forces might be even more powerful than previously assumed; and I was deeply impressed by the large number of officials and others in South Korea, Australia, Indonesia, Japan, Malaysia, the Philippines, Singapore, Taiwan, and Thailand who were urging us to stand firm militarily in East Asia. Consumed by rivalry with the Soviet Union, even the Chinese sometimes admitted concern about weakening of the American military presence.

I remember talking along these lines at lunch with Richard Holbrooke, the newly designated assistant secretary of state for East Asian and Pacific affairs. If he was agreeable, I was to be matched as the senior deputy to this ambitious, frequently brilliant, and always articulate highflier, some fifteen years my junior in age. But our meeting at the restaurant was awkward: Holbrooke, an independent spirit, was still furious after being told a few days earlier that he "had" to choose me as his deputy rather than make his own decision; I, in turn, was quite unaware of this power play within the new administration and innocently thought I was high on Holbrooke's list of candidates. Despite these inauspicious circumstances, Holbrooke and I sensed fairly quickly that we would balance each other and make a pretty good team. Unknowingly, I disarmed him by announcing comfortably (in answer to his question) that I would have no problem working for a man fifteen years younger than I. With the ice melted, Holbrooke relaxed. He wanted to know about my Asian experience, my knowledge of people, my willingness to speak up, and my comfort in working under the new administration. I was especially curious about his views on normalizing relations with China, the Korean problem, and American steadfastness in Asia. We seemed in basic agreement. To my relief, he emphatically denied rumors that he was responsible for Carter's ideas on troop withdrawal. We both assumed that Carter would have to modify his position once he faced realities as president of the United States. When we reviewed East Asian matters with secretary of state designate Cyrus Vance before Carter's inauguration, he also seemed to agree. All of us assumed that the president would be willing to examine the effect in and around the Korean peninsula before carrying out his pledge.

Ultimately, President Carter did modify his position on troops in Korea, but he did so under duress and after a two-and-a-half-year struggle within the executive branch and the Congress. The process was clearly painful for him and extremely uncomfortable for those of us working under him. The United States survived, not much the worse for wear and without giving much thought to the impact of this behavior on the Korean psyche. Korea also survived the buffeting. There were no rabble-rousing protests against the United States, and Korean officials behaved themselves carefully. With hardly an exception, however, they felt that Americans were once again toying lightly with their fate. It was less of a jolt for them than the combined effect of the United States withdrawing all of its forces from Korea in 1949 and Secretary of State Acheson's ill-advised statement in January 1950 defining America's vital defense perimeter to exclude Korea. But, inevitably, the new American president's determination left Koreans feeling that the United States was about to undermine one of the most critical aspects of their nation's deterrence against North Korean attack. Other East Asians were baffled and disturbed. Only North Koreans (and a few South Korean radicals) were briefly fascinated. For me, Carter's posture toward a wartime ally—and the attendant demonstration of ignorance and insensitivity about East Asia as well as the dangerous disregard for professional and political opinion at home—was one of the most unsettling experiences of my foreign service career.

Although President Park tried to convey a sense of calm and control over this threatening development, his inner anxieties were fairly apparent. They were intensified, moreover, when he learned that President Carter was equally determined to confront another sensitive issue. During his first meeting with a senior Korean official, Foreign Minister Park Tong Jin, in March 1977, Carter offered no reassurance that he would be careful in implementing his plan for troop withdrawals and instead emphasized that his administration was going to pressure Park to substantially improve human rights. Effectively, the executive branch was no longer going to serve as a brake on congressional demands, but rather as a facilitator and sometimes an initiator of pressure for human rights and political liberalization in Korea. This interventionist role, welcomed by some Koreans and resented by others, played a part in the unraveling of Park's regime in 1979.

Through no fault of the Carter administration, but adding to Korea's woes, the Koreagate scandal peaked during this same period, with attention focused more on the transgressions of Korean officials, especially Korean CIA agents, and businessmen who did the bribing than on members of Congress who accepted the dirty money. Congressional investigative committees—in one case guided by Leon Jaworsky, the bullying high-profile lawyer of Watergate fame—sought to obtain direct access to Korean officials, which the Korean government refused on diplomatic grounds, as would we. In fact, the administration allowed Congress to hammer the Koreans for investigative arrangements that would have violated many centuries of diplomatic practice. One representative was finally convicted of taking bribes, and several others chose to slide quietly out of the Congress, allowing their nervous colleagues to consider the matter closed. Koreagate evaporated after the 1978 congressional elections, but it poisoned U.S.-Korean relations for more than two years.

These developments brought U.S.-Korean relations to a low point in 1977. Americans tended to consider Korea a pariah state rather than an example of Asian success. Koreans, even some oppressed by their government, reacted with confusion, dismay, and barely concealed anger at being treated this way by their protector. Although the sour atmosphere worried me, it reinforced my determination to resolve the complicated tangle between the two countries.

Withdrawal of U.S. Ground Forces: The Beginning and Demise of a Flawed Policy

By the time of President Carter's inauguration in 1977, a substantial presence of U.S. ground forces had been a part of the Korean scene for twenty-seven years. In conditions of a contentious truce and no peace treaty after the Korean War, the United States initially kept a large force in Korea, not only to deter a North Korean attack but also to restrain President Syngman Rhee from undertaking a risky military adventure against the north. In Park Chung Hee's era, this latter concern eased, and for this, economic, and other reasons, the U.S. army presence was progressively reduced. By 1977 the South Korean army and, to a lesser extent, air force had been expanded and modernized to the point where they constituted the bulk of South Korea's first line of defense. The one remaining U.S. army division, the Second Infantry Division, along with powerful units of the U.S. air force were viewed as crucial reinforcements—tokens of the American commitment and a "trip wire" that would engage the United States militarily if North Korea should attack.

These American forces, 39,000 strong in 1977, were under the command of the four-star U.S. army general who headed the United Nations Command responsible for enforcing the armistice agreement. More important for the events I am about to discuss, he also headed the U.S.-Korean Combined Forces Command and, in this capacity, had operational control over all South Korean forces assigned to defend against North Korea. At the normal state of defense alert, this excluded two units important to domestic security in Korea: the Capital Security Command in Seoul and the highly mobile brigades of Special Warfare Forces. With these significant exceptions, all forces in South Korea deployed against the North Korean threat were clearly understood to be under operational control of the U.S. commander in chief.

Although Americans for the most part seemed to accept these deployments and command arrangements, there was always some controversy about the presence of U.S. forces in Korea. For a variety of reasons, several administrations conducted policy reviews and decided on significant force reductions, always, however, leaving a substantial force in Korea. There were also some abortive efforts to increase, weaken, or modify the U.S. presence. I recall, for example, that in the wake of the Vietnam experience, a few of my colleagues argued, illogically, I thought, that we would be safer if our forces were pulled south of Seoul, leaving only South Koreans near the line of confrontation with North Korea and making the trip-wire function of our forces less automatic in case of a North Korean attack.

Most of the controversy over troops came from dovish elements and human rights activists responding to Park Chung Hee's hard-line behavior in the early 1970s. During the Ford administration, a prominent minority of senators and representatives began to couple their complaints about human rights abuses in Korea with the force withdrawal issue. Reflecting muddled thinking more than indifference, they made little if any effort to explain how force withdrawals and the attendant decrease in security would advance the cause of human rights in Korea. In March 1976, Senator Cranston called for a reexamination of the U.S. alliance with the Republic of Korea. Shortly thereafter, more than 100 senators and representatives led by Senator Kennedy and Representative Fraser warned the administration that military support of South Korea made the United States an accomplice to Park's repression.

However, few of the representatives and senators joining this chorus out of personal conviction or constituent pressure were willing to endorse a more radical effort to force progressive withdrawal of U.S. forces from Korea. When, for example, Senator McGovern called for the withdrawal of U.S. forces and disassociation of the United States from the "disreputable tyrant" Park Chung Hee, he found few supporters. In subcommittee discussion of human rights abuses in Korea, some representatives pushed for a phased withdrawal of American forces, but they were blocked by the moderate leadership, who were responsive to the administration's objections. They were able, however, to insert language into the International Security and Arms Export Control Act of 1976 calling on the president over the next five years to review annually the "prospects for or implementation of phased reduction of U.S. armed forces in Korea." The Ford administration reluctantly accepted this reporting requirement as a way of deflecting more radical demands.

It was hard to judge the real mood of Congress in early 1977. General discomfort over Korea was pervasive, and almost all members seemed willing to criticize the Koreans for their bad behavior. An important minority, mostly Democrats, wanted the United States to help topple the Park regime, and a smaller faction among them favored using troop withdrawals as leverage. When the chips were down on security issues, however, a majority in the House as well as the Senate almost always rallied to support a firm military posture in Korea.

Anti-Korean fireworks in Congress, magnified by Korea bashing in the media, must have encouraged Carter to think he would have support for or at least acquiescence to his position on the troop issue. In any event, he failed to consult Congress before making up his mind. Similarly, he chose to confront rather than engage the executive branch machinery under his control, almost surely because he feared that the bureaucracy would emasculate his plans, if given a chance. Whatever the reasons, Carter seriously underestimated the obstacles he faced in Washington as well as in East Asia.

Shortly before the president's inauguration, the National Security Council met informally and identified Korea as one of the priority issues facing the administration. Holbrooke and I understood from Secretary of State Cyrus Vance, who attended the council meeting, that the review was to examine the feasibility as well as the modalities of troop withdrawal. The written instruction, Presidential Review Memorandum/National Security Council 13 (PRM-13), dated January 26, seemed to bear out our assumption. It ordered a broad review of policies toward the Korean peninsula, including "reductions in U.S. conventional force levels." An interagency group was formed under Holbrooke to conduct the review. As his deputy, I was responsible for coordinating the draft study. Just before or during our first organizational meeting with officers from the State Department, Defense Department, CIA, and National Security Council, we received an urgent message from Under Secretary Habib that jolted me. The White House had told Secretary Vance flatly that our review should not examine the consequences of proceeding with partial or complete troop withdrawals, only the manner of implementing the policy of complete withdrawals already publicly enunciated by the president. Angered by this news, we ended the first meeting with a mutinous argument about how to deal with this White House dictate. Some participants threatened to refuse to cooperate; others threatened to publicize the issue, perhaps by way of Congress. The angry, fractious session ended in bureaucratic chaos.

Carter's posture effectively forced members of the working group to accept the proposition that at least some degree of troop withdrawal could be undertaken without jeopardizing the U.S. national interest. If we could not accept this proposition, we could presumably try to resist, quit, or ride along with the president in violation of our convictions. While our group struggled privately over this dilemma, General John Singlaub, chief of staff of the United Nations Command in Seoul, polarized matters by choosing the path of open resistance. He publicly criticized Carter's decision and was swiftly recalled. Although many fellow officers disapproved of his public insubordination, almost all shared his views. They included General John Vessey Jr., the senior American commander in Korea, who behaved loyally but, along with Ambassador Richard Sneider, my predecessor in Seoul, never wavered in opposition to any significant cuts in U.S. combat forces in Korea.

Our group in Washington was constrained by our sense that we should remain engaged so as to influence the president. A few members insisted almost to the bitter end that the withdrawal study should include a "no withdrawal" option, contradicting White House orders. Most of us, both military and civilian, gradually concluded, however, that we could frame the study so that it would be consistent with the president's instructions, yet allow us to argue for a minimum of withdrawals. Over subsequent months, we found that the leaders of all the military services as well as virtually all the departments and agencies concerned shared our approach. With good contacts at all levels and informal coordination, we surrounded the president with a remarkably broad consensus regarding what should be done. We did not systematically set out to "conspire" against him, although he came to look on our behavior that way.

The consensus was to persuade the president to accept a policy option that would involve withdrawal of a largely symbolic number of combat forces along with a larger number of noncombat forces, followed by a careful review of the situation in Korea before any further withdrawals. Vance supported us fully; we knew through Deputy Assistant Secretary of Defense Morton Abramowitz that Secretary of Defense Brown and members of the Joint Chiefs of Staff agreed with us, and since our colleague, the senior staff member for East Asia at the National Security Council, Michael Armacost, was solidly on our side, we hoped the national security adviser, Zbigniew Brzezinski, would support us.

At a key meeting of the council on April 14, 1977, President Carter overruled both his secretary of state and secretary of defense (despite our preparatory efforts, Brzezinski refused to join them), reaffirming his original idea of a complete withdrawal of ground forces over four or five years, beginning in 1978. Shortly thereafter, he issued Presidential Decision 12, dated May 5, 1977, ordering the substantial withdrawals we were trying to prevent: one brigade of the second division (at least 6,000 troops) to be pulled out by the end of 1978; a second brigade and support units (at least 9,000 troops) to be pulled out by mid-year 1980; and complete removal of all ground forces by 1981–82. Carter did not call for any corresponding actions by North Korea, nor did he make his decision contingent on a satisfactory evolution in Korea's security environment.

Although the president's action was demoralizing, we kept struggling to find ways of softening its impact. I suspect we would have failed without help from three external developments. New American intelligence estimates reexamining existing data in greater detail suggested that North Korean forces were far larger than previously thought. Congressional opposition, which began rather quietly, grew into an insuperable obstacle. And President Park's skillful bargaining tactics reinforced the impact of both the intelligence data and congressional opposition. These developments, combined with an almost uniformly negative reaction throughout East Asia to Carter's plans, altered the debate within the executive branch and ultimately proved decisive in forcing the president to change his mind.

Although Carter raised the issue of troop withdrawals in a mid-February letter to Park, real consultations with the Koreans began only after the president had unilaterally decided on a withdrawal schedule in April and May. Once this was done, Under Secretary Habib and the chairman of the Joint Chiefs of Staff, General George Brown, were selected to deliver the news to President Park. Despite having reviewed most official conversations with Park on this subject and having myself discussed it with Park many times after my assignment to Seoul, I still do not know if this wily leader and veteran negotiator really expected a complete withdrawal of U.S. ground forces. Obviously, he was very concerned that it might happen, but he also was aware of pervasive dissent within the U.S. military and civilian hierarchies (including officials in Seoul) as well as in Congress. Wisely, he chose not to confront Carter directly, adopting instead a posture of "painful acceptance" of the president's risky decision. Emphasizing his fears for Korea's security, he proceeded skillfully to extract substantial compensation as well as a significant lengthening of the schedule for withdrawal of the second division. The United States agreed to give Korea the tanks, artillery, and other heavy equipment of the departing forces in addition to other military assistance. The withdrawal schedule was further back-loaded to leave two combat brigades and the division headquarters (8,000–9,000 troops) until the final tranche of withdrawals in 1981–82. The U.S. air force in Korea was to be strengthened, and the United States agreed to a significant increase in joint military exercises. (I have chosen not to address the issue of nuclear weapons in this book.)

As a practical political matter, no major troop withdrawals from Korea could have taken place without congressional acquiescence, and the arrangements worked out with President Park, particularly the turnover of U.S. army equipment, explicitly required congressional approval. Although aware of considerable discontent in conservative and liberal circles, the administration assumed that a majority of the House and Senate would probably go along with its proposed package of withdrawals and compensatory measures. Even though U.S. military officers were known to be uneasy about any withdrawals, the arrangements agreed to by President Park were publicly supported by the secretaries of defense and state as well as by members of the Joint Chiefs of Staff, because the withdrawals would be offset by very positive assistance to Korea, while the bulk of the second division would remain in Korea for several years. For most of these senior officials, the administration's package was, to be sure, a second-best outcome, but they accepted it as a tolerable compromise, and they defended it loyally in congressional hearings. Along with most of my colleagues in mid-1977, I too considered the arrangements the best that we could hope for given Carter's refusal to back off a bad policy. I suspect that most of us took greatest comfort from knowing that a significant U.S. combat presence would remain in Korea beyond 1980, virtually ensuring a thorough review of the withdrawal policy during the next U.S. presidential election.

The administration discovered quickly that it had miscalculated the odds in Congress. Reflecting anger that the president had embarked on a major policy shift with little if any effort to consult them, prominent members of the House and Senate, liberals as well as conservatives from both parties, progressively challenged the administration for embarking on a risky policy without a careful policy review. Steadily growing opposition from supporters of the status quo on one side of the political fence was reinforced on the other side by objections to any form of aid to a regime with Park's record of repressive political and human rights behavior. To make matters worse for the administration, the Koreagate investigations, going full blast at this time, virtually paralyzed legislative action on Korea. Members feared being tarred with the scandal's brush if they voted favorably for anything related to Korea.

More or less parallel with the growth of congressional opposition and eventually feeding it, the American intelligence community was exposed to increasing evidence that North Korean military forces were substantially stronger than previously assumed. An intensive, small-scale army study of aerial photography and electronic evidence concluded in late 1975 that North Korean tank forces were far larger than assumed. A subsequent, somewhat larger, study indicated that large numbers of previously undetected North Korean tank and artillery units not only existed but were well armed and forward deployed against the south. I first learned of this reappraisal effort in late 1976 while I was assigned to the National Security Council, and I became thoroughly entangled in it a few months later when our PRM-13 working group struggled to reach a consensus regarding the risks involved in various possible patterns of troop withdrawal.[1]

Before the president rejected his advisers' plan in the spring of 1977, our working group had patched together an uneasy intelligence consensus for the working group. Despite almost unanimous opposition to Carter's policy, a (bare) majority of us at that time believed that the small withdrawal of U.S. ground forces we were recommending would not jeopardize

1. When the second of two remaining U.S. army divisions was withdrawn from Korea in 1969–70, there was an assumption of general parity between North and South Korean forces. Over the next few years, while we were preoccupied with the Vietnam War, North Korea engaged in a substantial buildup of its forces, but the extent was not properly assessed, in part because so many of our intelligence resources were devoted to the effort in Vietnam. Beginning in 1975, however, there was a methodical effort to reappraise North Korean military strength, starting with a reexamination of existing data and concluding with the comprehensive army/CIA study. Although the results of this exercise were initially treated with some skepticism, by 1978–79 there was a rapidly growing consensus that North Korean forces were substantially larger than we had thought.

Korean security. Within just a few months, however, we were faced with cumulative evidence that undermined our assumption. The vehicle for this evidence was a comprehensive new army/CIA appraisal of North Korean forces. After being briefed informally in the spring of 1978 about the likely outcome of this study, I recall thinking that no reductions in U.S. combat forces from Korea could be justified any longer.

Knowledge of a sea change in the administration's risk assessment spread rapidly through Washington in late spring of 1978, leaving the president more and more isolated. He suspected that the intelligence community was warping its judgments to obstruct implementation of his policy, but he also recognized that he was cornered.[2] He did not, as many wanted him to, call off troop withdrawals pending final conclusions of the army/CIA study. Instead, on April 21, he reluctantly stretched out his withdrawal schedule, so that the first planned reduction of combat forces, one brigade of 6,000 soldiers in 1978, was cut to only one battalion of 800 (plus 2,600 noncombat personnel). This reduction, which fate perversely forced me to observe during a ceremonial visit to the second division in November 1978, was the only force withdrawal that actually took place under the Carter administration, and it had virtually no effect on American combat capabilities in Korea.

When I left Washington in mid-1978 to take up my new post as ambassador to Korea, my own anxiety about the troop issue had already eased substantially. Given the facts about North Korean deployments and the way the issue had developed in Washington, I assumed the president would surely use the occasion of the final army/CIA report on North Korean military strength to cancel or postpone consideration of any further withdrawals. The first months of my new assignment in Korea also reinforced my own views about what we should do, giving a new dimension to opinions formed in the relatively abstract debates of Washington. Although I was sometimes put off by the overzealousness of commanders at the front, I learned much from talking to a wide range of American and Korean officers as well as from visiting as many military units as possible. I was impressed by the near unanimity of views among key members of my embassy staff, including Thomas Stern, my deputy, and William Clark Jr., the political counselor. I listened with particular care to General Vessey's low-key explanations, because he impressed me as a man of integrity and good judgment. But it was Koreans who had the greatest effect on me. Koreans of almost all persuasions used meetings with me to register consternation with President Carter's

2. See Don Oberdorfer, *The Two Koreas* (Reading, Mass.: Addison-Wesley Press, 1997), p. 103.

policy. The regime's shrillest critics often seemed even more upset than the Korean president himself. None of this was new to me, but the direct exposure intensified my convictions.

While this was happening to me, events in Washington were moving toward a denouement. The criticism and great discomfort initially made public by two of the administration's most loyal supporters, Senator Humphrey and Senator Glenn, in their report of January 1978, continued to build in Congress. Korean policy was heatedly debated during consideration of the International Security Act of 1978, which was finally adopted late in the year. The legislation included the requested authorization for cost-free transfer of equipment to Korea, but it also encumbered the administration with new requirements for detailed reports and justification prior to any further withdrawal increments. The debate revealed widespread opposition to the president, especially in the Senate. In December the gist of the conclusions drawn in the definitive army/CIA study became public through a "leak" to the *Army Times*. People were waiting for the president to act.

Although, being in Seoul, I was spared the pain of trying to defend the administration's policy in Washington, I was exposed directly to the intense feelings of three prominent members of the Senate Armed Services Committee, two Democrats and one Republican, who visited Seoul in early January 1979 after a trip to China. During their call on President Park, they handled the troop withdrawal issue with great circumspection, but in private conversation with me before and afterward they were highly critical of President Carter for his failure to accommodate to the reality of new intelligence assessments. The conversation became extended when I joined the senators on their air force plane for a ride back to Washington. After dinner, they resumed their criticism of the president for failing to halt troop withdrawals at least until the entire question had been reviewed in light of the new intelligence. I said that I personally shared their views and hoped that the president would eventually reach the same conclusion. The uncomfortable conversation concluded with the senior senator pointedly warning me, as the president's senior representative in Korea, that if Carter failed to act by the time the Senate reconvened in January, the senator and his colleagues would go on the attack with strong public criticism of troop withdrawals. Since I was told explicitly to get the message to Carter, I quickly contacted Vance on my arrival in Washington. He promised to speak to the president.

Carter did not act before the Senate reconvened, and the senators held their fire, but on January 22, 1979, the president authorized a new policy review (PRM-45) to take account of the new intelligence estimates, and on February 9 he took the minimum action demanded by the senators. He publicly announced that he was holding further troop withdrawals in abeyance while the administration examined the impact of newly assessed North Korean military strength. General Vessey and I were kept informed in Seoul about the PRM-45 study, which was guided by Robert G. Rich Jr., country director for Korea in the State Department, and we were able to send in our separate, but similar, recommendations as to what we should do. While in Washington for a few days in early May, I attended the final National Security Council meeting on PRM-45 at which the president was supposed to preside. In fact, he did not, and Secretary Vance chaired the session, which left me feeling that we had seen the end of the withdrawal scheme. The president struggled for two more months before taking the bitter medicine of publicly backing down. On July 20, 1979, the White House finally told the press that withdrawals remained in abeyance and that there would be no further withdrawals until after a careful review of the military balance on the Korean peninsula in 1981. Despite the roundabout language, no one missed the point. The struggle was over.

Historians, armed with better documentation and more detachment than someone such as myself, will eventually sort out the full story of President Carter's attempt to withdraw American ground forces from Korea. Nothing I have read, heard, or observed to this day fully explains what Carter had in mind.[3] Obviously, he was bothered by polls and other evidence that many Americans would disapprove of fighting to defend Korea. Clearly, he thought the American people and Congress would endorse an effort to reduce military engagement on the Asian mainland. Presumably, he was convinced that American interests could still be protected if all our forces were withdrawn from Korea, even more so if only ground forces were removed. He accepted our treaty commitment to Korea, and he always contemplated strengthening South Korea's forces while withdrawing ours. He hoped that any heightened danger to South Korea resulting from withdrawals could be partly offset by Chinese and Soviet assurances that they would restrain North Korea. (However, nothing useful along these lines was ever elicited from either the Chinese or the Soviets.) More vaguely and secretively, he was toying with holding some sort of summit meeting with Kim Il Sung, apparently thinking that dramatic, high-level diplomacy might reduce North Korea's determination to best the south.

None of this was conveyed with any coherence or candor to the public or to those of us who were expected to implement his plans. The president

3. Oberdorfer has written the best analysis I have seen, drawing on his own experience as a reporter, record searches, and interviews, as well as an exchange of letters with the former president. See Oberdorfer, *The Two Koreas*, pp. 84–94 and 101–08.

seemed vague about his objectives and casual about the risks involved. He showed little concern about reactions in South Korea, North Korea, Japan, and other parts of noncommunist East Asia. And he rankled South Koreans by informing the Japanese of his intentions (a correct action) before beginning even the semblance of consultations with the Korean government (an inexcusable error). As a person deeply involved in the process, I found his behavior strange and troubling. Strange, because I could not comprehend a president reaching such a decision and pursuing it so rigidly in the face of realities, including the clearly articulated advice of so many senior advisers. Troubling, because a policy of such obvious importance to national security was pushed into implementation without expert examination of its impact and without prior consultation with Congress.

Fortunately, the policy was abandoned before it caused fundamental damage, and the safety valves of the American system of government performed impressively. The president's top advisers reached sensible conclusions on the basis of professional study, and they confronted the president as effectively as they could. Congress forced the president to permit a public debate, and along with the media it did a fair job of conducting a responsible review. To his credit, the president behaved responsibly by finally accepting the nation's judgment.

One ironic result of the president's stubbornness was to unify views among the motley crowd who served him. Among us were persons who openly supported his campaign promise about troop withdrawals or lacked courage to tell him it was a bad idea, many others who did not initially resist the president because they were not well informed, members of the bureaucracy who favored both a careful study and a careful response calibrated to security needs, and, which was important, the U.S. military officer corps, who tended to frown on any force reductions as dangerously risky. At the beginning there was considerable confusion as to who was on which side, and we were all working against a floating horizon determined by the course of presidential decisions. In the end, a huge majority of us sighed with relief when President Carter was forced to back down.

Target of Special Concern: Human Rights

The Carter administration pursued its human rights campaign with real fervor, and Korea was an obvious target for special attention. As a result of the Korean War and treaty commitments, Americans had good reason to be anxious about domestic events in Korea that might endanger stability. Habits formed during the early years of the relationship also left Americans with little inhibition about "lecturing" to Koreans and interfering rather freely in their domestic affairs. American media reporting on Korea highlighted the confrontation and drama of the nation's politics, while American missionaries, who were on the leading edge of Korea's human rights movement, effectively communicated with their supporters in America about the nature and extent of political repression. When Park Chung Hee clamped down hard on opposition and dissent in the early 1970s, church groups were in the forefront of the American protest movement. Along with labor activists and supporters in Congress, they called for American counteractions. Reluctant to antagonize an Asian ally, the Nixon and Ford administrations limited themselves to quiet diplomatic intervention.

By the time the Carter administration took office in 1977, Korea was sinking into a political morass. More and more people were demonstrating their weariness with Park's long rule, while Park himself was becoming erratic as well as increasingly authoritarian. Large numbers of students, dissidents, and opposition figures, including Kim Dae Jung, were in jail; the government was harassing its critics in the National Assembly and media; prisoners were often treated harshly; innocent people were branded procommunist; and strains were beginning to show in the structure of control. Although the majority of Koreans still supported Park as the father of development, political repression in Seoul and other cities had given Korea considerable notoriety abroad. This made Korea a prime target for a new American president who wanted to maintain a high profile on human rights and clearly intended to give these concerns great weight in relation to other interests.

Carter was zealous in human rights matters. He created new bureaucratic machinery, recruited highly focused and committed individuals (many drawn from the civil rights movement) to represent him in human rights questions, ordered close liaison with sympathetic groups in Congress, and let it be known that concern for human rights would be an important criterion for judging the performance of his officials. As a result, some of the past strain and argument between officials and special advocates for human rights moved from outside to inside the administration. The new human rights hierarchy in the State Department took issue with the judgments, methods, and even the dedication of both our embassy in Seoul and established parts of the Washington bureaucracy. The new people wanted a higher priority for gathering intelligence on human rights and injection of human rights concern into almost all representations made to the Korean government. As leverage against the Korean regime, they favored experimenting with relatively strong sanctions, and at least some of them questioned the overriding nature of our security concerns in Korea. Almost daily, they battered the Korean regime with condemnatory public comments.

Both in Washington and later in Seoul, I was on the firing line. Deputy Secretary of State Warren Christopher was a key figure on human rights policy. Within the Bureau of East Asian and Pacific Affairs, Holbrooke, who was very sensitive to the president's views, designated me as our bureau's normal liaison with the human rights group working under Christopher or the under secretary for political affairs. My negative reaction to the experience was intensified because I was responsible for dealing with all the East Asian human rights "offenders," particularly the Philippines, Indonesia, and Taiwan as well as Korea. Latin American countries were other favorite targets. African countries generally escaped criticism, as did China in those days, because normalization of relations was given overriding priority.

I shared the administration's concerns about political repression in Korea, and, unlike most of the newcomers, I had been engaged for several years in American efforts to soften it. In addition, experience over a longer period had convinced me that our military presence and defense commitment in Korea required political stability, while political stability in turn required some sense of progress among Koreans toward a more pluralistic society. In short, I considered myself on the side of the angels. Yet, the meetings of Christopher's group often left me feeling that I was the defendant in a court of western law where the judge and jury had already reached a verdict of "guilty."

My difficulty, not necessarily disagreement, was the issue of fairness and efficacy posed by many of the proposals made in the working group. Since most of the members were not familiar with Asia, in some cases not even with foreign affairs, they did not readily appreciate my view that in attacking the sins of these Asian regimes one should in fairness make allowance for the fact that many of them, certainly Korea, had done well in other respects by fostering the security, economic progress, equitable distribution of income, education, and social mobility of their citizens. From evidence available in 1977 (in contrast to circumstances at the end of the Chun regime ten years later), these accomplishments seemed more important to Korean farmers and workers than the individual political rights sought by Korea's small but growing middle class. I argued that effective American criticism had to acknowledge this progress, and my own efforts with the Koreans always did so.

But the most contentious problems concerned the efficacy of American actions. In theory the Carter administration had a huge assortment of tools for the enhancement of human rights in Korea: a security treaty, a large American military presence, foreign military sales credits, government and private loans, markets for Korea's exports, high-level visitors, supply of police equipment, assistance from international financial institutions, public criticism, and diplomatic representations. The inability to apply effectively this array of apparently massive influence created great frustration in our human rights circles as well as in opposition and dissident groups abroad. These people generally agreed that we could not threaten to pull out militarily or to cut access to our markets and private financing. But short of such drastic measures, they pressed for sanctions and downplayed the prospect that the Korean government would see these as threatening its survival and react with nationalistic defiance.

One of the most dangerous ideas that surfaced within the group was the suggestion that we attack President Park personally and publicly or signal in other ways that we were fundamentally dissatisfied with his conduct. I pointed out that American comments on such matters were studied with minute care and frequently misconstrued in Korea. Were we to be seen as lifting the mantle of legitimacy from Park, the consequence could conceivably be another coup and another military leader, not necessarily more enlightened than Park Chung Hee. Holbrooke backed me firmly, and senior members of the administration grasped the danger. The United States never mounted a personal assault on President Park. Yet the debate came back to haunt me after his assassination. Had the sum total of U.S. criticism of Park's regime unwittingly had the same effect?

During the initial debates in Washington, I tended to consider the views of the human rights specialists as naive; they in turn tended to consider me as defensive of Asian authoritarianism. Our clashing views were sometimes voiced with real anger. Over time, and especially after I became ambassador in Seoul, tensions moderated. More important, despite this battle of words and memos at lower levels, senior leaders of the administration never experimented with major sanctions. Apart from the apparent danger to our security and economic interests, Carter had already played his security card. He could not threaten to accelerate ground force withdrawals when these were proving highly controversial in Congress and objectionable to most Koreans—Kim Dae Jung and many of the human rights community were outspoken in their criticism of Carter's plans. Nor could he limit market access or governmental loans without heavy cost to the well-being of the

Korean people. Thus, after some symbolic actions, which had little effect, the administration resorted to traditional instruments of pressure: diplomatic representation and public criticism of Korea (not Park himself), making much greater use of the latter than preceding administrations.

The State Department and embassy in Seoul were necessarily the main channel for this effort. Although we were spurred to new efforts by the president's personal dedication and the omnipresence of his human rights lieutenants, we remained skeptical. As Americans, we believed that the relaxation of restrictions would ultimately enhance Korea's stability, but from our experience, we knew that Park Chung Hee was firmly convinced that more liberal policies would only embolden his opponents to challenge him more strongly. His sense of paranoia was intensified by tension over troop withdrawals and the Koreagate investigations. Nevertheless, we did not dispute the need to pressure the Korean government, and we tried loyally to make our actions as effective as possible.

Seeking, rather unsuccessfully, to limit public criticism and, more successfully, to be selective about our targets, we made serious representations to key officials, such as the foreign minister, the Korean CIA director, the secretary general, other presidential advisers in the Blue House, and occasionally the president himself.[4] U.S. Ambassadors in Seoul (first Sneider and then me), Holbrooke, and their staffs were the yeomen of this effort, but in almost every contact with senior Koreans, key U.S. cabinet officials raised human rights concerns. The president, of course, used every available occasion to weigh in, usually through letters to Park. Although a few representatives and senators broke ranks, many of them, including those identified as special friends of Korea, helped to reinforce the administration's message. Most of the bureaucratic skirmishes and battles on the American side were fought over application of symbolic sanctions, the degree of public criticism considered proper, and occasionally, the denial or granting of high-level recognition, particularly the treatment of senior Korean visitors and the holding of summit meetings. The sharpest break from traditional policy was the U.S. abstention on two loans for Korea from international financial institutions.

Park's response to this assault was tactical. He released some prisoners. His ministers decried and "investigated" reports of torture, which seemed to diminish. Yet EM-9, under which the government could detain anyone for

---

4. The Blue House refers to the Korean presidential complex, comparable to the White House in the United States.

the most minor slur, remained in full force, and people were still jailed for political crimes. American frustration continued to build.

A significant change occurred in the latter half of 1978. With guarded approval from Vance, Holbrooke and I began working cautiously toward a comprehensive new policy, which we informally labeled "normalization" of U.S.-Korean relations. Worried over the dangers of eroding goodwill in both countries, we argued that our security and other national interests required a more positive relationship with Korea, that this could be achieved, and that reconciliation might be more successful in our human rights endeavors than continued confrontation. By mid-1978 other strains with Korea were easing. The abrasive Koreagate investigations were near completion, and we hoped the controversy would drop out of the headlines after the November congressional elections. The new intelligence assessments of North Korean military strength, together with developments in Congress, appeared likely to slow or reverse Carter's earlier decision on troop withdrawals. This shifting context allowed us to contemplate what would have been unthinkable a year earlier: a Carter-Park summit in 1979 to clear the air and signify the beginning of a less strained, more fruitful era in U.S.-Korean relations.

In preparing for assignment to Korea mid-year, I talked to Holbrooke and Vance about my hope for a summit meeting. All three of us understood clearly that it would be impossible to reduce tensions over human rights without action by Park, and, short of suggesting a crude bargain, we wondered whether we could use the evolution of Carter's troop withdrawal policy as an incentive for making progress on human rights. I thought we could, and my first months in Seoul further convinced me. I found Park quite eager for a summit, considering a meeting beneficial to him personally as well as to Korea. With the secretary's permission, I broached the idea to President Park on October 25, 1978, touching on the easing of the strain caused by Koreagate and the troop issue and then engaging in a long review of our respective positions on human rights. Park reacted favorably. I think he understood the implicit tradeoff, but his exposition on human rights was an orthodox defense of his views: that is, Americans tended to apply American criteria to Korea, whereas Koreans had to take into account the stage of their development and the massive continuing threat from North Korea.

My strategy, set out clearly in messages to Washington, was to meet with Park periodically about human rights as one of many concerns, while my staff and I pressured members of his administration whom we understood to be relatively enlightened on the subject. I had many private lunches with Foreign Minister Park Tong Jin, whose obvious responsiveness allowed me to be increasingly frank with him. Robert G. Brewster, our senior intelligence representative, and I met with the Korean CIA director, Kim Chae Kyu, and he seemed taken with the approach. I also talked with key members of the president's staff in the Blue House. With a reward proffered for better Korean behavior, I hoped these advisers would be more willing than usual to convey our views to Park. When he was in Seoul for inauguration of the new Combined Forces Command in November, Secretary Brown moved the subject of summitry a notch forward by conveying to Park an informal invitation from Carter to meet sometime in 1979. A few months later in March 1979, Holbrooke, who was visiting Korea for his first extended trip, carried the process a stage further in his meetings with President Park and other officials. The context of our presentations implied, but did not promise, a favorable outcome on troop withdrawals. We were explicit, however, in stating that a successful summit required progress on human rights and consistently suggested that the most convincing signs of progress would be to lift EM-9 and release detainees.

Although other factors were obviously involved, the Korean government's behavior began to show a new sensitivity to American concerns. Park accepted the outcome of the December 1978 National Assembly elections in which the government party lost its majority of elected members, and many prominent political prisoners, including Kim Dae Jung, were released by year's end. Human rights conditions clearly improved, even though Kim remained under virtual house arrest and periodic new arrests took place under EM-9.

After his March visit, Holbrooke and I pressed hard to set the time and place of the summit, and on April 10 I was authorized to agree to a state visit to Seoul by President Carter following his visit to Japan at the end of June. Before giving me the final signal, however, the State Department subjected me to a rash of telegrams, asking whether we could obtain a significant gesture of human rights progress before the summit or at least get more solid assurance that there would be progress at the summit. In addition to our long-standing request for the lifting of EM-9 and release of detainees, there was special interest in asking the Koreans to free Kim Chi Ha, a well-known poet jailed many years earlier under harsh anticommunist laws. My impression from the distance of Seoul was that these messages and my replies were an effort to assuage the unhappiness of human rights activists when they first learned how much progress had been made toward the summit or, in most cases, when they first became aware that President Carter had many months earlier authorized summit negotiations with President Park. In any event, I was told that the president himself wanted a significant gesture in advance of issuing the summit invitation and might choose to make a meeting conditional on progress in human rights.

Carter's personal interest caused me to respond with particular care to these messages, sometimes with a secure phone message followed by a telegram for the record. I opposed a conditional invitation or demand for a major pre-summit gesture, arguing that the incentive of a successful summit was the most powerful instrument to get what we wanted in human rights. In a message to Holbrooke, dated April 3, 1979, I wrote (see also appendix, item 1):

> The Korean government knows very well that we would like a Carter-Park summit associated with progress in human rights and that we would be concerned about any setbacks. The "release" of Kim Dae Jung was probably viewed by them in this light, and their concern not to sour the summit atmosphere has undoubtedly constrained their natural proclivities in dealing with the dissident/opposition. Beyond this limited function, however, I do not believe the Korean desire for a summit meeting offers us much opportunity for extracting significant progress in human rights. President Park and his top officials clearly want a summit meeting, but not so badly that they will take actions they consider dangerous to their other interests, particularly political control. If we were to now make the summit meeting conditional on human rights progress or to chastise the South Korean government publicly for its human rights record before the summit meeting, I expect that the government—and once they found out, a majority of the people—would be confused and angry to find we were demanding something of Korea which we have properly downplayed in our Chinese, Soviet, and Middle Eastern summitry.

No one could accuse me of misleading the White House about what we could expect from the meeting with Park; in fact, I proved a bit too cautious. My final instructions regarding our agreement to the summit meeting were, as I wanted them, unconditional, even though they mentioned Carter's hope for a gesture of political liberalization. But, whether it was a delayed reaction by the human rights activists or second thoughts on the part of Carter himself, I was subjected to heavy pressure regarding human rights from some of my colleagues in Washington throughout preparation for the summit meeting. Carter's intense feelings on the subject before and during the summit kept me on edge until he was back on Air Force One.

4

The Carter-Park Summit Meeting

SUMMIT MEETINGS BETWEEN HEADS of state, particularly military allies, are normally expected to proceed smoothly in accordance with meticulous plans developed in advance through mutual agreement. The inherent concept of these occasions is to reflect agreement or enable constructive discussion, not provoke confrontation. While making allowance for some degree of spontaneity, little should be left to chance in the planning of such events.

In pushing for the Carter-Park summit, I was fully aware of these requirements and reasonably confident that we could meet them. With fingers crossed, I believed we were over the hump in getting President Carter to suspend his troop withdrawal plan, and I expected President Park to carry out his side of the bargain. Never did I question the wisdom of going ahead with the summit session, for which I was one of the architects. Yet the six weeks or so leading up to the summit were exceptionally stressful. Despite the plethora of messages, phone calls, and even a trip back to Washington, I felt out of touch with White House thinking. The embassy was under pressure to deliver more than we could on human rights. Despite the favorable trend on the troop issue, the White House seemed oblivious to the importance of giving the Koreans positive signals in advance, and I was almost swept off my feet by a last-minute White House lunge in American diplomacy toward North Korea.

Human Rights

Having more or less convinced my colleagues in Washington that they would have to live with "reasonable hopes" rather than reliable evidence of summit progress toward human rights, our preparatory work focused on the language of the communiqué and arrangements for President Carter to talk to a wide variety of Koreans, including some prominent opposition and dissident figures. After much haggling over language and many mind-numbing meetings, the Korean government finally accepted a brief but balanced statement on the importance of human rights issues, but it successfully resisted our vigorous effort to include more far-reaching language in the communiqué. The Koreans could not, however, stop President Carter from telling the state dinner guests gathered in the Blue House, "There is abundant evidence in Korea of the dramatic progress a capable and energetic people can achieve by working together. I believe that this achievement can be matched by similar progress through the realization of basic human aspirations in political and human rights." Although it is hard today to comprehend why he was so anxious, the foreign minister, who was seated near me, worried that these words would anger President Park. In fact, the course of the summit sessions earlier in the day left Park eager to contain signs of disagreement with Carter.

Although grudging about it, the Korean side also agreed to Carter's planned visit to the National Assembly, intended both to signify our support for representative politics and to provide an opportunity for Carter to meet with assemblymen from opposition as well as government parties. Similarly, the Koreans yielded to our firm insistence that the president meet with religious leaders and other critics of the regime. To ease the government's pain, we used the embassy residence, where the president was staying, as a neutral meeting site and invited a relatively noncontroversial group of people, the most prominent being Catholic Cardinal Kim Sou Hwan and Kim Kwan Suk, head of the Korean National Council of Churches. Although he enjoyed less respect among Koreans, the Reverend Billy Kim, a flamboyant Korean evangelist, was also present at President Carter's request.

As with many other targets of Park's repression, Kim Dae Jung was kept in the shadows and did not see the president. Nevertheless, concern about him suffused preparations for the summit, primarily because human rights advocates and Carter himself naturally wanted a meeting with Korea's most prominent human rights casualty. Since Kim's release from prison a few months earlier, the embassy had maintained quiet contact with Kim but refrained from high-profile actions, such as visits by me or my deputy, because we thought these would be counterproductive before Kim's "political rights" were finally restored. We were convinced that if Carter were to try to see Kim, the Korean government would react angrily and perhaps even physically block the meeting. Given our anxiety not to jeopardize the broader goals associated with Carter's visit, including human rights objectives, the embassy recommended firmly against pushing for a Carter-Kim session.

Washington never challenged this judgment directly, but people around the president were critical, and the issue continued to simmer in Carter's mind. A few days before the summit, I learned that the president had not completely excluded the possibility of meeting with Kim Dae Jung. I sent off an intemperate telegram, stating that if he should do so, the likelihood of the Korean visit being a large net plus "would be wiped out . . . the atmosphere would sour immediately . . . Park would consider our action a studied personal insult . . . He would clamp down on everything where we seek his assistance, including human rights issues." With hindsight, I would describe my reaction as excessive, but it helped to hold the line, which almost gave way at one point when Carter, in angry comments to Vance, threatened to scrub events with Park in favor of a session with Kim Dae Jung.

Troop Withdrawals

From our first private thoughts about a summit in 1978 to our agreement with the Koreans in 1979, we recognized that a meeting could succeed only if President Carter would agree to a major revision of his plan to withdraw U.S. ground forces from Korea. This seemed a reasonable hope when I was authorized to broach the summit with Park in October 1978, and most of us felt it was a sure bet when I conveyed Carter's formal acceptance of the proposal in April 1979. For Park, the anticipated shift in American troop policy was a prime incentive to agree to some relaxation of political constraints. For us, it appeared the most promising way to achieve some progress on human rights. Unfortunately, but unavoidably, a serious flaw on the American side handicapped consummation of the trade-off. Although Carter had authorized us to proceed toward a summit, he was still struggling to preserve a semblance of his policy on troop withdrawals.

Because of this, I had to walk a tightrope in the tricky process of encouraging President Park toward a tacit bargain over troops and human rights. Throughout the entire period, I was never authorized to promise Park anything specific about possible changes in the withdrawal policy, only to convey that we were reviewing the matter in light of disturbing new intelligence assessments, that we understood Korean concerns about the impact on security, and that "I," the U.S. ambassador, was confident of a mutually agreeable outcome. Nor, of course, could I encourage Park by telling him about the overwhelming number of people on our side who shared my objections to Carter's policy. I was forced instead to describe "favorable trends" in Washington, which were very promising for the summit, assuming that Park did his part for a successful meeting. Naturally, I resorted to the diplomatic practice of expressing my "personal views," conveying—perhaps occasionally exaggerating—optimism about force withdrawals.

My optimism about the evolution of Carter's policy was enough for President Park until we reached the final stage of negotiating the language of the summit communiqué. A new last-minute twist in our plans intensified his concerns about the risks of relaxing political controls. Our proposal to invite the Democratic People's Republic of Korea to a trilateral meeting would, he argued, expose South Korea to considerable danger from North Korea, unless it were handled with great care. Hence, he wanted positive assurances in the communiqué about the cessation of troop withdrawals. As late as June 26, four days before Carter's arrival, I cautioned Secretary Vance and Holbrooke, who were already in Tokyo with the president, that the Koreans failed to understand why we were so reticent on the troop withdrawal issue. I said that Park had made it very clear to me that any new diplomatic initiative must not be launched from "a security platform that appeared to him—and to the Korean populace—too shaky to withstand North Korean efforts to manipulate the troop withdrawal issue." Carter chose, nevertheless, to rebuff Park until the last day, almost tearing the summit apart.

Trilateral Meeting Proposal

Logically, the administration wanted the communiqué to include a positive statement about negotiations with North Korea. With so much attention focused on the American military presence in South Korea, common sense suggested a balanced statement on policy toward North Korea. Moreover, the idea of talks with the north retained some special appeal in the White House, despite an unfruitful exchange of messages with Kim Il Sung in early

1977 and North Korean propaganda complaining about the slowdown in troop withdrawals.[1] The South Koreans also wanted a statement on relations with the north. Since the beginning of the year, they had engaged in fitful efforts to establish a dialogue with North Korea but had found Pyongyang unyielding in demanding arrangements that would have implied greater legitimacy to the north than the south as well as interjected South Korean oppositionists and dissidents into the negotiating process. As part of the summit preparations, the embassy had formulated some ideas for possible consideration at the summit, and we were braced for a tangle with the Koreans over the language of the communiqué.

About the third week in May, my close colleague and immediate counterpart in Washington, Bob Rich, country director for Korea in the State Department, called me by secure phone with a staggering message. Without being able to tell me much about the context, he said the president wanted to invite President Kim Il Sung of the Democratic People's Republic of Korea to join him and President Park for a trilateral summit during his Seoul visit. If this could not be arranged for Seoul, he wanted to pursue a later tripartite meeting and would be sending Habib as his special emissary to explore the matter with Park. I exploded with surprise and anger, pointing out that such an effort would wipe out everything we were attempting to achieve with Park. In effect we would overwhelm the occasion, meant to symbolize successful "normalization" of relations with President Park, by a circus of events featuring Park's most feared enemy. Park would be shocked and furious. If President Carter persisted in the idea, I said, I would resign.

Rich, who shared my concern, explained that the White House might settle for a less horrendous version of the trilateral scheme, and he joshed me about making idle threats. I told him I was quite serious and that he should convey to Holbrooke the vehemence of my reaction. (In fact, I was not posturing and gave a lot of thought to two obvious questions: Would I publicly explain why I had resigned? Absolutely yes. Would I leave the foreign service? Probably.) In ensuing conversations with Rich and Holbrooke, I asked that Vance be told about my views, including my intent to resign. Holbrooke, who also discounted my threat, clearly did not want to brandish

---

1. Presumably enticed by presidential candidate Carter's position on troop withdrawals, Kim Il Sung sent President-elect Carter a message before the inauguration proposing talks, and, in a subsequent message to Vance through the same channel, he suggested peace talks. Having first informed the South Korean government, we expressed interest in talks, but only if South Korea were equally represented. Nothing came of this exchange, and Kim's special interest in President Carter waned with the slowdown in our troop withdrawals from the south.

it around the White House. One way or another, however, he let people know that I was extremely unhappy, and it was agreed that I should communicate directly with Vance, who was in London.

I did so immediately, stating that the proposal would destroy the repairs we had successfully made in our relations with Korea and would contradict some of our basic interests in Northeast Asia. If Habib were to tell Park, with or without assurances on the troop issue, that Carter wanted a trilateral meeting with Kim Il Sung during his Korean visit, we would

> stimulate paranoiac South Korean suspicion that we were taking the first steps—perhaps without full awareness—toward a Vietnamese solution for Korea. Park would not agree to our proposal; our action would poison the Seoul summit atmosphere; and there would be an extremely high risk that without making any advance on the north/south issue, we would find Americans blaming South Koreans for a problem of American making. The North Koreans might play along with us—at least I would, if I were they—but if they did, their prime interest would be to foster the rapid withdrawal of U.S. forces from the south and to unsettle U.S.-Korean relations rather than to reduce tensions.

I was more charitable about the idea of proposing a trilateral meeting subsequent to the Seoul summit. If Carter were to tell Park that we would accommodate his concerns by a significant alteration of our troop withdrawal plans, then on the basis of the confidence generated by such a declaration, we could tell him we wished to explore with him the possibility of announcing in Seoul a proposal for a trilateral summit at a later time. I concluded by asking that I be allowed to return to Washington to argue my case.

My alarm subsided a day or two later. In a slightly confusing sequence of events, Holbrooke informed me that the department had managed to get revised instructions for the Habib mission, which he hoped I would find acceptable, that Habib's mission had been scrubbed, that I was to be the messenger, and that, after making my presentation to Park, I could return briefly to Washington.

I was able to see President Park on June 4 just before leaving for Washington. With unusually careful preparation, I did my utmost to present our proposal as a reasonable effort, which, if successful, would test the prospects for reducing tensions with North Korea and, even if unsuccessful, would enhance our international positions. I noted that a tripartite meeting would build on Park's own initiative of January 19 in which he offered to meet with North Koreans at any place, any time, and any level. Although I could not be definitive on the troop withdrawal issue, I pushed my instructions to the limit and also stressed the constancy of our basic policy toward North Korea.

President Park appeared to take my presentation as a friendly, straightforward exploration, saying he had not given the matter enough thought to give me a careful response. On the basis of South Korea's recent experience and other evidence, however, he doubted whether North Korea was ready for a serious effort to reduce tensions. Pointedly emphasizing the need for firmness in coping with North Korea, he reminded me that almost all South Koreans shared his conviction that the United States should not withdraw any more ground forces. He also asked whether President Carter would be "on our side" or in the middle as a mediator, the way he functioned at Camp David during the negotiations between Egypt and Israel in September 1978.

Although extremely brief, my trip to Washington in early June was useful. I got some sense of the play around the trilateral proposal, and I witnessed the National Security Council's unanimous recommendation that the president suspend further troop withdrawals. I returned to Seoul wrongly confident that the president would deal forthrightly with the troop question at the summit. Even though my confidence proved "premature," it was important to me at the time, because I was faced with an uphill battle in Seoul over the concept of a trilateral meeting.

As soon as I got back, I went to work on key people who might influence Park's final decision, among them the foreign minister, the director of the Korean CIA, the chief of presidential security, the secretary general of the Blue House staff, and two key presidential advisers. I was surprised by the extent and vigor of their negative reactions. They all feared that the trilateral process would provide North Korea with the thin edge of a wedge to split America and South Korea. They all pointed to the example of Vietnam, and several of them suggested that we could not be counted on in the final analysis. Although I had predicted this sort of reaction if we had tried to transform the Seoul summit with Park into a trilateral one with Kim Il Sung, I was not prepared for such an emotional display over a far less controversial proposal. I spent many hours defending the honor and integrity of the United States, using rational argument, occasional anger, and even ridicule when it seemed called for. By far the most unpleasant contact was a debate with Cha Chi Chol, chief of presidential security, who was later killed along with President Park. I had hoped for a low-key private session. Instead I found myself the "guest of honor" at a long, elaborate luncheon where Cha, with an eye on his fawning subordinates and obviously convinced he was doing Park a favor, lectured me on my lack of experience in dealing with communists and other matters. After trying unsuccessfully to fill me with drink, Cha asked me where my next appointment was. I told him it was with the foreign minister. He signaled an aide and told him to tell Minister Park that Ambassador Gleysteen would be about an hour late and to please wait for him. Needless to say, I had a lot of explaining to do when I finally did see Minister Park.

When Ambassador Kim Young Shik in Washington delivered President Park's basically favorable reply ten days before the summit, this chorus of objection quieted. I am fairly sure the sentiments expressed were genuine, although they may have been exaggerated in hopes of pleasing Park. Only Park Chung Hee himself was confident enough to go along with Carter, calculating that a positive response would work to Korea's advantage on the troop issue. Carter's and Park's discussion of the matter at the summit was harmonious. The invitation to Kim Il Sung for a preparatory "meeting of senior representatives" was conveyed a few hours in advance to China, Japan, the Soviet Union, and Indonesia, the latter being the conduit for formal transmission to the Democratic People's Republic of Korea. The news did not make a big splash, and the North Koreans revealed through intermediaries that they would reject it. I must admit that there was a slapdash quality to the manner in which we conveyed this message to the North Koreans, but I doubt whether greater care would have altered the outcome.[2]

The Summit Sessions

By the time of President Carter's brief trip to Korea, June 29–July 1, 1979, the political tide at home had swept him into a surprising decision. His political advisers convinced him that he should spend one of his two nights in Korea visiting Camp Casey near the demilitarized zone so that he could

2. The final blow was administered a year and a half later by another American during preparations for President Reagan's summit meeting with Chun Doo Hwan at the White House in February 1980. The Koreans included a reference to the trilateral proposal in the draft communiqué. Secretary of State Haig, whose previous service coincided with hard-line South Korean policies, tossed it out as naive American thinking that might undermine an anticommunist ally. I was unable to convince him that for this summit it was a Korean idea, reflecting considerable evolution in Korean policy since his days in the White House. The Koreans, baffled by the American turnaround, decided not to argue.

mingle with the American troops he had tried so hard to send home. Thus, immediately after being greeted at Kimpo Airport, he helicoptered to Camp Casey with General Vessey. (Not having been included in this high-profile event, I remained in Seoul.) Although this irony of ironies pleased me, it also prevented me from speaking with the president before his first session with President Park, because his scheduled arrival back in Seoul was greatly delayed by fog. Corresponding to my advice to Park, I had intended to urge once again that he begin on a positive note, offering reassurances about security, before taking up human rights and political problems. In any event, I was expecting a highly successful summit meeting following in the grooves of careful, high-level preparation. In reality, fate brought us near disaster.

In a sense both Park, who led off during the first summit session at the Blue House on June 30, and Carter, who responded, handled themselves admirably by the standards of a debating society. They displayed skill and conviction in explaining their respective positions on bilateral, regional, and global concerns. However, Park almost immediately marred his performance as a statesman by delivering a long, schoolmarmish lecture on the North Korean threat. In what I described in my notes as a "very hard sell," he requested *no* further withdrawals of U.S. ground forces, emphasizing their importance not only for South Korea's ability to defend itself against North Korea but also for the security of Japan and all of East Asia. This hard line on the troop issue was exactly what we had tried to deflect, because we knew that Carter did not want to appear to be yielding to Korean pressure. Holbrooke had bluntly warned Ambassador Kim about this in Washington, and I had done so in my conversations with Park as well as with his staff. Whatever Park's reasons for ignoring our advice, his patronizing lecture on Asian security lit a fire within Carter. Harold Brown, who was sitting next to me, whispered that he could tell from Carter's face that he was furious. Indeed he was. I was very worried but did not yet sense disaster.

Deliberately or not, Carter, in turn, rubbed Park the wrong way. He defended his administration's effort to cope with various global and regional threats; he described the U.S.-Korean alliance and defense of Korea as part of our global commitment; and he agreed that the military balance had to be maintained and that the North Koreans should not be given an advantage. Instead of offering Park the assurances he expected on force reductions, Carter argued (quite disingenuously, given his sweeping initial plans) that he had only been planning to withdraw "3,000 of 40,000 troops in 1979" and that to equate the future of South Korea's security to this action, as Park had done, was "not accurate." He also chided Park for allowing North Korea, with its relatively small economy, to have gained such a large military lead over the far larger and far more prosperous South.

None of Carter's advisers felt that it was possible or wise to try to deflect him from this abrasive response to Park's provocation. Never before in numerous summit meetings I had attended in the past had I seen leaders mangle the process of communication the way these two men did that morning. Not only was I alarmed that all our efforts to repair U.S.-Korean relations were about to go down the drain, but, as the senior local U.S. official in Korea, I had a sense of personal failure. While I tried to maintain an even keel, I had a sinking feeling.

The effect of the presidential exchange was manifest during the break; Americans talked to Americans and Koreans to Koreans, with hardly any crossover. Then Park and Carter, each accompanied by a note-taker, met for a private session lasting almost the entire remainder of the Blue House meeting, while the foreign and defense ministers, secretaries of state and defense, national security adviser, Blue House secretary general, ambassadors, and note-takers cooled their heels. The wait was excruciating.

In private the two presidents continued their barbed argument, but they at least managed to conclude the session in a civil manner. President Carter criticized Park's insistence on a complete freeze of troop withdrawals, saying he could not promise this, and he continued to push for higher South Korean defense spending to reduce if not eliminate the military disparity between North and South. Although agreeing to an increased defense effort, Park explained that South Korea needed time to accomplish this and, unlike North Korea, had to operate within the country's economic, social, and political constraints. Finally, Carter brought up human rights, displaying finesse quite absent in the earlier discussion. Acknowledging Park's concern for stability and some useful Korean government actions over the past months, he described human rights as the most serious problem in American attitudes toward Korea, and he asked Park to lift EM-9. Blaming the North Korean threat, Park replied that it "would be difficult" to lift EM-9 in the near future, but that he would heed Carter's advice.

The feisty mood of the morning's meetings provoked an angry skirmish within the American camp. As he was leaving the Blue House, President Carter signaled me to join him, Vance, Brown, and Brzezinski for the ride back to the embassy residence. The president, Vance, and Brown were seated in the rear of the presidential limousine; Brzezinski and I were facing them on jump seats. Giving me virtually no context and clearly venting his anger on me, the president asked me why Park, in the face of North Korea's huge buildup, was unwilling to increase his country's defense expenditure at least to the American level of 6 percent of GDP and why Park was so resistant to some real measure of political liberalization.

I hesitated briefly while trying desperately to grasp the consequences of the summit's failure for our relations with Korea (and, of course, for my own future). The flash of these excited thoughts was replaced by a calm realization that the die was already cast. I told the president quite bluntly that, although Park's own behavior was ill advised, he was obviously upset by Carter's refusal to reassure him about the troop issue. Park was expecting, I said, to hear that the president was prepared to freeze further withdrawal of U.S. ground forces, which was important to both countries in light of North Korean military strength. As for defense expenditures, I pointed out that South Korea was already carrying a very heavy defense burden for a developing country and that in the past we had deliberately refrained from pushing Korea too hard on military expenditures for fear of strengthening the military and their authoritarian tendencies. The president bridled at this and went on to complain about Park's human rights record.

During the trip from the Blue House to the residence, I felt as if I were alone with the president, who deliberately focused his wrath on me. Not long after we came to a stop under the residence portico, with the engine and air conditioner working, Vance and Brown joined the fray, both firmly supporting me (Brzezinski remained silent). This high-level support eased anxieties about my immediate personal situation, but it did not stop the argument. After twenty or thirty minutes of the expanded dialogue, I finally asked the president what he wanted in return for satisfying Park on the troop issue. He suggested two measures: Park's agreement to spend at least 6 percent of GDP on defense and a significant move on human rights. I felt quite relieved and told him that we would do our best to reach an understanding before his departure from Korea. Carter seemed agreeable.

This angry debate, in which the president of the United States wagged his finger at me, did not go unnoticed. It was witnessed by Prime Minister Choi Kyu Ha who was waiting to pay a courtesy call, the foreign minister, Dick Holbrooke, Nick Platt, Bob Rich, the Korean press, and many others who were huddled around, some fiendishly eager to know what had caused this spectacle lasting almost half an hour. Limousines stretched behind us down the driveway and into the street. Observing the scene, Platt said to Holbrooke, "There goes your Korea policy; it's all being decided there now!"

While sharing a sandwich, Secretary Vance, Holbrooke, and I agreed on a strategy of using two parallel approaches to President Park. Vance and

Holbrooke would work through Ambassador Kim Young Shik, their sympathetic and influential contact with Korea in Washington, while I would go to the Blue House Secretary General and Park's interpreter to request "clarifications" of Park's comments on defense expenditures and human rights. The reaction was swift. By mid-afternoon, I got a phone call from Secretary General Kim saying that President Park wanted to see Secretary Vance and me late Sunday morning after Carter's visit to the National Assembly. He told me that we could expect good news, and I immediately informed all concerned that I considered this an authoritative, favorable response from President Park. Vance talked to Carter, and when I passed through the receiving line at the state dinner, I made a point of saying to President Carter, in an exchange interpreted for Park, that we had very good news for him. I also thanked President Park, who was finally displaying some cheer. The mood softened further with the appearance of more than fifty angelic looking children who sang beautifully. Both the president and Mrs. Carter were deeply impressed.

With the mood of the summit greatly improved, the Sunday functions were completely free of the previous day's wrangling. When Vance and I called on him, President Park all but committed himself to spend more than 6 percent of GDP on defense and said that he "understood" President Carter's views on human rights and would take liberalization measures as rapidly as he could. President Carter's farewell courtesy call at the Blue House, which we originally viewed as a time-consuming formality, proved very cordial and quite substantive. I was the only American staff member present. After signaling his satisfaction on Korea's future defense spending, President Carter commented that he could deal "satisfactorily" with the military question when he got back to Washington, keeping in mind Park's request that the second division and Combined Forces Command be kept in Korea. This was the music Park had been waiting so long to hear. Toward the end of the meeting, Carter emphasized the importance of doing something to relieve the human rights situation, which he again described as the most serious problem of our relationship. Noting his intention to move "in a liberal direction," Park promised to do his best to satisfy Carter, even though he could not identify any specific step at the moment.

Despite the initial setback, Park's positive signal to Carter left us feeling that the president had achieved a fair success on human rights during his visit. We were equally pleased with the president's other meetings. At the National Assembly, we won points from the opposition and provoked vociferous complaints from the government side when, with Carter's eager collaboration and physical blocking by Bill Clark, I violated the agreed rules so as to allow a disproportionate amount of time for Kim Young Sam (later to become president of Korea) and his opposition colleagues to talk frankly with Carter. Kim, who had boycotted the state dinner the previous evening, was grateful (even though he thought he should have been given equal time with Park Chung Hee).

The meeting with religious leaders and oppositionists at the residence also was quite successful. President Carter, obviously in his element, indulged his guests with extra time. When Cardinal Kim, clearly annoyed that Reverend Billy Kim had monopolized the president for most of the discussion, excused himself to leave, Carter saw him to the gate, and then, while the remainder of the group waited for a picture, the press seized their opportunity for an unscheduled press conference. I feared that something might unzip in the heady garden atmosphere, but nothing did. Carter was delighted with the attention and offered a number of frank, unrehearsed comments to spice up the bland material provided by our spokesmen.

During the departure motorcade to the airport, the hundreds of thousands of Koreans who had been on hand to greet the president of the United States on his arrival miraculously became millions of cheering citizens.[3] Carter liked it. The turn for the better in their relationship also emboldened Carter to suggest that Park consider conversion to Christianity. I assume that Park masked his real reaction to this startling proposal. After Air Force One was airborne, Park, normally rather dour and distant in manner, looked at me, laughed in appreciation, and gave me a big bear hug, an act of spontaneity that astounded his attendants. Park carried out his part of the tacit bargain a few days later when he sent Korean CIA Director Kim Chae Kyu to see me on July 5 with a message for Carter stating that he would release 180 political prisoners over the next six months. Carter carried out his part of the bargain on July 20 in Washington when he finally announced the freeze on troop withdrawals.

3. The day before on the way in from the airport President Carter stopped the motorcade at Seoul Plaza in the center of the city and in American presidential style got out of his limousine to shake hands with flag-waving Koreans. With visible discomfort, Park Chung Hee followed along, doing the same. Although the crowds that day were relatively small, they were huge in contrast to those in Tokyo, where police, for reasons of security, routinely prevented people from massing along the route. Despite the government's heavy hand in producing Seoul crowds, I suspect that most of the Korean greeters were demonstrating genuine respect for the president of the United States of America, the country so central to their safety and well-being. Some of them, mostly students as I recall, also chanted approval of Brzezinski, who was in the car, probably because he had been played up in the Korean press as an anti-Soviet cold war hawk.

Dashed Hopes

President Park's decision to release a surprisingly large number of political prisoners beginning in July was widely welcomed in Korea, even by the political opposition and some dissident groups, leading to a brief interlude of cautious optimism. It was not enough, however, to narrow the rift between Park and his hard-line opponents, and in the final weeks of his life Park bungled management of a crisis largely of his own making.

After a few weeks of post-summit relaxation, labor activists, students, dissidents, and left-leaning politicians resumed their protest efforts. They posed only a modest threat to Park's regime, but in the summer of 1979 they broadened their appeal, particularly in urban industrial areas, by exploiting widespread concern over the deteriorating economy. Normally Park's major asset, the Korean economy was suffering from relatively high rates of inflation and stalled growth, largely the result of escalated international oil prices as well as ill-advised and excessive investment in heavy and defense industries. In the face of this resumed protest, and perhaps assuming that the United States would once again pressure Park to make further concessions, some normally moderate political leaders got swept up in a rising swell of antigovernment activity. In particular, Kim Young Sam, president of the opposition New Democratic party, became noticeably more militant in the National Assembly and elsewhere, and his boldness was reinforced by his determination not to yield leadership of the opposition to his rival, Kim Dae Jung. Although still handicapped by restrictions on his political activity, Kim Dae Jung was working vigorously behind the scenes, drawing on his semi-martyr stature as a man who had almost defeated Park in the 1971 election and survived a ruthless kidnapping by Koreans in Tokyo.

Confronted by these forces, President Park abandoned his tactics of patience. Rather than indulging his opposition with further concessions, he sided with hard-liners on his staff, cracking down hard on protesters. In a widely reported incident during August, the police crushed a militant strike by clothing workers who had been guided by outside activists and befriended by opposition politicians. Kim Young Sam's high profile in these activities, which resulted in the death of a union worker, infuriated President Park. Exercising singularly bad judgment, he first toyed seriously in late September with arresting Kim, but settled for having him thrown out of the National Assembly on concocted legal grounds—grossly violating democratic and constitutional procedures.

Because we had repeatedly warned Park against such actions, the United

States took the unusual action (among allies) of both publicly criticizing Park's high-handed behavior and publicly recalling me to Washington for "consultations." Meanwhile, Park resorted to even harsher measures, ultimately declaring "partial martial law," to suppress student and worker protests that mushroomed in the economically depressed cities of Masan and Pusan, Kim's home base and center of his political support. In three short months, the gains of the Carter-Park summit had completely dissipated, and Park was widely seen as having lost his touch.

These ugly circumstances faced Park in October when I returned from Washington to Korea with Secretary of Defense Harold Brown and accompanied him to a meeting with the president on October 18, 1979. Under instruction from President Carter, Brown cautioned Park about the costs of political repression. Park, in turn, complained sharply about our public criticism, especially my recall and the publicity stimulated by our background comments to the media. Although Park defended his administration, he seemed uncharacteristically ambivalent about how to deal with the unrest, probably reflecting sharp disagreement among his key advisers. His ambivalence gave me a peculiar feeling. I had never before seen the president in such a state. I myself could see no way out of his troubles except through actions I knew he would never take. In any event, he did not want advice from Secretary Brown or me. The hard-liners were in the ascendancy. Cha Chi Chol, chief of presidential security, seemed to have achieved dominance among the presidential advisers. This infuriated his rival, Kim Chae Kyu, director of the powerful Korean CIA, and apparently triggered Kim's decision to assassinate the president and Cha.

5

President Park's Assassination and Its Aftermath

KOREA WAS QUIET but tense on Friday, October 26, 1979. As a symbol of solidarity for the democratic process, I had invited Kim Young Sam and Political Counselor Clark for lunch at my residence. During the long, dismal discussion, which was briefly drowned out by the overhead din of President Park's helicopters returning from a rural visit, Kim angrily predicted to us that the Korean people would rise up and overthrow Park's regime. I understood his anger and, though skeptical, could not entirely dismiss his sweeping prediction. Korea was indeed undergoing severe turmoil, but I did not sense a mortal threat to the regime.

Later that day, around midnight, Lieutenant General Rosencrans, acting commander of U.S. Forces, Korea, alerted me by phone to signs of unusual activity, and a little later our senior intelligence representative, Bob Brewster, told me of Korean military movements that seemed preparatory to the imposition of martial law. While I was mobilizing key officers to meet at the embassy, General Lew Byong Hion, acting commander of the Combined Forces Command, came with Rosencrans to my residence with the shocking news that President Park had been killed. He said that as a precaution the authorities planned to declare martial law and wanted a U.S. statement warning North Korea not to exploit the situation. Rosencrans, who offered me all possible assistance in coping with the emergency, said that he and his staff had no amplifying details about what had happened to Park, but confirmed that the Korean army had properly notified the United Nations Command of military redeployments and plans to declare martial law before dawn.

Having asked others to join me, I went quickly to the embassy, my head awash with thoughts about the implications of Park's death and the urgent tasks facing us. My most immediate anxieties were to communicate with Washington, contact the emerging civilian and military leadership, and make sure that the embassy, intelligence staff, and U.S. military used all available means to determine whether Park had been killed as a result of a military coup or some other conspiracy. Two other concerns were on my mind: North Korea's potential reaction and the safety of our citizens. Although I favored a vigilant defense posture, I expected North Korea to react cautiously, at least initially. I did not foresee special danger for Americans in Korea, but for their own protection, they obviously needed a candid explanation about the assassination and why martial law was being imposed.

At the embassy, I talked by secure phone with David Aaron of the National Security Council in Washington, D.C. I told him about Park's death, impending martial law, and the Korean desire for a "hands-off" warning to North Korea, which I strongly endorsed. I commented that I feared a coup might be under way, but in my follow-up telegram a little later I refrained from repeating this speculation, which was not corroborated by the scattered intelligence we were beginning to receive. My communications, along with parallel messages from our military and intelligence headquarters, happened to coincide with a White House meeting of key members of the National Security Council, so we got a swift response. The United States issued a firm statement about our treaty commitment to the defense of the Republic of Korea, and as a further precaution, the president ordered an aircraft carrier and airborne warning planes to Korea.

My anxieties eased somewhat after the early morning hours of October 27, because Korean comments and behavior were forming a rather reassuring pattern. Despite General Lew's "top-secret" whisper to me that the president had been killed by "a small group that has been eliminated," there were few signs of a coup or major conspiracy. As far as we could determine, channels of communication were functioning normally, including those for contact between our respective military and intelligence services. Korean military officers showed concern for constitutional procedures and appeared to accept Prime Minister Choi in his new capacity as acting president. Choi, in turn, concurred with the declaration of martial law and with the designation of Army Chief of Staff Chong Seung Hua as the administrator. Koreans praised the firmness and swiftness of the U.S. government's public affirmation of the security commitment as well as the attendant military precautions. Korean military authorities were keeping us informed about the implementation of martial law and seemed fully aware of the need to minimize inconvenience to the civilian population. The general populace was reacting cautiously. As the people learned of Park's death, they seemed skeptical of initial explanations, and surprisingly few grieved for their former leader, but they were subdued. Military deployments in the city provoked no significant protest.

Political Counselor Clark and I called on the acting president as early as we could (7 a.m., October 27) to offer condolences for Park's death and signify U.S. support for Choi as his constitutional successor. Choi and Foreign Minister Park Tong Jin, who accompanied him, showed the trauma of the night's events, but they were quite coherent. Choi emphasized that the military had agreed to a declaration of "partial martial law" (excluding the province of Cheju), leaving him rather than the armed forces ultimately in charge. Although their account of the night's turmoil was fascinating, Choi and Park did not know whether President Park had been killed accidentally, what had motivated Korean CIA Director Kim Chae Kyu, or whether there were other important accomplices.

Over the next few days, we worked with little sleep to find out exactly what had happened on the night of October 26 and why. General Wickham, who returned urgently from a trip abroad, and I both talked at length with General Lew, our principal channel to the Korean army. Bob Brewster and his staff gleaned what they could from Korean CIA officials, obviously demoralized by the behavior of their director, while I talked further with cabinet members who had attended the key meetings.

Basic Events

Within a day or so, the basic events of the assassination became fairly clear. With short notice on October 26 President Park requested Korean CIA Director Kim Chae Kyu, Presidential Security Chief Cha Chi Chol, and Blue House Secretary General Kim Kye Won to dine with him near the Blue House. Before this sudden request, Kim Chae Kyu had previously invited Army Chief of Staff General Chong Seung Hua to dinner for the same evening. Rather than disinvite Chong, Kim asked him to dine in the same complex, with one of his deputies serving as host. Kim then joined the president's dinner. During a heated argument with President Park and Cha Chi Chol about the adequacy of his performance as intelligence chief, Kim Chae Kyu drew a pistol (actually he ran out of ammunition and had to complete his murderous attack with a second pistol) and killed both the president and Cha. Kim Kye Won was left unscathed.

After the assassination, Kim Chae Kyu returned excitedly to his other dinner. Without mentioning his role, Kim told Chong that something terrible had happened to the president and urged Chong to join him at Korean CIA headquarters where they could arrange to declare martial law. Chong insisted instead on returning to his own headquarters, managing to get Kim to accompany him. At the army bunker, Chong convened the military hierarchy, and they were eventually joined there by Acting President Choi Kyu Ha and other cabinet members. Kim hid his guilt for several hours, confessing only after he was finally accused by Secretary General Kim Kye Won, the only other surviving dinner guest.

On hearing early accounts of this meeting, I was puzzled by the near-paralysis manifested at this powerful gathering, but the behavior of the attendees became more understandable as I gradually pieced together the circumstances of their meeting. Only two participants, Kim Chae Kyu and Kim Kye Won, had witnessed the assassination, and neither disclosed the killer—the former for obvious reasons and the latter perhaps out of fear or complicity. Without an explanation from these two, the others present were left to speculate whether the killings were truly accidental, organized by North Koreans, or perpetrated as part of a South Korean conspiracy, large or small. They could not rule out the possibility that some among them in the bunker were part of a plot. Without knowing the balance of power, both civilian ministers and military officers worried about making a wrong move and decided to play it safe. Toward the end, some began to suspect Kim Chae Kyu, because he was so strident in opposing disclosure of Park's death as well as in calling for "full," as opposed to "partial," martial law, which would have put military and security forces in a better position to manipulate the situation. Nevertheless, no one confronted Kim Chae Kyu until Secretary General Kim Kye Won finally identified him as the killer, having inexcusably withheld this critical intelligence for almost four hours.

Progressive disclosure of the bare facts regarding the assassination dampened public speculation about a coup d'état, but it did not erase questions about why Kim Chae Kyu killed Park, whether he had any reason to expect cooperation from the army chief of staff, and why Kim Kye Won had taken so long to identify the assassin. Over the next week or so, I concluded that there were probably no major conspirators linked with Kim and that, even if the killing had been triggered by an irrational surge of anger, Kim Chae Kyu might well have been contemplating treacherous action against Park. As chief of intelligence, he was acutely aware of Park's weakened position and may have believed dementedly that the assassination could be explained to the Korean people and Korean army as a heroic action. Conceivably, he saw himself as a possible successor to Park. This speculation would also explain why Kim tried so hard to enlist the army chief of staff to join him. Yet, whatever Kim may have hoped, it always seemed to me that General Chong Seung Hua's behavior was logical and honorable. Many others shared my opinion about Chong's innocence, and history might have taken quite a different turn if the circumstances of Park's death had been investigated by someone other than the head of the Defense Security Command, Major General Chun Doo Hwan. At the time, I knew that Chun was considered an active Park Chung Hee loyalist, and I also was aware from intelligence sources and journalists that he was carefully reviewing any possibility of collaboration between Kim and Chong. However, I had no reason to anticipate that this ambitious officer would warp the investigation to destroy a senior official and advance his own career. I found it hard to believe that Kim Kye Won, a man whom I had known modestly well over a number of years, was a co-conspirator, but in any event his behavior appeared reprehensible.

America's Role in Park's Demise

Many Koreans, and some Americans, suspected U.S. complicity in President Park's death. The most prevalent view was that U.S. criticism of Park contributed significantly to his demise, but some people entertained more radical ideas. Among Park's critics, for example, numbers of people in dissident, church, and student circles believed, in some cases approvingly, that we had conspired with the assassin, Kim Chae Kyu. From the opposite side of the political fence, some of the late president's conservative cronies worried that we were somehow involved in the killing.

Korean suspicions were fed by ignorance of the facts and the circumstances of Park's death, particularly the mystery of why Kim, one of Park's most trusted lieutenants, killed him and whether other powerful figures were involved, particularly Army Chief of Staff General Chong Seung Hua. For the first few days, the authorities, often quite ignorant themselves, provided nothing except sketchy and sometimes contradictory descriptions, and the first comprehensive report by the Defense Security Command was not released until November 6, ten days after the killing. As a result, Seoul seethed with speculation, which often dovetailed with communist propaganda and gained credence from foreign reporting. A number of Japanese and American papers circulated stories alleging that the U.S. government's criticism of Park had sent a deliberate signal to would-be coup makers and saviors of the nation.

To counter this baseless speculation, we conducted a vigorous educational effort in Seoul and Washington, supplying the facts as we knew them to foreign governments and the public. In contacts with diplomatic colleagues and numerous background briefings for Korean and foreign journalists, we flatly denied charges of conspiracy and candidly reviewed our imperfect knowledge of what had happened. Although these efforts and belated publication of the Korean government's investigative reports checked the spiraling growth of conspiracy theories, the problem did not disappear.

During my briefing for Secretary Vance and other members of the American delegation to Park's funeral in early November, I found Representative Clement Zablocki, chairman of the House International Relations Committee, transfixed by the issue. This important man, with whom I had considerable contact, asked me with a great deal of hostility whether there was "blood on American hands." I assured him there was not, although some of Park's Korean supporters complained that our steady public criticism of his regime contributed to his fall. Explaining that he suspected conspiratorial action on our part, Zablocki went on to ask about possible CIA involvement of which I might be unaware. I told him I was confident that I knew about significant U.S. government activity in Korea, and I reiterated my initial response. Despite firm reinforcement from Vance, our senior intelligence representative, our top military commander, and others, Zablocki said, "I don't believe it," and I think he left Seoul still suspicious.

A few weeks later, I received a military intelligence report stating that Kim Chae Kyu alleged during his interrogation that "a former American ambassador" told him that President Park "had been in power too long." After reviewing the record of my own contacts with Kim and double-checking with Ambassador Sneider about his earlier talks, I brought the issue to Washington's attention, stating flatly that neither Sneider nor I ever had signaled to Kim Chae Kyu or any other Korean that we thought the Park government's days were numbered or that we would condone Park's removal from office. When complaining about human rights and political problems, both of us had always demonstrated continuing U.S. cooperation with the Park government.

Yet I was not surprised that Kim had apparently tried to implicate us or that he, like some other Koreans, might have misconstrued our words and actions to mean that we anticipated the end of Park's rule and would not be unhappy to see him depart the scene. In my message to Washington (see appendix, item 3), I speculated retrospectively that this might have been the way Kim interpreted a conversation he had with Bob Brewster and me on September 26 in the midst of rising tension between Park and his many critics. At the end of a long conversation about this confrontation, Kim asked me for my views about future domestic political developments. I spoke of two concerns. One was the danger of growing political polarization, which could seriously divide the nation and create political instability. The other was the ability of the current constitution and political institutions to ensure a peaceful transition of power. Contrasting the Korean situation to upheaval in Iran, however, I emphasized my optimism about Korea, which had the advantage of domestic strengths and common values. Kim endorsed my judgments as "very accurate" and concluded the discussion by stressing the need to protect political stability.

Brewster and I hoped the conversation with Kim would encourage him to urge Park toward moderation when he next talked with the president, but in my report to Washington, I certainly did not characterize him as a "closet liberal." I commented that Kim probably hoped that the opposition forces would exercise some restraint and that the government would, in turn, continue to be selective in choosing its targets for tough deterrent actions. Would I have answered Kim Chae Kyu differently on September 26 had I sensed traces of hostility toward Park, let alone detected a demented man about to kill his leader? Obviously, I would have, but at the time neither Brewster nor I had the slightest premonition that Kim was about to turn against his longtime benefactor.

Chun Doo Hwan's seizure of power on December 12 resuscitated talk about a conspiracy. In forcibly arresting General Chong Seung Hua, the martial law commander, and army chief of staff, Chun justified his brazen act of insubordination on grounds that Chong refused to cooperate with a Defense Security Command investigation, which had implicated Chong in Park's death. Chun provided no credible evidence to support his allegations and denied access to sources of objective information. Chong was courtmartialed in secret and jailed. The public also was denied an objective review of evidence from the trials of Kim Chae Kyu and Blue House Secretary General Kim Kye Won, the only other official who survived Kim Chae Kyu's gun. The former was tried, found guilty of the assassination, and executed without full public disclosure about his possible motivation. The latter also was tried and jailed for his ambiguous role and failure immediately to identify the assassin.

After Chun's move we were subjected to one more round of misinformation and allegations of American complicity. In my first conversation with Chun Doo Hwan on December 14, I naturally focused on his actions on the night of December 12. Partly as a defensive tactic against my criticism, Chun brought up the assassination, saying he had the impression I had met with the assassin on the day of Park's death. He mentioned persistent rumors in Seoul about American CIA involvement in the assassination as well as reports that Kim Chae Kyu would escape punishment for his crime because of U.S. pressures. I snapped back at him, stating that rumors of the CIA's or my own involvement were completely untrue and mirrored the communist line taken by Radio Pyongyang and Radio Moscow. I corrected his impression about my meeting with Kim Chae Kyu, pointing out that it occurred a month earlier on September 26, not October 26, and I flatly denied that we had in any way worked to obtain leniency for Kim.

Some weeks later, in January 1980, I met with the new director of the Joint Chiefs of Staff who had presided over the initial court martial of Kim Chae Kyu. In response to my blunt question, he replied that during the proceedings Kim Chae Kyu claimed that I had spoken to him about "overturning the *Yushin* system." I carefully explained that I had never said such a thing to Kim Chae Kyu. To reinforce the point, I gave him a brief account of my last conversation with Kim and also asked Bob Brewster to provide the record to Chun Doo Hwan.

These discussions with the military never became public, and the matter was never raised as an issue between the Korean and U.S. governments. The last reference I remember was in March 1980, when Chun Doo Hwan— perhaps in angry reaction to the obstacles we had put in his way—spoke critically about us to some of his information officers, saying that Kim Chae Kyu had implicated the U.S. government in Park's death.

Although informed Koreans seemed skeptical about Chun's charges, few dared challenge him. In effect, the conspiracy theory became official doctrine for seven years until Chong Seung Hua was finally in a position to debunk the trumped-up charges that he had colluded with the Korean CIA director against Park. Far greater problems preoccupied my dealings with Chun, but I had concluded by the time of our December 14 conversation that his case against Chong was contrived. Commenting that I would be shocked to learn that Chong had, in fact, been part of a plot, I stressed the importance of conducting the investigation thoroughly and fairly, which Chun correctly interpreted to mean that they must not resort to torture.

Today I think most Koreans understand that the United States was not involved in a conspiracy with anyone to unseat President Park. More Koreans also appreciate that the U.S. government did not intend its criticism of his regime to be construed as unwillingness to cooperate with Park, and many of them share my view that Park probably sealed his own fate by the excesses of his own actions in the early 1970s. Yet Americans still need to ask themselves whether the sum total of U.S. actions and words unwittingly contributed in a significant way to Park's downfall.

It is fairly apparent from my account of events leading to the assassination that I believe our behavior had this effect, adding rather thoughtlessly to Park's problems and reducing his room for maneuver. Americans paid little attention to how Nixon's Guam Doctrine and the sudden change in China policy would aggravate Park's sense of insecurity. The indiscriminate criticism of Korea that accompanied the Koreagate bribery scandal certainly added to his feelings of paranoia. And Carter's stubborn effort to withdraw U.S. ground forces from Korea in the wake of our retreat from Vietnam amounted to rubbing salt in Park's wounds. I am less certain about American efforts on behalf of human rights, because American intervention often contributed to moderation in Korea, while Park always rebuffed any of our demands that would have jeopardized his continued rule. One possible exception was the summit meeting with Carter and Park's agreement to release many political prisoners. This move, which we warmly welcomed, emboldened Park's opposition and may have accelerated the day of reckoning, but it did not cause Park's death.

Whatever the role played by the United States, there is no question in my mind that Park Chung Hee's assassination stripped Korea of an extraordinary leader. Park came to power illegally by coup d'état. In his public personality, he was dour and utterly lacking in charisma. At his best, he was an enlightened autocrat; at his worst, he was a heavy-handed ruler who was out of touch with political change. Yet Park was a brilliant man with strategic vision. He not only understood what Korea could become but also had the intelligence, skill, and drive to achieve his country's modernization with stunning speed. For all his sins as a tough authoritarian leader, he lived simply, empathized with the common man, and hewed closely to the priorities and values of most Koreans. Unfortunately, these qualities were overshadowed by faulty judgment and paranoia in his final years. When historians strike the balance, I suspect that they will rate Park as the most important Korean leader of modern times.

Basic Considerations in the Evolution of U.S. Policy

Park Chung Hee's assassination presented the United States with difficult choices and a degree of tension that transformed life for me and other senior members of our country team, including General John A. Wickham Jr., who had just replaced General Vessey as commander of the Combined Forces Command, and Bob Brewster, the senior intelligence representative. This will be apparent as I sort through the complicated events that led ultimately to Major General Chun Doo Hwan's becoming president of the Republic of Korea on September 3, 1980.

Beyond the tension pervading our lives, there were more troubling features of the new situation in Korea. Instead of the relatively predictable behavior of the Park regime, we suddenly found ourselves in a volatile environment of uncertainty, where various forces engaged in a protracted test of strength among themselves and sometimes with us. Instead of fairly good intelligence about who was doing what to whom, we now frequently lacked the basic knowledge necessary to make sound decisions. Instead of relatively good access to the governing authorities and people of Korea, we were denied contact with key leaders at critical points, and we were obstructed in our efforts to convey basic factual information as well as American views to the Korean people. In short, we were faced with a new game, many new players, and new rules, often bringing us into a raw and abrasive confrontation with the new authorities.

Although I had experienced other periods of crisis, this was my first as ambassador and senior American official, responsible for making sound decisions in Korea. When events were cascading around us, I must admit there were moments when I had a sense of helplessness or of events reeling out of control. But the feeling never lasted long, because we were under pressure to act swiftly, and, fortunately, I was confident that our superiors would respect our judgment. Thanks to a running dialogue with colleagues in Seoul and Washington, I knew there was widespread support for the guidelines we were using. Although I doubt I ever wrote them down, I remember them well:

—Guard against North Korean efforts to exploit the weakness in South Korea's governing structure,

—Deter fighting between South Korean military units,

—Prevent hostile confrontation between U.S. forces and Korean troops or civilians,

—Communicate with effective authorities but refrain from premature endorsement of self-appointed leaders,

—Support the process of constitutional change, even through a flawed constitution,

—Stress that long-term stability in Korea requires discernible progress toward political liberalization,

—Sustain economic stability,

—Keep in mind that U.S. influence is a marginal factor in Korean domestic struggles, and

—Try not to be on the wrong side of an issue from the majority of the Korean people.

These were conservative principles designed to limit damage, not a prescription for heroic American efforts to force Korean soldiers back to their barracks or to mandate the course of Korea's political development.

After Park's death, the importance of local context became more obvious, and people in Washington were more willing to defer to those of us participating in events in Korea. Typically, but not always, I would learn of an emergency from Wickham or Brewster, and the two or three of us would either meet urgently or consult by phone to decide on initial actions. At the beginning of these tense occasions, we often were alone, but we were soon joined by our staffs, and we always communicated quickly with our civilian and military counterparts at the state and defense departments, the CIA, and the National Security Council. Washington usually approved our recommendations rapidly, rarely trying to second-guess us. Its reactions were generally constructive, often identifying significant issues we overlooked in haste and providing us with critically important information about reactions in the executive branch as well as Congress.

The inherent importance of Korean stability combined with strategic developments elsewhere gave American officials in Seoul a rather long tether from Washington headquarters. Hard-line Soviet behavior around much of the globe as well as the Iranian hostage crisis preoccupied the Carter administration, which, in contrast to the cantankerous struggles over human rights and troop withdrawals, now wanted to minimize tension with Korea. President Carter himself was no longer straining to change our policy.

The phases of U.S. policy that I am about to describe amount to a painful accommodation to hard realities in Korea—more or less paralleling the grudging way the Korean people themselves adjusted to a new regime. President Park's assassination left governing control within the same group that had supported him, and Chun cunningly seized power within that group. Neither the Korean army nor any major segment of the Korean people was prepared in 1979–80 to contest the power Chun was able to array around himself. Although the United States did not prevent Chun's accession to the presidency, we were given credit in many quarters for consistent criticism of political repression, for admonitions that helped to moderate the regime's behavior, and for efforts to educate the new rulers to the world around them. In the process, the United States earned much respect among Koreans, even though this positive reaction was confused or muffled for many years by emotions and misinformation that mushroomed after the Kwangju uprising in the spring of 1980.

Embassy Seoul's voluminous communications with Washington over the course of this accommodation provide an accurate record of U.S. behavior, and they also convey some sense of the premises underlying our decisions. But they do not spell out some of the most basic considerations that governed our policy, nor do they give today's reader an adequate grasp of the practical constraints under which we were operating. Highlighting some of these issues at this point may clarify the discussion in subsequent chapters.

First and most important, the big levers of influence theoretically available to the United States were blunt instruments. The most powerful was the American commitment to the security of the Republic of Korea. If the United States had significantly compromised this treaty commitment in trying to force a domestic change in South Korea, we would have risked inviting North Korean adventure, reminiscent of our ambivalent actions on security before the Korean War. A threat to renew the troop withdrawal scheme in such circumstances would have run similar risks and would have antagonized the majority of the South Korean people. Using American military forces to block insubordinate Korean units would have posed completely unacceptable military risks, given the relative size of Korean forces, and it would likely have invited a nasty nationalistic backlash by angry Korean soldiers and citizens. Cutting South Korea's access to American economic credits or threatening to disregard its sensitivities in order to normalize our relations with North Korea would have punished the South Korean people for the sins of the coup makers.

In an effort to ward off military encroachment into the civilian sphere, the United States consistently supported Korea's interim constitutional leader,

President Choi Kyu Ha. This was a correct, almost inescapable, feature of American policy, yet it also meant that Choi was often the arbiter of what we should and should not do. The president was an honorable and intelligent man, a career bureaucrat with little experience in the rough world of politics, whom Park had selected to grace the office of prime minister in a powerful presidential system. When Choi was suddenly thrust near the center of power, his cautious instincts and conservative tendencies dominated his actions. Although often more courageous than he was given credit for, he instinctively shied away from bold challenges. Perhaps wisely, he was unwilling to enlist popular support against Chun, and although he deeply appreciated our support, he was uncomfortable with our efforts to steer events in the military or civilian sector.

Despite these powerful restraints, there were times when our frustration and anger led us to review the case for radical action. Not infrequently, we played around the edge of the abyss, for example by warning Chun Doo Hwan that his actions might undermine the willingness of the American people to sustain the defense commitment and force presence. But there was a virtually complete consensus among American officials in Seoul and Washington that pulling the big levers would endanger our most basic interests. During the Kwangju crisis, for example, President Carter voiced this consensus with a note of realpolitik when he told an American television audience forthrightly that human rights issues had to be subordinated to security concerns.

Another sometimes humiliating restraint on our actions was inadequate intelligence of tactical developments. On many occasions, we were caught by surprise and crippled by basic ignorance. When General Wickham and I arrived at the eighth army bunker on the evening of December 12, we both suspected that a coup was under way, but we could not identify the perpetrators or the forces they controlled. We suspected that Chun was the leader, but he cleverly refused direct contact with us until his forces were in effective control. My parallel effort to communicate urgently with President Choi also was obstructed for several hours.

Given our ignorance of military loyalties and the balance of forces until the deed was largely done, the only sensible course for us was to warn against the grave danger to the nation of fighting within the Korean army. Through skillfully organized surprise and clever suborning of key officers in units dominating the Seoul region, Chun outwitted his superiors and presented the United States with a fait accompli that could only be undone at very high risk.

A concomitant restraint on our behavior was the new regime's abusive control of the media, which allowed it to distort the Korean people's understanding of what we were doing. Apart from his tendency to paint me and American policy in unflattering terms, Chun Doo Hwan on more than one occasion completely distorted the nature of our policy when talking to journalists, telling them, for example, that we supported the extension of emergency martial law and the arrest of political leaders when, in fact, I had vigorously protested both events in meetings with President Choi and the martial law commander. The most severe instance was the disinformation about us purveyed during the Kwangju uprising. The spread of lies about us in this incendiary situation had disastrous effects on attitudes toward the United States in the Cholla region. To be sure, we had some limited means of communicating with our American citizens and members of the Korean elite, but it would have been hard to mount even a cautious challenge against Chun in conditions where we were denied access to the mass of the Korean people.

These considerations did not leave us helpless, because it was transparent to General Chun and most of his group that the Korean people, including soldiers and officers of the Korean army, cared about the attitude of the United States and did not want to jeopardize the relationship with us. Koreans had a visceral desire for American approval or at least American understanding, and this need provided us considerable leverage.

The Immediate Aftermath of Park's Death

Even though weary from lack of sleep for thirty-six hours, I forced myself to send a message to Washington on the night of October 27, 1979, assessing the situation after President Park's assassination and suggesting broad policy guidelines. I pointed out that, although the assassination was a stunning event and a new source of great uncertainty, it was not revolutionary. The key players, I wrote, "are still the previous establishment forces—above all the military who, even if we can encourage them toward more liberal directions, have not changed their spots and comfort in working within an authoritarian structure." I assumed that the governing structure would hold together short of chaos, in part because of the North Korean threat, but I worried that the political opposition "will almost surely seek more reform than they are likely to achieve, and if they push too hard too soon, we may see a rapid return to political polarization," possibly triggering a coup.

Although ignorant of who would come out on top in this contest and pessimistic about early political progress, I urged that we adopt a benign posture toward the new regime—providing reassurance against the threat of the north, urging observance of the constitutional process, working gently through all channels toward political liberalization, while avoiding public criticism and punishing actions—at least until the new leaders blotted their copybook (see appendix, item 2).

Reflecting these views, I conveyed a balanced message in my first extended private conversation with Foreign Minister Park on October 31. I told him I thought it terribly important that the acting president promptly consult various elements of society, including the political opposition and even some of the dissidents. After such consultation, the Korean government could then indicate its determination, whatever the decision on specific constitutional steps, to introduce in an orderly way a greater degree of political participation into the government and to allow freer expression. Park reacted positively to this formulation, and over the next few weeks I became progressively more optimistic as we discovered more and more Koreans who favored revision and liberalization of the harsh *Yushin* Constitution. Although officials were more cautious than the general populace, they seemed to appreciate that some political relaxation was necessary for Korea's stability. The cautious acting president and even senior military officers also appeared ready to take some careful first steps in that direction.

I also was reassured to find that Washington agreed with my policy recommendations. President Park's funeral, held November 3, 1979, to which we sent a distinguished delegation headed by Secretary Vance, provided an early occasion to demonstrate our posture and formulate specific objectives under the rubric of "broadening the base" of the government. Dick Holbrooke, who was already in Asia at a conference in the Philippines, came a day early and had a good talk with the foreign minister. On his way to Seoul, Vance commented publicly that we hoped political growth in the Republic of Korea would be "commensurate with economic and social progress." In Seoul he assured the foreign minister and the acting president that the United States would reinforce Korea's external security, refrain from public criticism, and offer realistic advice "when asked." He strongly urged that Choi's government move in a liberalizing direction and offered to encourage moderation among opposition forces.

Without waiting to be asked, we used various occasions over the next few weeks to identify what we considered the principal challenges facing the government: constitutional reform, cancellation of EM-9, freeing of political prisoners, reconvening of the National Assembly, easing of censorship, and ending of martial law. We argued that Korean citizens would be disappointed by a dilatory approach to these matters; opposition forces would surely cause trouble if they concluded that Choi was simply perpetuating Park's authoritarian regime. Hoping to ease the polarization of Korean society, we pressed Choi hard to provide his fellow countrymen with a reasonably prompt schedule for political change as well as to consult a broad spectrum of political figures.

Throughout this period, we paralleled this advice to the government with a countermessage to the wide circle of our political contacts. We encouraged all groups to exercise patience and give President Choi some running room in his effort to ease political controls. In particular we sought out opposition leaders and influential figures in dissident circles and warned them that excessive demands and aggressive protest activity would reinforce hard-line tendencies in the government's apparatus of control rather than advance the cause of democracy.

This American advice was offered politely and discreetly on both sides of the political fence, but it was, nevertheless, a rather high-pressure operation. On the government side, we used multiple channels to convey our message. I had two long, very frank meetings with President Choi (one with no one else present), many private sessions with Foreign Minister Park, who was part of Choi's inner circle, miscellaneous talks with a variety of military officers, and one brief but highly focused discussion with General Chong, the martial law administrator, during a social affair at Wickham's home. General Wickham paralleled my efforts through meetings with the minister of defense and the military hierarchy, while Bob Brewster met with Chun Doo Hwan and other security and intelligence officials. Given the influence of the military and security groups, we deliberately informed the minister of defense and his senior generals about our contacts with civilian officials as well as key politicians. I told the president why we were doing this and kept him generally informed of our efforts in other channels. Understandably, he did not want me dealing directly with military and security officials about political matters, but he seemed appreciative of our missionary efforts to soften resistance among hard-line elements over whom he had little control.

My own sense of the popular mood in Korea was that Choi would find a substantial reservoir of goodwill so long as he demonstrated enough resolve. Rural people and many of the laborers were known to be conservative, but they also were responsive to firm leadership and did not pose a real obstacle to liberalization. At the same time, fair numbers of students, labor activists, and religious dissidents were quite radical in their demands and hardened by years of struggle. However, the extremism of their demands and aggressiveness of their tactics tended to isolate them. My impression, right or wrong, was that large numbers of urban Koreans, particularly the growing middle class, appeared ready to support Choi if he moved to ease controls.

I worried that the acting president's instinctively cautious approach would undermine his credibility as an interim leader capable of reform. Choi acknowledged the danger, but he agonized over his political weakness. He told me that he needed to move deliberately, in piecemeal fashion toward a consensus. If the people were calm, he would move further; if students or opposition leaders got too far out of line, he would have to pull back. This was an understandable stance for a very conservative man, motivated less by his democratic instincts than by a rational awareness that urban Koreans craved some degree of political relaxation. In any event, Choi's sudden and unexpected elevation to leadership left him with little power to shift the authoritarian style of the regime he inherited from Park. Time after time, I found him unwilling to use his authority to run a real risk and actively push for change.

Even so, I was pleased by President Choi's first statement to the Korean people on the state of the nation, made on November 10, because he addressed the central political issue and committed himself to moving toward liberalization:

> In parallel with our economic and social growth, we ought to promote progress in the political field. I understand this is what the majority of the people desire today . . . I believe the new president to be elected ought not to exhaust the remaining tenure of office stipulated in the current constitution but [should], at the earliest possible date, sound out a wide spectrum of opinion of all sectors and layers of society, amend the constitution, and conduct elections in compliance with the amended constitution.

The foreign minister told me that this formulation reflected our advice, and he added that the government was going to hold the presidential election in early December, well before the ninety-day deadline stipulated in the constitution, as well as lift EM-9 at an early date. The government expected that the people would welcome the combination of these actions.

While welcoming this start, we complained that it was flawed in two respects: opposition leaders were not consulted in advance, and the program did not specify the reforms being contemplated or offer a sense of when they would be implemented. Beginning with my own and, even more emphatically, with Secretary Vance's conversations, we had stressed the crucial importance of Choi's consulting opposition forces in hopes of engaging their cooperation, at least for a limited period of time. In my own talks with various figures, I also argued strongly for identifying specific reforms, together with a schedule for implementing them. In answer to Choi's concern about committing himself publicly to loosen controls and then running into unrest stirred up by students and others, I suggested that he qualify his promised schedule by saying that the timing of implementation would depend on public cooperation and the maintenance of public order. In my boldest—almost brazen—bit of advice, I encouraged Choi to use the occasion of his inauguration (as the "interim" as opposed to "acting" president) to state that he would only serve about one year. If more than one year were required to revise the *Yushin* Constitution, the extension should, I said, be agreed through consensus of the government and opposition parties.

These efforts were not productive, and Choi proceeded in a most deliberate fashion. He postponed meeting with the principal opposition figure, Kim Young Sam, until almost two weeks after he had publicly announced his reform program; he avoided publicizing the specifics of his reform plans; and he chose not to declare a specific limit on his presidential term (in part for fear of becoming a lame duck). Yet progress was made. Over the next few months, many political prisoners were released; EM-9 was lifted; censorship was eased; political activity was allowed to resume; and schedules were set for reopening the schools that had been closed under martial law on October 27.

Choi's task was complicated by the desire of Korea's foremost political leaders to be front and center while the nation selected Park's successor. The requirement under the *Yushin* Constitution for an indirect presidential election within ninety days of Park's incapacitation further complicated matters. In mid-November, the collective leadership around Choi Kyu Ha decided to hold the rather pro forma election on December 6, 1979, with Choi running for president and serving until the constitution was revised—in effect extending his service as a neutral interim leader. The United States assumed that most Koreans would go along with this arbitrary but realistic arrangement. We refrained from criticism, focusing instead on the importance of lifting martial law and revising the constitution so that a free direct election could be held within a reasonable period of time.

However, Kim Jong Pil, perhaps the strongest candidate ultimately to succeed Park, threw a monkey wrench into the works by threatening to contest Choi for the interim job. This veteran insider, who had served Park in a number of capacities, including prime minister, had already grasped control of the government party in the National Assembly, and, if he were able to be elected under the old constitution, he would have a great advantage in continuing under a new constitution. The collective leadership centered around Choi, particularly the military hierarchy, objected to Kim's taking over in this fashion and used its muscle to have him withdraw. Choi was duly elected president on December 6, but Kim Jong Pil remained a major complication in his plans.

Two less conservative leaders added to Choi's difficulties. Kim Young Sam, head of the main opposition party, almost immediately demanded publicly that Choi agree to revise the constitution within the ninety days before a new election was required. Rebuffed in this impractical demand, he then pressed for constitutional revision and elections by the fall of 1980, a much more reasonable position, despite the undesirable feature of a deadline. However, Kim also pushed to have the National Assembly control the drafting of the new constitution, something Choi was not willing to accept, and he maintained an impatient public drumbeat for immediate easing of political restrictions. Privately, I found him more reasonable, and he eventually adopted more realistic public positions, but at this early stage Kim Young Sam appeared to believe that a confrontational position, just to the right of the dissident community, would help him retain leadership of the main opposition party, thus enhancing his chance to succeed Park.

Kim Young Sam's calculations were obviously influenced by expectations that his rival, Kim Dae Jung, would soon be freed to compete for leadership of the opposition. Although Kim Dae Jung's political rights were not yet restored, he had been "partially" freed from house arrest for some time, and after Park's death he was effectively back in the political arena. He was behaving carefully, but obviously positioning himself with various groups, among other things criticizing the United States for being "soft" on President Choi Kyu Ha. At the time, few people felt he would ever be successful in a quest for the presidency, but no one doubted his ambition to run.

I was not particularly surprised by the behavior of these political leaders, who at least understood the danger of provoking the military/security authorities and demonstrated some willingness to be patient during the transitional period. For me, the greatest spoilers were the dissidents, consisting mostly of radical religious, labor, and student groups. Some of them barely paused to reflect on what had happened. They demanded immediate revocation of the *Yushin*-era political controls, complained about martial law and censorship, and generally carried on as though Park Chung Hee were still in the Blue House. Some student activists, instead of welcoming the impending return of colleagues previously barred from the universities for EM-9 violations, agitated for punishment of academic authorities who co-operated with the Park regime. More generally, these groups complained about martial law and lack of political progress. They organized demonstrations in violation of martial law and, when deterred by the threat of arrest, used subterfuge to get around the regulations. Government authorities initially used a rather light hand in dealing with them, but as they became more strident began arresting them. Ironically, arrests of these disaffected people took place almost simultaneously with the release of hundreds of detainees held under EM-9.

The American and international human rights communities, while disturbed by this confrontation, generally refrained from identifying overly with the radical cause. Less for reasons of sympathy than to prevent a tear in the fabric of public order, my colleagues and I made a substantial effort to urge both sides toward restraint. We talked to dissident leaders themselves, but we focused primarily on moderate intermediaries who enjoyed the confidence of the disaffected, urging that protesters give Choi a chance to deal with a complicated problem. Wickham and Brewster repeatedly asked their counterparts not to overreact or let a small fraction of the Korean people obstruct progress toward liberalization. In many conversations with officials and politicians, my embassy colleagues and I argued that the government should not be overly sensitive to criticism and should instead bolster moderate elements by explicitly declaring its intention to cancel EM-9, release political prisoners, and end martial law if the public would cooperate in maintaining public order. I made the same points to General Chong Seung Hua.

Although no serious incidents occurred during this period, it was apparent to me that martial law authorities were losing patience. They frequently voiced their frustration about the radicals, the number of arrests increased, and tensions rose several notches when General Chong Seung Hua made critical remarks within earshot of reporters about the American role as well as threatened to lead a coup if the "communist" Kim Dae Jung were ever to come to power. But military officers, including Chong himself, still professed to support liberalization of the *Yushin* regime.

At the end of November 1979, about a month after Park's assassination, I sent a second assessment to Washington, stating that the Republic of Korea was "in much better shape than many Koreans and outsiders would have assumed." I praised thoughtful Koreans for being quick to grasp the central issue facing them: "how to liberalize the structure fast enough to satisfy popular expectations but steadily enough to avoid the danger of over-reaching themselves or scaring military elements into a military takeover." I was relatively confident that the government would lift EM-9, free political prisoners, including Kim Dae Jung, ease censorship, and probably end martial law so long as it was not faced with widespread or violent unrest.

Ducking firm predictions, I speculated that Choi might preside fairly successfully over a period of constitutional bickering, which might be more or less tolerable to the opposition, or that his government might proceed so ineffectively that the opposition would be drawn into greater and greater confrontation by popular dissatisfaction. I added, quite incorrectly it turned out, that a military coup "is not very likely unless and until there is a substantial deterioration in public order." More presciently, I complained that, although I was more optimistic about the republic's political future than during the last months of Park's rule, I was also more discouraged than two weeks earlier, primarily because of the extreme wing of the dissident/opposition "who seem unwilling to experiment with compromise, continue to lean into the wind when it may be no longer blowing, and characterize the situation to their following in ways that may prove a self-fulfilling prophecy." Of course, unbeknown to me, my American military colleagues, and almost all Koreans, a coup was being planned for reasons more selfish than the nation's welfare.

One good by-product of this period, which came to such a bitter and disappointing end the night of December 12, 1979, was the evolution of well-coordinated American behavior in Seoul and Washington. President Park's assassination jolted us into an alert mode, and the intervening events until December 12 provided us with a kind of dry run for the much more difficult challenges we were going to face. In the process, I had impressive support in Washington as well as Seoul.

Although we enjoyed firm support from Washington, I recall three relatively minor issues during this period where Washington was more exercised about events than those of us nearer the source of action.

First, Holbrooke and others in Washington were apparently more worried than we in Seoul that opposition and disaffected elements would write off the new government and take to the streets within a relatively short period of time. Thus he reacted more strongly than I to President Choi's failure to consult any opposition leaders before announcing his plans to revise

Of the many people in Washington responsible for constructive support of our work in Seoul, two individuals controlled my lifeline. One was Bob Rich, the extraordinarily effective Korean country director, who always exercised good judgment and dealt efficiently with the tasks we dumped on him. The other was my immediate boss, Dick Holbrooke, whose grasp of the Korean issue and deft political skills helped to ensure the support of senior officials and, if necessary, the president himself. Holbrooke was very effective in his relationships with Secretary Vance and Deputy Secretary Christopher, and, assisted by Rich, he worked almost as impressively with the Defense Department and White House, usually through Morton Abramowitz, Michael Armacost, and Nicholas Platt, top-notch foreign service officers seconded to those institutions.

Without an understanding commander of U.S. Forces, Korea, I would have been severely handicapped, since political events so often forced my intrusion into military matters. John Wickham—a smart, youngish, four-star general known as a modernizer and respected for his combat command in Vietnam—accepted me as the senior U.S. official in Korea (except for military operations and command). He conformed to agreed policy, did not play games or undercut me, and, on the contrary, went out of his way to boost my standing with Korean military officers. I, in turn, reciprocated by including him in my inner circle. Wickham and I were acutely aware that relations between U.S. ambassadors and military commanders in chief had sometimes been fractious in the past. We both worked hard to keep ours cooperative.

I was equally well served by our senior intelligence representative, Robert Brewster, who fell ill and died not long after the crisis. Brewster was one of the most cooperative individuals with whom I was associated during my foreign service career. Not only straight in the way he worked with me, he was savvy and adept in his dealings with the new players on the scene, including Chun Doo Hwan.

Three embassy officers played a crucial role in our crisis management, helping me think through policy dilemmas, debating with me, extending my reach during emergencies, substituting for me when I was absent, and keeping the embassy running efficiently through remarkably difficult times. I had strong deputies, initially Thomas Stern, who orchestrated the complex Carter-Park summit meeting, and later John C. Monjo, to whom I constantly turned for help during the tumult. Stern, Monjo, and I received much of our hands-on education about the Korean scene from our sensible and tough-minded political counselor, William Clark Jr. All of these officers worked harmoniously with their American military and intelligence counterparts, contributing significantly to the comfort of my relations with Wickham and Brewster.

the constitution, and he urged that I, together with Wickham, mount an even more vigorous campaign to educate Choi and the generals about the dangers of being too cautious. We did so through our respective channels, even though we did not believe that large-scale street protests were an imminent threat. Our systematic missionary work probably contributed to some helpful government decisions over the next few weeks, but it also created resentment, especially in military circles, so much so that I informed Holbrooke on December 7 that as a result of careful review with Wickham and Brewster I was temporarily going to tone down delivery of political messages through military channels.

Second, the State Department usefully reminded me on November 22 that I should be doing something about reestablishing embassy contact with Kim Dae Jung. Throughout his house arrest, the embassy had kept in touch with Kim by telephone, and we frequently pressed officials about full restoration of his political rights. In my response to Washington, I said that I expected Kim, who was still under partial house arrest, to be completely freed in the near future. I promised to have one of our political officers visit him right away as well as to call on him myself once he was completely free from house arrest. Although Kim's political rights were not fully restored until March 1, 1980, I met with him for the first time on December 12, 1979, the same day Chun made his move. From then on, I made a point of inviting Kim to social functions at my residence along with senior civilian and military leaders.

Third, Holbrooke made a bold suggestion to me on December 4 designed to discourage Korea's disaffected community from the unruly behavior that jeopardized prospects for democratic evolution. He proposed that I send the Christian dissidents a clear message from the U.S. government, possibly by way of moderate church leaders. I was to say that we considered their street demonstrations a throwback to an earlier era and a threat to democratic progress. In short, they could not count on American government support as in times past; although we favored the lifting of martial law and EM-9, we did not favor direct challenges to martial law at this time. Before delivering this message, I was to approach the civilian and military hierarchy and tell them what I was about to do and stress that our willingness to speak this way to troublemakers was linked directly to the commitment of the Korean leadership to move toward liberalization.

In asking for my reaction, Holbrooke said that he recognized this was a "delicate operation." Politely, I told him of my very serious reservations. I reminded him that we were already doing much of what he proposed. As

Vance had promised President Choi, we had directly warned the dissidents against provocation as well as sought help from moderate Christian leaders in hopes of getting a respite from dissident challenges to the ruling authorities. Not only had we told the government in advance of these actions, but we had also reported back to them after making our approaches. We had stopped short, however, of threatening the dissident leaders with nonsupport or formalizing our Faustian bargain with the government. If we were to do so, I doubted that the moderate leaders would continue to help us and suspected that the Christian dissidents would tell American human rights activists that they had been sold out by American officials in Seoul. Holbrooke accepted my point, and the proposal was dropped.

In the year-long crisis that followed Park's death, American influence was probably at its high point during this seven-week period before General Chun's coup on December 12. At a moment of great uncertainty, we provided South Koreans with a basic sense of security—economic as well as military—without which they would have felt dangerously exposed. Moreover, many, if not most, Koreans associated the United States with the general political direction in which they wished to go. During these few weeks, the radicals on the left were unable to generate much public sympathy for their impatience, while the military/security establishment on the right was open to some cautious experimentation with political relaxation. The United States was very active in its efforts to enhance the liberal trend and used quite sophisticated tactics. We restrained ourselves from public criticism, but we continued to advance our views privately with considerable vigor. The occasional boldness of our advice was tempered by the discreet manner in which it was offered.

Could Korea's experiment in democracy possibly have succeeded in the circumstances of 1979–80? Could President Choi have isolated the radical and disaffected elements of Korean society who were so hardened by years of struggle against Park that they could not appreciate opportunity for change? Could he have kept a tight rein on hard-liners on the right, especially the security apparatus that instinctively exaggerated all threats to the regime, and if so, would the "three Kims" have agreed to cooperate with him? We will never know, because General Chun Doo Hwan undermined the democratic experiment, beginning on the night of December 12, 1979.

6

Chun Doo Hwan's Coup d'État and Choi Kyu Ha's Interim Presidency

CHUN DOO HWAN'S power grab within the Korean army on December 12, 1979, abruptly transformed the relatively benign atmosphere of the preceding seven weeks and severely strained U.S.-Korean relations. The stealth and insubordination with which a faction of army officers usurped military leadership shattered the sense of trust girding the security relationship; the deliberate blockage of operational intelligence and communications limited the ways in which the United States could respond to a situation affecting its vital national interests; and blatant manipulation of the media began to distort popular Korean perceptions of American policy, causing long-term damage to the American image in the case of Kwangju. The implication for security was an immediate worry. The threat to constitutional rule and democratic evolution was deeply disturbing.

U.S. policymakers were torn between, on the one hand, a powerful instinct to threaten (and if necessary apply) major sanctions against the new power holders and, on the other hand, realistic awareness that heavy sanctions might not be effective and posed great risks to American political as well as security interests in Korea. The outcome of this dilemma was an inherently contradictory policy: a vigorous effort to sustain political liberalization and civilian rule combined with a willingness to deal, where necessary, with the new military authorities through normal channels. Despite a few months of cautious optimism in early 1980, this approach failed to prevent Korea's new military strongman from encroaching progressively into the political realm.

A Coup in All but Name

Early in the evening of December 12, General Wickham called me about a sensitive development that he could not discuss on the regular phone. I agreed to meet him as quickly as possible at his headquarters in Yongsan, driving my personal car and managing to get through the Namsan tunnel just before troops sealed it off to public traffic. I joined Wickham at about 7:30 p.m. in the eighth army bunker, where he told me about reports of unusual troop movements and shots fired. Both of us sensed that a coup was under way, but neither we nor General Lew, Wickham's four-star Korean deputy at the Combined Forces Command, had reliable clues about what was happening. Events seemed to center around the Defense Security Command, suggesting that the commander, Major General Chun Doo Hwan, was involved. I tried to get in touch with him through Bob Brewster, our regular liaison, but it soon became clear that Chun did not want to talk to us. I was also given the runaround in my efforts to get hold of President Choi.

The crisis lost its abstract quality when the minister of defense, Roh Jae Hyun, and the chairman of the Joint Chiefs of Staff, General Kim Chong Huan, together with a small entourage, barged in on us around 9 p.m., seeking refuge and using our facilities to check the availability and loyalty of forces supposedly under their control. Wickham ordered a substantial reinforcement of the American unit guarding the bunker, because we could hear sporadic small arms fire in the vicinity, and tension was building rapidly.

Wickham, Brewster, and I—along with the Korean military establishment—were all caught by complete surprise that night, victims of a painful intelligence failure. Wickham had received a report in early December of unrest among eleventh- and twelfth-class graduates of the Korean Military Academy. When he mentioned it to Minister Roh and General Lew, they dismissed it as a rumor. About the same time, a U.S. intelligence source learned of plotting by General Chun and others for some kind of action, but no American official received the report until the day after Chun's move. What we learned over the next few days was that a cabal of officers secretly organized by Chun had a careful plan to seize control of the Korean army. The cabal consisted of about forty officers mostly from the Kyongsan area in southeastern Korea and graduates of the eleventh, twelfth, and thirteenth classes of the Korean Military Academy, the first to receive the full four-year curriculum. These officers—too young to have fought in the Korean War, but in some cases having served in Vietnam—not only tended to discount the quality of older officers who received abbreviated training but also resented the way their elders monopolized senior jobs. Minister Roh, for example, had been occupying a top position as a minister or four-star army officer for twenty years.

Nine officers within the group, who constituted an inner core, were longstanding friends, classmates, or workmates. Most, like their mentor Park Chung Hee, were natives of the southeastern city of Taegu, and many, including Chun himself, were known within the army as Park loyalists. Although they may have more or less shared Chun's suspicion that Martial Law Commander and Army Chief of Staff Chong Seung Hua was part of a conspiracy to assassinate Park, I believe from the design of their plan as well as from what some of them later told me that they were motivated primarily by "young turk" sentiment and by ambition to advance their careers. In Chun's own case, knowledge that Chong considered him a troublemaker and was apparently planning to exile him to a distant post may have prompted him to step up the timing of his insubordination. In any event, Chun brimmed with ambition to advance himself within the army, and I strongly suspect that even grander thoughts were already going through his cunning mind.

Whatever the exact nature of their appeals, Chun's group successfully enlisted enough corps and division commanders to join them as well as to get brigade and battalion commanders in other units to turn on their leaders, thus creating a sufficient mass to seize control in Seoul—and throughout the country—within less than twelve hours and without extensive fighting. In the process, they effectively immobilized the Capital Security Command, blocked all tunnels as well as the heavily trafficked bridges over the Han River, and—completely disregarding the authority of the Combined Forces Command—brought an armored regiment from the front-line Ninth Division down to Seoul. Concern about how their actions would affect relations with the United States was apparently downplayed. Similarly, the cabal displayed little observable concern about the possible effect on North Korean behavior. If they had any anxiety about these matters, they probably overcame it on the assumption that they could present the United States and North Korea, as well as the Korean government and Korean public, with a fait accompli.

The pretext to initiate this sweeping act of insubordination was Chun's assertion that his official investigation of Park's assassination required interrogation of the martial law commander. Carefully arranged to catch everyone by surprise, Chun sent forces to fetch Chong Seung Hua around 6:30 p.m. on December 12, and when Chong's bodyguards opened fire, reinforcements arrested Chong after a firefight.

Capture of the martial law commander was almost complete before Chun went to the president's office to seek Choi's approval for his extraordinary action. Choi refused unless the minister of defense concurred, creating a stalemate since the minister had fled to our bunker. By phone Chun urged Minister Roh to join him with the president to discuss the matter, but Roh refused for fear of being ambushed. Meanwhile, in hopes of minimizing the possibility of combat, he accepted Wickham's firm advice to hold off ordering any troop countermovements into Seoul at least until daybreak. After more communications with individuals of dubious loyalty and for reasons never clear to me, Minister Roh and General Kim decided, against Wickham's and my advice, to leave the bunker and go to their headquarters at the Ministry of National Defense, where they were trapped by insurgent forces who captured the building in a firefight during the early morning hours. A few hours later, the minister met with the new prime minister and then the president to give his "concurrence" in Chong's arrest. With constitutional form preserved, under duress, President Choi finally gave Chun what he wanted.

Perhaps Minister Roh and President Choi will some day clarify their decision to yield to Chun on that fateful morning. In the absence of authoritative information, I assume that they did so from a realistic calculation that they had been cornered by (at least locally) superior forces. As conservatives, I doubt it ever crossed their minds to appeal for popular support against the usurpers. An appeal for a military or civilian countermove at that point would have been extremely risky, if not quixotic. However, both men could have complicated Chun's plans if they had simply refused to concur.

Unaware of Chun's plan and ignorant of who was doing what to whom, we were forced to be cautious and defensive during the night of December 12. We used every conceivable source to discover what was going on, and we struggled to communicate with all elements suspected of involvement. Our message was simple: do not allow serious fighting between South Korean military units, which might embolden North Korea, and do not disrupt the civilian government and plans for political progress. I admired Wickham's handling of the situation, particularly his stalling for time before moving any counterforces into Seoul, and his demonstration of outrage over violations of the command structure. My own manner was calm, but my mind was racing while trying to determine our best course, given our ignorance and the studied effort of the coup forces to keep us at arm's length. The possibility of major unit confrontations within the Korean army was particularly alarming to me because it could lead to great bloodshed and weaken deterrence against North Korea.

Although my thoughts did not suddenly come together in neat focus, I remember concluding fairly quickly that we should concentrate on damage control; that is, we should use our obviously limited influence to underscore the dangers of a major military confrontation or serious damage to the political process. Subconsciously, I was conditioned by my rather critical reaction to our handling of Park Chung Hee's coup eighteen years earlier. I was honestly worried that night—far more than at any previous time—about North Korean adventurism, but in my contacts with Korean generals and officials I allowed myself to exaggerate this danger in hopes it would have a restraining effect. The other instrument of restraint was to warn all parties about jeopardizing continued American support. Again I was willing to indulge in some exaggeration, because we could not hope to influence events without brandishing a serious warning to all concerned. From our running discussions, I knew that Wickham and others in the bunker generally agreed with these views, and once we were able to convey some sense of what was happening through situation reports and secure phone conversations, Washington seemed to be reaching similar conclusions.[1]

Consultations over a proposed public statement proved to be a vehicle for catching the attention of Chun's group. After being rebuffed in efforts to communicate directly with Chun and President Choi, I drafted a public statement reflecting American views and allowed both sides to see it in advance. The tactic worked. Although the insurgents were in position to block the embassy from disseminating the message in Korea, they obviously read the draft and became slightly more responsive, promising me (through word from the Korean CIA director to Bob Brewster) eventual contact with Chun. I also was able to get through to Secretary General Choi Kwang Soo, my normal liaison with the Blue House. Without being able to explain why, he said that the president could not talk to me, but he asked that I dictate the

---

1. I remember being surprised and annoyed by my old friend and mentor Phil Habib, who at one point told me simplistically to get hold of Chun Doo Hwan and "tell him to get back in line" or words to that effect. With lots of others listening through speaker connections, I intemperately told Habib that he did not know what he was talking about. I said I could not very well communicate with a man who refused contact, and I did not have the power to force him back in line. To Habib's credit, he backed down once I explained our circumstances.

statement to him. Some time later, he called me with suggestions that I am sure reflected the president's opinion and perhaps Chun's as well.

Although I agreed to some changes, I firmly rejected efforts by Choi and General Lew to strip away virtually all content except the warning to North Korea. Since the best medium for having a wide impact in Korea was the Voice of America, we asked that Washington release the following statement through that medium, which it did very promptly:

> During the past few weeks we had been encouraged by the orderly procedures adopted by the Republic of Korea to develop a broadly based government following the assassination of President Park. As a result of events today in Korea, we have instructed our ambassador and the commander of U.S. Forces in Korea to point out to all concerned that any forces within the Republic of Korea which disrupt this progress should bear in mind the seriously adverse impact their actions would have on Korea's relations with the United States. At the same time, any forces outside the Republic of Korea which might seek to exploit the current situation in Seoul should bear in mind our warning of October 27.

General Lew accompanied Minister Roh and General Kim when they left the bunker for the Ministry of Defense between 11 p.m. and 12 a.m. He returned alone two or three hours later after his colleagues were trapped by the insurgent forces. Presumably freed because he was the deputy in a joint U.S.-Korean command, he was unusually taciturn about the incident, which concluded the first phase of Chun's ascension to higher office. After a gloomy breakfast with Wickham and Lew, I scraped the ice off my car and returned to the embassy. Our warnings about the dangers of fighting and damage to the security relationship did not deter the usurpers; the United States was effectively marginalized the night of December 12.

Bitter U.S. Protests

To highlight our anger over the night's events and signify our continued support for the constitutional regime, I thought it important and urgent to call on the president, who agreed to see me the morning of December 13. I emphasized to him the need for continued, orderly political progress and the importance of his continuing in the presidency, notwithstanding the night's deeply disturbing events. I described the cabal's behavior as a grave breach of command arrangements, divisive within the Korean army, and potentially enhancing to the North Korean threat. After handing him a copy of our statement and explaining in blunt terms why we had issued it, I commented that copies also were passed to General Chun and General Lee Hui Song, the Korean CIA director who had already been designated the new army chief of staff (effectively the most coveted position within the armed forces) and martial law administrator. In our contacts with the military, I said that General Wickham and I would underscore the full meaning of our statement about "the seriously adverse impact" on U.S.-Korean relations.

Choi reacted gracefully to my presentation. Following a long, unrevealing account of his own role, he admitted that the actions of the "young turk" military challengers were indeed both serious and disturbing, and he promised to convey my points to the new army chief of staff immediately after our meeting.

This session with the president was the first of a new pattern, strikingly different from the candid contacts of the previous few weeks. Beginning with this meeting, Political Counselor Clark and I would appear at each juncture in the progressive erosion of Choi's presidency to make a strong protest, which the president knew would be less important than our parallel presentations to the real power holders. Choi would always hear us out and provide a rationalization that we (and probably he) found unconvincing. He was polite, despite the painfully blunt comments I felt forced to make. I suspect that he often agreed with me but could not say so, and I know he sometimes quoted me when talking to Chun and others. Nevertheless, he seemed to have a high tolerance for being pushed around by powerful Koreans, so long as the people pushing followed proper procedures and forms.

Before collapsing into sleep on the night of December 13, I sent Washington my groggy conclusion that "we have been through a coup in all but name" (see appendix, item 4):

> The flabby facade of civilian government remains, but almost all signs point to a carefully planned takeover of military power positions by a group of "young turk" officers. . . .
>
> The December 12 incident is bad news from our point of view. The military of Korea who have remained remarkably united for eighteen years under the firm, authoritarian hand of Park Chung Hee have now engaged in actions of insubordination which have not only generated animosities that may take years to work their way out but have also set a precedent for others to follow. In doing so they totally ignored the Combined Forces Command's responsibilities, either ignoring the impact on the United States

or coolly calculating that it would not make any difference. By their actions they have also run a serious risk vis-à-vis North Korea without giving it much thought.

Ultimately our real influence is going to stem from Korean awareness that they are significantly dependent on the United States in both the military and economic area . . . .

General Wickham and I and others will obviously make opportunities over the next few days to convey to the new military group our concern over the danger of insubordination, particularly in light of the North Korean threat, the importance of sustaining constitutional civilian government, and the dangers of disappointing popular expectations of political evolution. Without threatening, we can point out that any one of these issues could mushroom into a serious problem in U.S./Korean relations with damaging effects in both countries.

At the same time, I do not think we should treat the new military hierarchy as so bad that we risk seriously alienating them.

The next day, December 14, 1979, I had my first meeting with Chun Doo Hwan at my request. He came to the embassy residence in combat gear accompanied by a few aides and a contingent of about forty armed soldiers, presumably to make sure I was not up to any tricks. In any event, if trouble had broken out, my only companion, Bob Brewster, and I were no match for his firepower. With his huge contingent of bodyguards arrayed all around the grounds of our residence, Chun strode into the Korean-style building as though he were a victorious battlefield commander—brusque, self-confident, and clearly relishing his new role as the center of attention. I greeted him in businesslike fashion at the door and led him through the large reception room, whose elegance contrasted with his coarse camouflage, into a smaller room where we met for about two hours. We looked each other over intently for a few seconds before beginning our session. In fact, if I had not been so worried about dangerous uncertainties, I would have enjoyed the fascination of finally meeting the actor in a rugged drama. I remained fiercely alert throughout the meeting, cynical about the "explanations" I was hearing, determined to appear stern, yet not wanting to alienate the new force on the stage. Chun, equally intent, looked as though he had a matching set of concerns. The atmosphere of the meeting was civil but tense.

I elaborated the reasons for our great anxiety over the events of December 12, specifying the dangers even more bluntly than in my talk with President Choi. I argued that for reasons of political stability Korea had to maintain a civilian government and could not afford to lose the support of the U.S. military and business community. Like me, these Americans were deeply disturbed and angered by what had happened. Chun did not dispute these points, asserting that he too was concerned about the ramifications. He denied that his actions amounted to a coup or revolution. They were motivated entirely by his investigation of the assassination; he had no personal ambitions; he supported President Choi's program of liberalization; and, although Chong's supporters might cause trouble for a few weeks, unity within the Korean military would be restored within a month. Chun's long, self-serving account of his actions on December 12 made them appear reactive or spontaneous, in sharp contrast to my own impression of what had happened and other information we were receiving.

Rather than challenge Chun's disingenuous remarks, I simply noted that I had heard many interpretations of the incident and firmly reiterated our concern about the threat to development of a broadly based constitutional government under civilian leadership. The only time I remember letting my anger show was when I smacked down his baseless accusation that the U.S. government was linked to Park's assassin. In my brief comment to Washington, I highlighted three aspects of the conversation: the disparity between Chun's account and evidence that the move against Chong had been carefully planned over at least a ten-day period; Chun's defensiveness about the risks his group had run; and his ominous reminder that there was a danger of further struggle within the Korean army. Chun's comment on the army reinforced my existing concern. I cautioned Washington that we might be faced with some extremely tricky choices in the weeks and months ahead.

Because I considered him the strongest figure in the frail civilian government, the third man I talked to urgently was the new prime minister, Shin Hyon Hwack, who was designated after Choi was elected president. With extensive service in both government and business, including a stint as deputy prime minister and economic czar under Park Chung Hee, Shin was considered smart, middle-of-the-road, candid, and tough. I felt that if I could communicate effectively with him, we could work together to shore up the civilian establishment and demonstrate its importance to military leaders.

I called on Shin on December 18, appearing alone and speaking from notes to underscore the seriousness of my message. I reiterated the points I had made to Choi and Chun about the events of December 12–13. I warned that Korea could not survive without ties to the outer world and that, if the American military and business communities ceased supporting Korea, the result would be devastating. I offered to be helpful in counseling patience in opposition and dissident circles, urging the Korean military to focus on its basic function of defending the country, and advertising our support of the civilian government so long as it worked to receive the support of the Korean people. The two most urgent problems seemed to me to be preventing further infighting among the Korean military and signaling clearly, perhaps through Choi's inaugural address, that the government would get on with the process of political liberalization.

Shin agreed that Chun's actions on December 12 were improper, regrettable, and dangerous, but he said he was reasonably confident there would be no repetition, and he assured me that they would have no adverse effect on Choi's announced program. In answer to his question, I told Shin that I personally thought one year would be a reasonable period for completion of constitutional and electoral reform. He said "officially and personally I agree with you."[2] I left somewhat cheered by the meeting.

U.S. Policy Response

Immediately after Chun's move on December 12, General Wickham and I had a rare disagreement, which reflected differences in our tactical concerns and responsibilities more than a real divergence of views. Along with our respective staffs, we assessed the new situation in remarkably similar ways; we both favored a tough policy to contain Chun against further encroachment into the political realm. At this early stage, however, Wickham favored a somewhat harder line toward Chun and his co-conspirators than I did. His views were influenced by the real fury and sense of betrayal seething through the ranks of American officers as a result of the cabal's blatant violation of command arrangements. As the senior American military official in Korea, he was also understandably uneasy about my meeting directly with any Korean military commanders in an official capacity. For these and other reasons, he argued strongly against my seeing Chun, at least at this early point.

I, however, felt it essential to convey the extent of our concern quickly, bluntly, and directly to Chun, since he and his crowd seemed in effective control of the Korean army and cast such a large shadow over the civilian government. Thus, despite great discomfort in doing so, I overrode Wickham's concerns. My colleagues in the embassy concurred with my judgment, as did Bob Brewster, who had been dealing with Chun in his intelli-

---

2. Shin's optimism helped me answer Holbrooke, who had stressed correctly the importance of President Choi's setting a date for completion of this process. In fact, Choi did signal the continuity of his political program in his inaugural address delivered on December 21.

gence capacity. After the event I also received the comfort of being told by Washington that they had approval "at the highest levels" to instruct me to do what I had already done (see appendix, item 5).

I was fully aware that Chun would try to portray our meeting as an indication that the United States accepted the legitimacy of his group's seizure of power, but having delivered my message, I did not intend to make meetings with him a normal practice. Quite the contrary, I planned to go out of my way to make it clear to him that we still considered President Choi the leader of Korea. I wanted Brewster and Wickham to deal with Chun on intelligence and military matters, respectively, while I maintained contact with President Choi and other civilian officials. Wickham and Brewster were comfortable with this plan. Over the next several months, I avoided all (but one social) contact with General Chun. Wickham had his first meeting with him in mid-February, while Bob Brewster saw him more frequently, several times at my request. Although the approach was effective in conveying American policy to Chun as well as the military in general, it annoyed and frustrated Chun, who soon tried to get around me in ways that I describe below.

Wickham and I also struggled with striking the right balance in our effort to keep the new military leaders away from politics. We agreed that we should say and do certain things to warn the new group about further misbehavior—for example, dropping or delaying certain plans for new types of positive cooperation between our forces—but we were concerned not to threaten measures that would jeopardize deterrence against North Korea or effectively punish Koreans in general for the sins of a few. Influenced by our handling of Park Chung Hee's coup in 1961 and even more by my experience with Carter's efforts to withdraw our troops, I was determined not to threaten sweeping moves that the United States should not—and was unlikely to—carry out. Although agreeing fully in substance with my point, Wickham was less inhibited in his language. In his first encounter with the new army chief of staff, General Lee Hui Song, on December 17 he suggested that the policy on troop withdrawals might be among those reappraised as a result of December 12. But this and a few similar references did no harm, and within a few weeks we had worked out a well-coordinated approach.[3]

3. Wickham remained less concerned than I about using the troop withdrawal issue to reinforce our admonitions to Korea's soldiers. In his second meeting with Chun Doo Hwan on March 14, 1980, Wickham cautioned that when the United States reviewed the withdrawal issue in 1981 it would consider the Korean army's record of military stability and political neutrality in addition to the state of tension and military balance with North Korea. I did not advise Wickham to do this, but neither did I object. As far as I can recall, I never introduced the subject in any of my own discussions with Chun or other Koreans.

To ensure no public doubt or confusion over our position or views, Political Counselor Clark conducted frequent meetings with U.S. media representatives, who were the main sources of public knowledge in the United States of events in Korea. I sometimes did the same.

In my second, somewhat less groggy, assessment, which I sent to Washington on December 28, I was forced to revise my initial assertion that "we have been through a coup in all but name," but said that I was still convinced that the December 12 incident was a planned power grab by a group of officers who at a minimum expected to play a powerful background role as mentors of a weak civilian government, even if they did not currently intend to take full power into their own hands. The Korean people were hunkered down, more worried by Chun's action than Park's assassination, but remaining quiet.

Although I described myself as "neither optimistic nor deeply pessimistic" about future events, I discounted the cabal's declarations of democratic intent, because its key members shared Park Chung Hee's *Yushin* mentality. A serious test of their intentions would be whether they would agree to lift martial law or would leave it to become Korea's new EM-9, and whether they would allow the soldiers to return to their defense role or to continue playing policemen. However, I acknowledged that widespread fear and unease among the Korean people had been partly offset by the absence, up to then, of any challenge to the new military authorities as well as by President's Choi's willingness to announce a timetable for political reform in his inaugural speech.

Reflecting views I had vetted thoroughly with my colleagues in Seoul, I recommended that the United States:

—Use its considerable influence to strongly support the Choi government so long as it did not become either a puppet of the military cabal or a simple perpetuation of the *Yushin* system;

—Deal with the new Korean army authorities through normal military channels, continuing to convey our distress over recent events, but not giving the impression that we expected a return to the status quo ante; and

—Encourage unity of the armed forces, maintenance of civilian government, and moderation in the political realm, all in hopes of preserving progress toward political liberalization.

About a week earlier, General Wickham recommended to his superiors that we adopt what sounded like a tougher policy to make certain that Korean leaders recognized the depth of U.S. outrage, that we would not tolerate any repetition of December 12 events, and that we would not accept the influence of the insurgent group. He recommended that we:

—Contain if not diminish the influence of the insurgent group and make unequivocally clear the risks of further insurgent activity, and

—Refrain from dealing directly with leaders of the insurgent group, unless necessary, and take no action to dignify or legitimize their control of events.

Although his tone was harsher than mine, this was consistent with what I proposed to do. In practical terms, moreover, Wickham and I found ourselves in close agreement as we struggled to minimize dealings with a group of Korean officers whose influence was steadily permeating the entire military establishment.

The final official U.S. remonstrance about the December 12 affair was a crisp letter from President Carter to President Choi that I received on January 9, 1980, and delivered the next day. After warmly applauding Choi for his statements of political conciliation and constitutional reform, Carter complained sharply about the events of December 12. Noting his deep distress over the gross violation of agreed channels of command, the president warned that similar occurrences in the future would have "serious consequences for our close cooperation." I told President Choi that we were providing copies of the letter to Chun and the army chief of staff. Since the letter was a succinct, authoritative summation of our stand, we subsequently circulated it throughout the military hierarchy.

This was the note on which we ended phase one of Chun Doo Hwan's ascendancy to the presidency. During the immediate events on the night of December 12, we found ourselves caught by surprise, unable to mobilize counterforces without great risk of internecine fighting or North Korean exploitation, and humiliated by our inability to communicate effectively with the insurgents or the Korean people. Subsequently, we were inhibited from threatening the insurgents with major military or economic sanctions, both because we doubted they would be effective and because we knew they would punish the Korean people along with the insurgents. The scope of possible American action was also circumscribed by Korea's constitutional leaders as well as its citizens, who, at least initially, chose not to contest the new military authorities. Few Koreans at the time criticized American behavior. Most of them seemed to understand the limits of what the United States could do, and many felt that we had helped to prevent even greater damage to Korea's democratic prospects.

Pushing for Democratic Reform

After my first conversation with Chun Doo Hwan, I never doubted that he was determined to become the controlling figure in Korea. The only uncertainty was whether he would succeed and how he would exercise power. Right after December 12, I described Chun's action as a "coup in all but name." Then, as a result of encouraging events in January and February, I wondered whether he might be content, at least temporarily, to play a powerful "shogun" role behind the scenes with a weak president serving as the "emperor." And by mid-April, Chun's behavior caused me to speak of a "rolling coup," one that began within the Korean army on December 12 and was to be completed nine months later when Chun assumed the presidency. When I talked in these terms with informed Americans and Koreans, I found much agreement.

In the absence of major resistance within the Korean army, civilian government, or Korean public, I was never optimistic that actions of the United States could effectively stop Chun: the instruments of our power were too blunt to be used without incurring enormous risk. On the night of December 12, I felt forced to accommodate to realities in Seoul, and although there were later times when I thought seriously about taking a more forceful posture, I eventually returned to my same cautious conclusion. Few Americans voiced coherent opposition to this process of accommodation, nor did many Koreans at the time. To be sure, there were citizens of both countries who assailed us for not ordering the U.S. Second Division into Seoul or called on us to take other heroic actions that neither the president of Korea nor large portions of the Korean populace would have condoned or supported.

This American accommodation to Korean realities was gradual and grudging. Until the polarization caused by the Kwangju affair, we did not completely rule out the possibility of achieving some democratic progress, despite the shadow cast by Chun and his cohorts. With this in mind, we sought to get the Korean army back to its assigned task of national defense, to slow if not stop Chun's encroachment into the political arena, and to energize President Choi to push ahead with democratic reforms. Although these were difficult objectives, they did not seem hopeless. Even if unsuccessful in the short run, we saw the effort as having the long-term advantage of putting the United States on the "right side of history" in the eyes of many Koreans.

General Wickham and his fellow officers carried the brunt of the missionary effort within the Korean military community, keeping the embassy informed and occasionally including us in meetings. They used every opportunity with the minister of defense and other new military leaders to rub in the message conveyed by President Carter's letter. They also spread the word broadly to other important officers, many of whom were responsive and perhaps capable of influencing Chun's group. Such was the zeal of this effort that, after a while, Wickham got my agreement to tone it down for fear it would destroy the spirit of comradeship necessary among allies.

To give some bite to our complaints, we sorted carefully through the variety of sanctions we might adopt to underscore our unhappiness over Chun's actions. As candidates for delay or elimination, Wickham informed Washington that he was reviewing U.S. programs in Korea where reliability was an especially important consideration, such as technology cooperation, missile development, intelligence sharing, and the plan to place peacetime operational control of U.S. forces in Korea under the Combined Forces Command, something very much desired by the Koreans. Other possibilities were large programs for Korean co-production of F5-E and purchase of F-16 aircraft as well as the annual security consultative meeting, an event always attended by the defense ministers and particularly prized by Korean officers.

When Washington queried us about possible sanctions, Wickham and I responded in coordinated messages through our respective channels. In my reply I cautioned against measures that would appear to the Korean public as "anti-Korean" as opposed to "anti–December 12." I strongly endorsed Wickham's recommendation that we not tamper with agreed programs for supplying F5-E and F-16 aircraft to Korea. I said that it would be crazy to modify peacetime operational control of U.S. forces as the Koreans desired while we were in the process of trying to discipline Chun's group for its cavalier treatment on December 12 of both the Combined Forces Command and operational control. Short of a final recommendation, I noted my attraction to the idea of delaying or even canceling the next security consultative meeting.

Washington generally agreed with our approach, and the United States refrained from imposing major sanctions. President Carter sent his sharp letter to President Choi; our officers undertook their vigorous cautionary campaign regarding command and cooperation; we postponed further changes in operational control; we slowed certain programs of cooperation; and we delayed scheduling the security consultative meeting. Although these measures were modest in nature, their impact was magnified by our coolness toward Chun. We kept him at arm's length, using pre–December 12 channels for all business. Wickham, for example, postponed his first meeting with Chun for almost two months.

Annoyed and unhappy about this coolness, Chun tried to conduct an end run around troublesome American officials in Seoul. Using a well-regarded officer as his messenger, he sent letters to General Vessey (by this time army vice chief of staff in Washington) and other senior American military officers proposing either a Vessey visit to Seoul or a Chun visit to Washington. On learning about this, Wickham asked Vessey not to indulge Chun. I also weighed in, pointing out that a visit in either direction would imply U.S. acceptance of Chun's behavior and amount to a vote of no confidence in Wickham and me. Vessey put a quick end to the exercise by telling Chun's emissary that Chun should stay out of politics and get himself reassigned at an opportune moment.[4]

Drawing primarily on the officers of the political section and the information service, the embassy launched a major effort to spread the word among Koreans about American policy. Our targets were leaders of the government, political parties, news media, business, churches, labor unions, and universities. Although we adjusted our message to the audience, we criticized December 12 as a dangerous event and potential threat to constitutional government as well as democratic progress. On the government side, we warned against further instability in the armed forces, stressed the importance of civilian leadership, and urged orderly political reform, including prompt revision of the constitution, consultation with politicians, an easing of censorship, the lifting of martial law, and the full restoration of political rights to Kim Dae Jung. On the other side, we explained what we were asking of the government and counseled patience and moderation. We did this through meetings with relatively confrontational members of the opposition and dissident community as well as with established political leaders. I made myself available to speak to correspondents, both Korean and foreign, as well as to fellow diplomats who were often ill-informed. At

---

4. "End runs" and "emissaries" were a periodic problem for us in Seoul. Rebuffed on this first occasion, Chun carried on with many American visitors who came to Seoul, and during the election campaign in 1980 he short-circuited dealings with the Carter administration by maintaining active contact with the Republican party. With few exceptions, however, his American interlocutors behaved correctly and did not undercut official policy. Some of our American associates in Washington subjected us to similar worries by periodically proposing that they visit Seoul as special emissaries to underscore this or that. I welcomed "visitors" who would reinforce what Wickham and I were doing. Not wanting to have our wings clipped, I usually, but not always, objected to "special emissaries."

the suggestion of our information service, I began conducting weekly background sessions with Korean columnists and editors, a practice the regime disliked but never dared snuff out.

A number of American visitors in January and February underscored the American consensus. Holbrooke and Armacost from the State Department, the new commander in chief, Pacific, Admiral Robert Long, and a bipartisan congressional delegation led by Lester Wolf all spoke forcefully to President Choi and others, impressing on them the consistency of American reactions, whether civilian or military, congressional, or executive branch. Defense Secretary Brown contributed to this process from offshore by asking me to come over and brief him in Tokyo before his visit to Beijing, where among other things he sought Chinese help in discouraging any North Korean thoughts of exploiting leadership instability in South Korea. We made sure none of our visitors called on General Chun.

Whatever the impact of this campaign, public anxiety in Korea about a military takeover of the government eased somewhat in January and February 1980, in part because of President's Choi's declared intention to proceed with reforms, the rhetorical support that the new military leaders proffered to the civilian government and democracy, and the relative quiet among dissatisfied students and workers. In fact, a degree of political optimism reappeared in late winter, leading some people to speak of a "Seoul Spring." Before examining this phenomenon, I want first to describe how we handled a most sensitive development we suddenly faced in late January.

Abortive Plans for a Counter-Coup

When I spoke to Chun Doo Hwan on December 14, 1979, about the danger of further infighting in the Korean army, he displayed what I thought was real anxiety about "unsettled conditions" in the army but asserted that unity would be restored within a month. With surprising speed and apparent ease, his group proceeded to place sympathizers in all key positions of control, and although we heard grumbling and resentment against Chun from significant numbers of officers in Seoul and along the front line, we had no early indication of attempted counteractions.

In the last week of January 1980, however, we received a message indicating that about thirty general officers, apparently triggered into action by Chun's unsuccessful effort to have himself promoted to lieutenant general, were planning an effort to remove Chun.[5] A few days later we were approached by an official, who had previously served as one of Korea's senior combat commanders. He told us that a few weeks after Park's assassination former chief of staff Chong Seung Hua and former minister of defense Roh Jae Hyun discovered that thirteen general officers, including Chun Doo Hwan, planned to take over the government. To prevent this, they decided in early December 1979 to phase Chun and cohorts out of the army, gradually and quietly. However, knowledge of their decision leaked to Chun, who quickly preempted them by his actions on December 12.

According to our interlocutor, Chun's original plan was to take power first within the army and then within the government, but he decided to defer the latter move in view of the strong U.S. reaction. Identifying himself as in sympathy with the disgruntled officers but not their leader, this official depicted the Korean army officer corps as rife with resentment. He claimed that more than 90 percent of officers who had not graduated from the Korean Military Academy and 50 percent of academy graduates opposed Chun. Even two of Chun's closest comrades were allegedly disenchanted with him and might turn on him. If a counterstrike were mounted, he said, deputy commanders would neutralize commanders installed by the Chun hierarchy. Alluding elliptically to U.S. support, the official asserted that the United States should either have opposed Chun much more forcefully on December 12 or, if unwilling to do so, have acquiesced in his takeover. From other contacts, we knew that the disgruntled group expressly wanted our support and considered the official to be their leader. They hoped to energize us into action by highlighting Chun's latent threat to civilian rule and the possibility of exploiting dissent within his ranks.

Wickham, Brewster, and I realized that we were faced with a tricky situation that could have devastating results if not handled carefully. We limited access to the information within our own staffs, alerted Washington, tried to find out more about the plan, and spent many hours discussing what we should do. I remember a number of long conversations with Wickham, the crucial one taking place in the security of his car after we had returned from the south by helicopter.

Given Chun's behavior and our constant thoughts about how we might obstruct his ambitions, none of us had any moral inhibition against dealing with plotters seeking his removal. But we were severely constrained by practical considerations. We did not know enough about the identities and ori-

5. President Choi decided that his promotion was premature and postponed final action until later. Choi did not hold out for long, acquiescing in the promotion on March 22.

entation of the plotters. Although the official and other interlocutors firmly identified themselves with us and our objectives, we knew little about the group and could not be certain that they were not primarily a dissatisfied faction trying to borrow our influence to advance their careers. Above all, we were unable to estimate how many troops the generals could muster. In short, the odds of success seemed slim, and the dangers of permanently antagonizing significant portions of the military hierarchy seemed high.

On February 1, 1980, I asked Washington for instructions about how we should respond to the rebellious officers, warning that we had been sent a message that, if not answered properly, could drag us into an eruption far more serious than that of December 12. It was crucial, I said, to make clear to all concerned that the U.S. government believed it would be potentially disastrous for Korea if either a rebellious group within the army were to try to undo the events of December 12 or Chun's group were to aggrandize its position further, perhaps to the point of a full military takeover of the government. With my agreement, Wickham had already made these points in a general way to the minister of defense and General Lew (by this time chairman of the Joint Chiefs of Staff), and I had asked Brewster to do the same with General Chun.

My colleagues in Washington were more hesitant than I had expected, in part because they were considering an American initiative to get Chun moved away from the scene of action in Seoul. Although they recognized the obstacles and risks of trying to stage-manage such an effort, they were less aware of them than were those of us in direct contact with the Koreans. In addition they were understandably bothered by one element of my proposal for sending matching messages to both sides: while warning Chun to restrain himself from encroaching on the civilian government, we would effectively alert him to the existence of plotters. Wickham, Brewster, and I shared this discomfort but saw no way we could damp down the danger of armed strife without approaching both sides.

After a long, secure phone conversation with Holbrooke and others, I thought we had reached a consensus, but, to be doubly sure, I recorded my phone comments in a written message, arguing that:

—We did not have enough intelligence about the forces involved or enough power over the Korean scene to guide and manipulate the Korean establishment in hopes of heading off a potential government takeover by Chun;

—Chun's support within the military not only made it difficult to envisage how he could be removed from the scene but also raised the question of who would step in to fill his shoes as the strongman;

—Given Korean skepticism that we would damage our own vital interests by pulling out of Korea, we should be careful in dealing with Chun not to have our bluff called; and

—Logically there was no way to dissuade the disgruntled officers from challenging the December 12 group without appearing to protect Chun Doo Hwan to some degree. However, if we made sure the officers understood that our warning to them was matched by one to Chun, we would take much of the curse off our action.

I concluded that:

> We will probably have to settle for a policy of containing the dangers of a coup and living with one if it occurs. Our containment measures should consist of shoring up those civilians and military officers who agree with us, warnings to those who underestimate the dangers of further strife, and perhaps some carefully considered, discreet efforts to manipulate events— if the opportunity arises. One of our greatest dangers is that Chun or his enemies will seize on public unrest to justify a grab.

Washington quickly accepted our position and instructed me to proceed with representations, including carefully phrased warnings about the danger of undermining Korea's ability to finance its large balance of payments deficit as well as to defend against North Korea. Brewster had already spoken along these lines to Chun. Using the same channel as before, we replied separately to the disgruntled officers and the official. Naturally, they were disappointed. The official expressed doubt that the disgruntled officers could be stopped and urged unsuccessfully that we meet with one of the group, but it was clear that he understood our negative position.

Once these messages were delivered, I met on February 6 with President Choi, who commented that he had no corroborating intelligence about unrest but respected our capabilities and accepted the wisdom of what we had done. On Wickham's return from a trip to Washington about a week later, we decided that it would be prudent for him to meet directly with the disgruntled official to reinforce the message. By the time Wickham did so on February 14, the official indicated clearly that the plotters were backing off. Two days later Wickham also used the occasion of his first meeting with Chun Doo Hwan at the Combined Forces Command headquarters to stress the danger of further instability from any quarter. He described how firmly we had responded to officers who were restless in reaction to December 12, and he warned Chun to keep military hands off the civilian government. As he had with both Brewster and me, Chun disavowed any political interest and asked that we judge him by his future actions.

Within three weeks the disgruntled official was transferred to another job. I assume that the careers of some of his colleagues were also affected, although I do not recall any reports of disciplinary actions. From subsequent intelligence on this affair, I concluded that the plotters were probably less well placed and militarily weaker than we had first assumed. Moreover, the official's motivation struck me as not entirely disinterested; he apparently had his eye on the army chief of staff position, the plum of jobs in the Korean armed forces.

Although I believed at the time, and continue to believe, that we were absolutely correct in the cold-blooded way in which we handled this potential "counter-coup," few events of these crisis years except the Kwangju uprising caused me as much personal anguish. I deeply regretted having to blight an effort designed to "correct" December 12 but felt that to encourage a struggle within the Korean army would have been madness. Few people were aware of the abortive operation, so it had no effect on burgeoning optimism in political circles.

Growing Strain in our Relations with Chun

Not surprisingly, our relations with the new military leadership of Korea remained prickly because of the vigor and frequency with which we had been admonishing Korean officers about the dangers of insubordination and violation of command arrangements on December 12. This was a necessary process but also an unpleasant one, especially when conducted by American officers still smarting from feelings of betrayal. Similarly, my own blunt remarks and cool behavior toward Chun Doo Hwan inevitably annoyed him and his colleagues. In addition to feeling irritated and occasionally angry over this treatment, Chun's group was also uneasy about our access to information, in particular how we had become aware of the abortive plotting within the army. Although Chun and colleagues were presumably relieved to learn we had discouraged the rebellion, they clearly felt uncomfortable with our knowledge of strains within the Korean army.

While having some beneficial effect, our criticism of the new military hierarchy also provoked distinctly negative reactions. Korean officers began to display an understandable but unhelpful caution toward their American counterparts. More revealing of inner attitudes than a source of real harm,

Chun Doo Hwan and his supporters semi-publicly attacked American intervention in general and me in particular for conduct allegedly reminiscent of a "colonial governor general." And after the abortive counter-coup, Chun called for tightened security procedures within Korean units, presumably to limit our knowledge of politically sensitive information. General Wickham and Senior Intelligence Representative Brewster were particularly concerned about this latter development, because it threatened to undermine military and intelligence cooperation basic to an allied relationship.

When we decided in March to ease some of our pressure on the Korean military, Wickham suggested that I join him (as I often did) at one of his periodic conferences with his U.S. commanding officers. We used the occasion to tell these officers to pursue their assigned tasks in a normal cooperative spirit, leaving the essentially political messages to Wickham and me. Subsequently, both Wickham and Brewster made a point of telling their Korean counterparts about this "normalization" of our behavior and suggesting corresponding action on the part of Koreans. In a March 14 conversation with General Chun, Wickham stressed the need to encourage openness between counterparts, particularly from the Korean side, because secrecy would lead to suspicion. About two weeks later, I raised the subject with Blue House Secretary General Choi Kwang Soo, who had been urging us to accept the "reality" of Chun's role. I told him that since the American side had taken steps to restore normalcy in military contacts, I wanted him to inform President Choi that we expected the Korean government to do the same. I mentioned that Secretary Brown was upset when he learned of strictures limiting Korean cooperation in policy and intelligence matters and suggested that the problem be cleared up before the security consultative meeting (then scheduled in about two months).

7

False Optimism: The Seoul Spring

GIVEN THE WAY he was pushed around on December 12, I was mildly surprised by President Choi's determination to pick up the pieces of his political reform program. In addition to announcing a reasonable schedule for constitutional reform during his inaugural address on December 21, 1979, he made several good cabinet selections (at least from my point of view), choosing a strong figure, Shin Hyon Hwack, as his prime minister, retaining a realistic liberal, Park Tong Jin, as foreign minister, and including a woman, Kim Ok Gil, as the new education minister. Through her leadership of Ewha University, the preeminent women's institution in a society of male chauvinists, Kim was admired for her ability to balance enlightened ideas with practical considerations. I hoped that she could help cool hotheads in the student community while pressing the authorities to loosen restrictions. There were, of course, less helpful appointments where the president had little choice. In security affairs, for example, Choo Young Bock, the new minister of defense and former air force chief of staff, had neither the weight to control the Korean army nor the stature to tangle with General Chun.

The government also seemed to be picking up momentum in pursuing a reform agenda. Prime Minister Shin spoke of completing the constitutional revision so that elections could be held in early 1981; President Choi stepped up the pace of consultations, including a long talk with opposition leader Kim Young Sam; censorship was eased; universities were allowed to reopen on March 1 under conditions granting students some of the rights of protest and autonomy they were demanding; and Kim Dae Jung was progressively freed, with restoration of his full civil rights on March 1. President Choi seemed more responsive than he was before December 12 to arguments in favor of lifting martial law early enough to allow free debate over constitutional revision, even though he deferred to the military hierarchy, which wanted to postpone a decision until after the spurt of protest expected from students and workers in the spring.

In contrast to their mood a few months later, we also found most established political leaders somewhat less concerned than expected about the potential fallout from December 12. Kim Dae Jung, in particular, seemed surprisingly optimistic about the new military leadership and political situation. As a prime victim of the Park regime, he obviously shed no tears for members of the old guard who were swept out by Park's assassination and Chun's seizure of power, and over the winter months he continued to talk in relatively confident tones. Along with other elected politicians, he was, of course, frustrated by continued martial law as well as by the pervasive distrust he met in civilian and military circles. Yet he found Choi's political timetable "tolerable," and he thought the Korean people, specifically including students, would be patient so long as the government maintained democratic progress.

Kim Young Sam and Kim Jong Pil, respectively presidents of the main opposition and government parties, displayed more anxiety over December 12, but by mid-February 1980 they too agreed that student and worker unrest would probably not get out of hand if the government kept proceeding with reforms. All three Kims were focused intensely on their prospects for becoming the next president. Kim Jong Pil, although less ebullient than before December 12 because of his vulnerability to corruption charges of an earlier era, was still hopeful that he might win the presidency, if Kim Young Sam and Kim Dae Jung split the opposition vote. Kim Young Sam was determined to use the advantages of incumbency to hold onto the presidency of the New Democratic party, while Kim Dae Jung was equally determined to use his popularity as a reformist to wrest control of the opposition as he had once before. Although Kim Young Sam and Kim Dae Jung each saw the other as his main antagonist, they both attacked the government, especially the security forces, for fomenting factionalism in the opposition as a way to get a conservative elected.

To their credit, political leaders were counseling their followers to exercise restraint so as to enhance the prospects for democratic progress and head off the threat of political encroachment by the military. Almost instinctively, the populace agreed with them during this late winter period in 1980, when Korea was suffering severe economic problems largely brought on by misguided investment decisions and the energy crisis. Despite the erosion of their income from inflation, workers did not repeat the large-scale protests of the previous fall, effectively accepting reductions in real income as the government devalued the currency and imposed energy price increases. Students were restive but still relatively quiet when schools reopened in March. Minister Kim Ok Gil successfully prodded the government to reinstate faculty and students expelled in the Park era, to modify the highly unpopular student self-defense corps, and to allow nonviolent protests so long as they did not spill off the campuses. Wickham and I both tried to help Minister Kim, supporting her vigorously in our discussions with the president, prime minister, minister of defense, and senior military commanders. She and her bold tactics survived, but barely, and as the tension mounted in subsequent weeks, she was attacked by forces of the left and right. Although student restraint was tenuous because of the challenge from hardline elements, parents, politicians, and many other voices of society were urging patience and warning about the dangers of violent confrontation.

Similar restraint marked the struggle for control over the process of constitutional reform. Led by Kim Young Sam's public statements after Park's demise, elected political leaders tended to favor relatively swift action, arguing that the National Assembly should lead, if not control, the drafting of the new constitution. By mid-February the elected government and opposition parties had both tabled drafts of a new constitution similar enough to allow prompt reconciliation within a short period. President Choi and Prime Minister Shin remained quietly determined, however, to keep their hand in the process, drawing on bureaucratic expertise and public hearings to shape the final draft before it was put to the people in a referendum. Politicians accused them of dragging their feet and of "reactionary" proclivities, while Choi and Shin were convinced that "fractious politicians" could not reach a consensus without a long period of deadlock.

Cautious behavior by most players on the Korean scene and the general mood of restraint among the people contributed to a sense of optimism in Seoul, a mood that struck me as more positive than the one before December 12. The high point for me of this rather romantic interlude was the night of February 25, 1980, when I was invited along with the Japanese and Canadian ambassadors to an unprecedented "historic" dinner arranged for Kim Jong Pil, Kim Young Sam, and Kim Dae Jung by Kim Sang Man, chairman of *Dong A Ilbo*, a major Korean newspaper. Our host staged his "happening" for the three presidential contenders in sumptuous style at home and managed the event with considerable grace and heavy media coverage. I rather enjoyed myself, but I commented sarcastically to Washington that:

> Each of us present felt a good deal of tension until the press withdrew and the players sheathed their swords for the evening. While Kim Sang Man had his moment of glory, the bureaucratic and military guardians of public morality may have viewed the affair in a less sentimental light. It may have reinforced their feeling that the best thing for Korea would be an arrangement under which none of the Kims were to come to power.

My sour remark reflected very real concern that incumbent conservatives within the government and military would by one means or another prevent a fair exercise of democracy in Korea. Before December 12 we worried that Kim Jong Pil might "slide" into the presidency through collusion of the military/security complex. This did not occur. After December 12 we worried first about political aggrandizement by Chun's group and, when this seemed at least temporarily deterred, about the possibility that Chun might try to rule through a surrogate, either President Choi or an "elected" successor. We did our best in Washington and in Seoul to prod Korea toward genuinely democratic elections in which the three Kims (and possibly others) could all run freely without the restrictions of martial law. Yet I remember thinking (mostly to myself) that we could live with something less perfect so long as it was tolerable to the Korean people. Given Korea's circumstances at the time, I did not feel it would be a disaster if a strong, relatively moderate figure, such as Kim Jong Pil or Prime Minister Shin, were to come to power under less than ideal conditions.

While I was thinking these thoughts in early February, I received a sharp message from the State Department suggesting that President Choi might be flirting with the idea that he or Prime Minister Shin could be elected the new president of Korea under a status quo political machine backed by Chun Doo Hwan and certain business conglomerates. "We need not emphasize to you," the department warned, "the obvious and adverse consequences an 'arranged' political outcome of this sort would have upon Korean-U.S. relations." In my interim reply, I defended President Choi, stating that I did not think he was pulling a fast one on us, but commented that Shin might be toying with the idea of entering the political fray at some point.

Shortly thereafter, I invited the prime minister to a private lunch at the residence where I raised the subject of a "third party" at the end of a very frank conversation during which I reviewed the firm way we had responded to the disgruntled military officers as well as our concern about the sweeping powers amassed by Chun Doo Hwan. In answer to my point-blank question about a third-party movement, Shin denied any involvement whatsoever in such a scheme that would, as I had suggested, divide conservative forces to the advantage of the opposition. However, he implied that he might be willing to play some future role in developing and leading political arrangements to "solve the confusion" he and the president expected over the next few months. From this conversation, I concluded that, although the prime minister did not appear to be involved in any crude arrangement to "front" for Chun Doo Hwan, he nevertheless considered himself a good compromise candidate for leadership if the political parties and military reached a stalemate.

In mid-March, toward the end of this apparently promising period, I sent Washington a thorough, rather verbose, assessment of the Korean scene along with separate policy recommendations. In one of my poorest political forecasts, I asserted bravely, "The prospects for stability and democratic-mindedness through 1980 are not bad. The odds of a dangerous disruption, such as a military coup or massive student/worker uprising, do not seem high." Notwithstanding this badly flawed judgment, my analysis was comprehensive and balanced. I singled out students as potential spoilers of stability, and I underscored my concern about the great power accumulated by Chun Doo Hwan, who "has already won the battle for his third star, extended his intelligence security net throughout the armed services by means of a commissar system, and set about dealing with all kinds of people in a manner suggestive of a national leader rather than a security officer. Generally, he gives the impression of a man biding his time to take over power—either directly or behind a civilian facade." I even noted, presciently it turned out, that if Chun should try to extend his formal power to include the Korean CIA or manipulate the structure of the next elections, he could precipitate dangerous public unrest and reactivate stresses within the Korean army.

The policy recommendations, written a few days later, had some of the same flavor:

> Since the Choi government's program for "orderly democratization" appears acceptable to the majority of Koreans ... I favor continuation of our avuncular and occasionally schoolmarmish role to warn various elements of Korean society of the dangers of slipping off course and the need for internal accommodations.

In a significant change reflecting the cooling of tempers and reality of Chun's power, I recommended shifting our general behavior from emergency to long-haul measures. If we were to deal effectively with Korean counterparts, particularly military ones, we needed to include periodic praise as well as exercise care in the way we complained. Obviously, the most delicate aspect of this process was finding ways to work with General Chun without condoning his actions of December 12. I noted that both Wickham's and Brewster's contacts with him were becoming more frequent and talked of my having a second conversation with him.

This comment about our general behavior was aimed in particular at Holbrooke, who questioned our new stance on grounds that it would appear to accept Chun's spreading power and might give the impression that we were "actively courting him." I did not consider this a fair description of our posture. From the beginning, on the night of December 12, I had felt forced in one sense to accept the reality of Chun's actions, but directly or indirectly I never left Chun in doubt about U.S. disapproval. Although I knew he might try to exploit our eased stance as evidence of American approval, I thought we could continue to counter this in various ways. In any event, I had no intention of allowing any warmth to develop in our dealings with him.

The remainder of my message discussed contingencies we might face. I doubted we need worry about chaotic unrest spiraling to the point where we would be compelled to reconsider our security relationship. However, the Korean military might take some action clearly out of keeping with the national consensus, ranging from political manipulation to a coup. To deter such behavior, I urged continuing to make clear to all parties that such developments would pose "severe problems" in U.S.-Korean relations. But even if there were a military coup or if Chun Doo Hwan should somehow manage to come out on top, I firmly opposed threatening a change in our basic security relationship or policy toward North Korea, because I was convinced these steps would alienate the Korean people and damage our presence throughout East Asia.

Since the idea still seemed to intrigue a few people in Washington, I also used this occasion to reiterate my opposition to an attempt to maneuver actively within the Korean army for the removal of Chun and other officers, because:

As a practical matter we have been so unsuccessful in other efforts—for example, in Korea during the Rhee era and later in Vietnam. The odds of being exposed are great, and anyone being hurt in the process could stir up a virulent nationalistic reaction. Above all, I doubt we would find any completely reliable white hats to replace the black hats which we wished to remove.

These were hardheaded recommendations, but the tone of my appraisal was complacent. Within a few weeks I was embarrassed to discover that my colleagues and I had indulged ourselves in a brief bout of unjustified optimism. Thoughts about a "Seoul Spring" were washed away by the massive student protest movement and sweeping political crackdown that, in turn, triggered the Kwangju uprising and the collapse of President's Choi's flabby regime.

8

Political Protests and Military Crackdown

A MILITARY CRACKDOWN was, of course, one of the contingencies we had reviewed carefully with Washington, and we had enough warning signs to be braced for trouble. Yet crude, violent repression was obviously not the outcome I expected when I prepared my assessment in mid-March 1980 or even when I wrote a more sober one a month later. Tension was building in a worrisome way, but most of us—Koreans as well as foreigners—did not sense an imminent explosion.

I am not certain why the Korean situation deteriorated so precipitously in the spring of 1980. North Korea was not a major factor, although quite a few student and radical labor leaders were pro–North Korean at least in their rhetoric, and presumably some real North Korean agents were on the scene. Years of confrontation with the Park regime had also pushed many other students into sympathizing with North Korea, even with Kim Il Sung's peculiar ideas, but this was usually nothing more than angry attraction to the enemy of their enemy, Park Chung Hee. For most students and workers, fascination with North Korea was skin-deep, and I am convinced the struggle in Seoul was essentially a confrontation among South Koreans. Nor do I agree with the conspiracy theory that Chun Doo Hwan and his cohorts organized and orchestrated the mounting challenge, even though they obviously saw it coming and seized the opportunity to take complete control.

I believe the principal reasons for the unrest were the reopening of the universities in March 1980, the dynamics of impatience within opposition groups, the hard-line core within the governing structure, the indecisiveness of the Choi regime and the fuzziness of its program, severe economic malaise throughout Korea, and, above all, Chun Doo Hwan's fateful decision to extend his direct control to the Korean CIA.

Building Tension

Students, like most other elements of society, were relatively cautious in their protest about the sins of the regime when they first returned to the universities at the beginning of March. So much so that in a conversation with General Wickham on March 19, 1980, Chun Doo Hwan was quite confident that student and worker unrest could easily be contained by local authorities. Yet six weeks later, students at Seoul National University and many other schools were almost completely preoccupied with strident protest activity. This strong reassertion by students of their historical role as a kind of national conscience was prompted in part by their understandable impatience with the behavior of a hesitant regime, especially its failure to lift martial law and censorship five months after Park's death. But it also reflected the impressive organizing skills and radical tendencies of Park-era protesters who had been reinstated on campuses.

Incidents of labor unrest also were multiplying as people began to feel the full pain of economic recession and severe inflation. Workers were experimenting with bold strikes for large wage increases. A more fractious tone once again characterized the political scene, with politicians resuming sharp criticism of the Choi regime. They accused the president of procrastinating in the reform program, usurping the National Assembly's role in revising the constitution, and plotting to extend authoritarian rule through a cabal of bureaucratic, business, and military interests. President Choi and Prime Minister Shin did not help matters by resisting the calls for faster action and sometimes leaving the impression that they were comfortable remaining Korea's leaders for an indefinite period. More than anyone else, the public security forces eroded the government's support among moderate people by blocking efforts to end martial law, ease censorship, and give the people, including students, a longer tether in their protest activities.

Political dynamics within opposition quarters contributed significantly to the upward ratcheting of political tension. Kim Dae Jung had returned to full political participation, convinced (with some justification) that he was not only the natural leader of the opposition but also the people's logical choice for a democratically elected president of Korea. However, he was handicapped by not being a member of the National Assembly and even more by Kim Young Sam's unyielding determination to hang onto the presidency of the opposition party. The resulting struggle for power locked these oppositionists into an antigovernment posture. Despite assertions to the contrary, I do not think that either Kim Dae Jung or Kim Young Sam instigated unrest. Both usually reminded their followers to refrain from violence. These bitter rivals were, nevertheless, extremely reluctant to risk loss of support on their left flanks by urging students and laborers to remain cool. Increasingly, they adopted uncompromising public positions (even though they might strike a more reasonable stance privately with persons such as myself).

Another Lunge by Chun

In the midst of this building tension, Chun Doo Hwan contrived to have President Choi appoint him acting director of the Korean CIA in addition to his job as head of the Defense Security Command, thus giving him extraordinary power. Defending himself, the president argued that, in the face of growing student and labor unrest, his government needed a competent head of the intelligence structure capable of providing both information and organizational skill to reinforce the police without resorting to military intervention. This rationalization did not impress me, because it was so obvious that the move would be highly controversial and would fan the flames of confrontation. In any event, Choi's capitulation allowed Chun to lunge into the civilian sphere through leadership of the most powerful and ubiquitous mechanism of control in Korean society. To me, this sudden, illadvised move was by far the most important reason that tensions escalated, erupting four weeks later in mid-May.

Presumably to prevent us from trying to block it, the Korean authorities gave us only thirty minutes' advance notice of Chun's promotion (we had heard rumors of it about four hours earlier). When Blue House Secretary General Choi Kwang Soo officially informed me of it on April 14, 1980, I told him bluntly that I feared that the common, if unspoken, reaction of Koreans would be similar to mine: this was an aggrandizement of power by an officer who had arrested his chief of staff and martial law commander, gotten himself promoted to lieutenant general, and was now taking over the principal agency for monitoring domestic politics. I explained that I would have reacted less negatively if Chun had first resigned from the army and the Defense Security Command.

To Washington I reported that Chun's action was an "adverse if not entirely unexpected move" demonstrating his intention to become president or the power behind the throne: "Overnight he has gone from the official obscurity maintained since December 12 to front-page news and Davy Crockett–style descriptions of his noble character." While acknowledging that some of the military leadership, bureaucracy, and business community might welcome the reimposition of "political order," I warned that the most obvious danger was renewed confrontation in Korean society, with political leaders less willing to play a moderating role and students more likely to join the fray.

The U.S. Response

General Wickham and Senior Intelligence Representative Brewster agreed with me that the United States would be seen as a paper tiger unless we registered opposition to Chun's move. We favored doing this firmly but without damaging our basic interests. A direct public attack on Chun struck us as dangerous, because we thought it would invite instability within the army. We were even more firmly opposed to threats of a change in our security relationship or other actions damaging to the Korean people. After some argument, we jointly recommended to Washington that the United States postpone the security consultative meeting and, among other things, cancel the impending visit to Korea of our director of central intelligence.

Although symbolic, this response was intended to convey a strong message to the Korean authorities. Postponing the meeting of defense ministers would discount for Korea the annual seal of approval we had been extending to the Korean armed forces. In fact, these meetings had become a kind of comfort blanket for the Korean officer corps since the rugged days of President Carter's effort to withdraw U.S. ground forces. When we initially delayed scheduling the security consultative meeting in response to the December 12 incident, virtually all officers, even Chun's critics within the officer corps, complained sharply. The Koreans were then relieved to find us easing our stance in the more cheerful atmosphere of late spring. At that time we had tentatively scheduled the meeting for June 1980, making clear, however, that this was conditional on the Korean military's not interfering in the political process.

In addition to formal notice of the postponement, we asked that I be authorized to meet with Chun in a neutral place where I could deliver the message directly the way I had after his activities on December 12. Unlike his reaction to my first meeting with Chun on December 14, 1979, Wickham was in full agreement on the wisdom of a second meeting. The departments of state and defense concurred in our judgment, instructing me to deliver the news to President Choi about the same time that General Wickham notified Defense Minister Choo. Endorsing our opposition to a frontal public attack on Chun, Washington cautioned me not to pursue my idea of venting our views indirectly through press backgrounders.

During my long meeting on April 18 with President Choi, I carefully spelled out the reasons we were so concerned by the extension of Chun's role into the civilian sphere. Although noting that we would neither publicize our decision nor reduce support to Korea, I said we hoped our largely symbolic warning would be considered carefully by the president himself, General Chun, and his military colleagues. Criticizing us for moving too hastily, the president emphasized his need to shore up his weak administration. If not checked, the radical trend in student and labor unrest could provoke a reaction from the extreme right that would destroy all hopes of political progress. Chun would, the president asserted, help to maintain control by putting some spine into the police. I reiterated my less benign view of Chun's intentions and suggested that we should both perhaps worry less about extremists and more about moderate citizens. If the president proved right, we would take any favorable developments into account in reviewing our position over the next few months. In reporting to Washington, I described the president as a beleaguered leader trying to rationalize a decision where his hand had been forced.

General Wickham was subjected to the same line of argument when he notified the minister of defense about our decision regarding the security consultative meeting. Minister Choo, however, appeared more exercised than the president and tried harder to get us to reconsider. He complained that we were turning on our friends in the military and inviting trouble from the radicals.

These rather blunt exchanges reflected little room for compromise. Although we refrained, as promised, from publicizing our concerns, most members of Korea's elite learned rather quickly that the United States disapproved of the extension of Chun's control into the civilian sector, and it was not long before they heard news of the security consultative meeting's postponement by way of press leaks from Japan. Korean authorities complained bitterly to us about this unintended publicity, which sparked a nationalistic reaction among Korean military officers. I had the impression, but cannot prove, that Chun's group encouraged this in an attempt to deflect Korean anger away from Chun himself and onto the United States. Minister Choo, for example, told Wickham that our treatment of the security consultative meeting amounted to intervention in Korean domestic politics, and he spoke of a nationalistic backlash against Americans. Many of our closest Korean military contacts came to us with a similar message. Ambassador Kim Young Shik and Korean CIA station chief in Washington, General Sohn Jang Nae, complained to the state and defense departments. Even the foreign minister was enlisted as a most unlikely messenger to deliver these points to me.

This feisty tone in our relationship reinforced my desire to speak directly with Chun. However, my apparent eagerness to do so played into his hands. I first asked Washington for permission to meet with him on April 15 and, hearing nothing, reiterated my request on April 18, finally receiving authorization on April 22. My appointment with General Chun was set for April 25, but on that day I was told he was "busy," necessitating a delay of another week. In the meantime Ambassador Kim and Station Chief Sohn were instructed to urge my colleagues in Washington to reverse the decision on the security consultative meeting and, failing that, to agree to a visit by General Lew Byong Hion, chairman of the Joint Chiefs of Staff, who would "explain" Chun's appointment to the Korean CIA and seek to reschedule the security consultative meeting. Sohn and some other retired Korean generals also contacted former U.S. commanders in Korea, urging them to weigh in with the Pentagon against advice from Wickham and me. Fortunately, our colleagues in Washington handled this flurry of Korean activity with impressive unity. They eventually agreed to a visit by Lew but made clear that the security consultative meeting was not going to be rescheduled and complained about Chun's delay in seeing me.

By May 6 we decided to stop pushing for the meeting with Chun, and, no sooner had we done so than Chun agreed to see me. The meeting was finally set for May 9, three and a half weeks after the precipitating event and an unprecedented two and a half weeks after my request. Although I was highly annoyed and embarrassed by this treatment (which Chun and some other Koreans undoubtedly felt I deserved), the long delay forced a major shift in my approach. Whereas I originally intended to focus on why we objected to his appointment, tension over student and labor unrest had mushroomed to the point where I needed to concentrate on how the government intended to deal with the impending crisis.

Protests Turn Militant

Not surprisingly, the Korean public reacted negatively to Chun's promotion, seeing it for what it was: military encroachment into civilian affairs, dimming hopes for political liberalization. Although still peaceful, student protests expanded rapidly in terms of numbers, institutions, and stridency. Skillfully encouraged by hard-line leaders, students refused to engage in military training activities, and they began openly criticizing government leaders, specifically the president, prime minister, and eventually Chun himself. Prime Minister Shin took a heavy beating, because he was often the key government spokesman, reminding protesters and politicians about the need for "law and order." He also featured in most rumors about the efforts of an alleged bureaucratic-business-military cabal to usurp the presidency. More and more students were clamoring to take their protest efforts off campus and into the streets, in violation of explicit martial law decrees.

Fortunately, radical student leaders were unable to create and lead a classic alliance of leftist forces, but, even without "help" from students, workers were becoming more responsive to confrontational tactics favored by some labor union activists. Militant strikes took place in Seoul clothing factories as well as at four major industrial plants in Inchon, Seoul, and Pusan. In one highly publicized incident at an isolated coal mine near the east coast in late April, police reinforcements and army special forces units had to be dispatched to restore order when workers seized and held a police box for several days.

Student and worker protests encouraged members of the dissident community to step up the sometimes flamboyant challenges to martial law that they had pursued without much success since Park's assassination. Far more serious, the protests tempted or forced opposition politicians to raise the profile of their struggle, meeting with students and workers in forums that were technically out of bounds under martial law. Kim Dae Jung, for example, addressed some huge crowds, not inciting people with his words but clearly trying to ride the wave of protest.

Up to this point I felt the authorities were exercising self-restraint in their response. The strikes were handled with care, and students were still free to engage in quite provocative activity on campus, such as calling for the resignation of Prime Minister Shin and even of Chun. But the increasing appearance of politicians among students generated real anxiety among martial law monitors. Singling them out, the Martial Law Command warned on May 1, "We will take stern action when necessary in the event illegal activities continue." With a residue of fairness soon to disappear, however, the command still asserted its hopes that political development would continue and promised that the military would return to their barracks after martial law duties were accomplished. The warning had little effect. The protest movement became more aggressive, the police became more forceful in their measures of control, but few instances of violence were reported.

Shortly before the crest of student upheaval, many politicians, especially leaders of the opposition, appeared less cautious and more eager to identify themselves with the protesters' goals. In particular, Kim Young Sam called a press conference on May 9 at which he read a hard-hitting statement, chastising the president for failing in his duty as transitional leader. Kim went on to list many demands, among them the immediate lifting of martial law, acceptance of the National Assembly's draft constitution without further deliberation by the government's Committee for Constitutional Revision, and the transfer of power to a newly elected government within the year of 1980. "I will not sit idly by while any form of oppression is practiced against students." Students echoed these demands, threatening to march off campus if martial law was not lifted by May 14.

I was deeply troubled by what appeared to me at the time to be a shift in tactics by some opposition leaders. Although I was in the forefront of those criticizing Chun Doo Hwan's latest move and sympathized with many campus demands, I was also fearful that if students pushed too hard, they would provoke a possibly disastrous clash with the police and military units. All senior American officials were engaged along with me in a vigorous effort to encourage continuing restraint by the public security forces, and it was obviously discouraging to find influential politicians reluctant if not unwilling to call for a parallel restraint on the campuses. In later conversations with me, both Kim Young Sam and Kim Dae Jung claimed they had, in fact, spoken out strongly against excesses and violence, but that press coverage of their remarks was censored by martial law controllers who wanted to besmirch their reputations. There was circumstantial evidence supporting their assertion, and as the crisis began to peak I believe both men understood the danger and resumed their efforts to counsel restraint. In any event, after experiencing the full force of the student protest in Seoul and Kwangju, I later came to realize that we had perhaps asked too much of leaders whose political survival was at stake. However, at this point in early May 1980, the only reassuring factors were the government's continued patience and scattered evidence that most of Seoul's population was not going to join the student protest, even if the protesters were their own children.

Massive Student-Police Confrontation

Just before I saw Chun, Richard Holbrooke asked me several questions
prompted by an interagency Korea policy meeting that he chaired in Washington on May 2.[1] In particular he wanted my judgment as to what our
political objectives should be and whether "the disintegrative process we
have long feared may be starting." Promising a more careful reply in a few
days, I sent him some hasty one-sentence answers:

(a) Our basic political objective should be to help bring about whatever
degree of political relaxation is necessary for the maintenance of political
stability, leaving to the Koreans the question of deciding how much relaxation is required and how it is to be accomplished. (b) Regarding Chun
Doo Hwan, our objective should be to slow him down so he does not go
beyond what the Korean people, and even the Korean military, consider
tolerable. And (c) like you, I am more anxious than I was before Chun's
latest move and worrisome student/labor unrest.

Having concluded in this message that I was "not inclined to describe the
current situation as the beginning of a disintegrative process," I appeared to
contradict myself a day later. On May 8, I warned Holbrooke about "multiplying signs that tensions are rising over the student issue, which in turn is
activating many other dynamics in the situation." I explained that students
were proceeding remorselessly with their challenge to law and order and
appeared to be doing so with a great deal of coordination and direction.
Although highly conscious of the enormous dangers involved, the government seemed equally determined to preserve order, if necessary with troops.
Referring to my separate meetings scheduled with Chun Doo Hwan and
Blue House Secretary General Choi the next day, I made a comment that
has been taken out of context and misconstrued in recent years:

In none of our discussions [with Chun and Blue House officials] will we in
any way suggest that the U.S. government opposes Korean government

1. The meeting reached a number of sensible decisions, including support for Wickham and
me on the security consultative meeting issue, recognition that the next president of Korea might
well be someone other than the "three Kims," and realization that there was not enough organized
support within Korea for us to pressure the Choi regime to accelerate its schedule for political
reform.

contingency plans to maintain law and order, if absolutely necessary by reinforcing the police with the army. If I were to suggest any complaint on this score, I believe we would lose all our friends within the civilian and military leadership.

Holbrooke's colleagues, Mike Armacost and Bob Rich, with whom I had been discussing my proposed approach to Chun, understandably seized on these words, accepting my point but cautioning me to remind Chun Doo Hwan and Secretary General Choi about "the danger of escalation if law enforcement responsibilities are not carried out with care and restraint." Although I always intended to do so, I did not object to the reminder, and I appreciated their tactical advice to minimize abrasiveness in my meeting with Chun.[2]

My meeting with General Chun on May 9 was businesslike and far less tense than our first encounter after the December 12 coup. We met in the same "safe house" where President Park had been gunned down six months earlier, and I have never figured out what, if any, message Chun was trying to convey through this choice. Despite the ominous note, I could not hide my curiosity. Chun noticed this, and we acknowledged mutual awareness of where we were meeting. Politely, I stated our conviction that to maintain stability in Korea required that the people have a sense of orderly progress toward political liberalization. Although we had been encouraged by the political evolution begun under President Choi's program, we were concerned about "other developments" that had led many to suspect that political development would be frustrated. In short, it was essential that the Korean government adhere to its program for constitutional change and political liberalization. I also urged that we not engage in acrimonious public debate, because nationalistic reactions in both countries could be extremely damaging to our mutual interests. Concluding my sermon, I told Chun that the decision on the security consultative meeting had been made at the highest levels in the U.S. government, not by our military, although they supported it. Although he made a cutting reference to the way we abandoned our alliance with South Vietnam, Chun did not argue with me.

---

2. Some critics of our policy used these and other words taken out of context to insinuate that I effectively endorsed the Korean mind-set and military deployments that led to the Kwangju killings. Having spent so much of my time in Seoul counseling restraint and moderation, I find such accusations offensive. As an example, see Tim Shorrock, "U.S. Leaders Knew of South Korean Crackdown," *Journal of Commerce*, February 27, 1996.

Most of our long session focused on student and labor unrest, which Chun described as "very serious but not yet critical" (he was more alarmed when he saw General Wickham a week later, accusing North Korea of being the hidden hand behind the students and raising the possibility of a North Korean attack on the south). He blamed the student threat to take to the streets on May 14 on a small number of "ringleader students and faculty" as well as "ambitious politicians." Making clear that the government would take all necessary action to maintain law and order, he outlined a number of steps beginning with exhortation and possibly leading to the arrest of ringleaders and the temporary closing of schools. Only as a last resort would the military be engaged. If they were, he recognized that the situation would be extremely dangerous and perhaps chaotic. I interjected that in dealing with a few troublemakers the government had to be careful not to antagonize the majority of students or the general populace. Agreeing that the government had to be ready to maintain law and order, I warned about the risk of using the army and the chaos that might occur if anyone were killed. Since Chun had spoken of them critically, I also emphasized the danger of arresting politicians and told him about my strenuous efforts to encourage key leaders to counsel moderation among their followers. Chun nodded approval.

In my subsequent meeting with the Blue House secretary general I made the same points. Choi told me that although contingency plans had been made, the president was determined to do his utmost to avoid the use of army units and hoped that the combat police, who had been heavily reinforced, would be able to handle the students. In reporting these conversations to Washington, I commented that the authorities had adopted a "sensible, prudent approach" to the student problem. "They have given it a good deal of thought, and they are very aware of the danger of overreaction and use of military force." Referring to my discussion of the problem with Chun, I said, "I think he probably found my attitude sympathetic."[3]

I found Chun considerably more assured than during the tense confrontation of our first meeting on December 14, 1979. To the State Department, I described him as "a strong, vital, and highly ambitious individual" who had a somewhat coarse look intensified by a direct manner and lack of ceremony. But he was obviously bright and displayed a politician's ability to

---

3. This sentence has also been misconstrued by the same critics mentioned in the previous footnote. If I had known at the time that my hasty messages would be subject to random public scrutiny, I would have explained the context more carefully.

adjust his pitch to his audience. Above all, I was impressed at the time by his almost childish pleasure at finding himself at the center of power.

More or less parallel to my efforts, General Wickham covered much the same ground in discussions with the defense minister, with the chairman of the Joint Chiefs of Staff, and with Chun himself on May 13, just before the students burst off their campuses in Seoul.

From the extent and thoroughness of these discussions, I am certain the senior Korean leadership—military as well as civilian—was thoroughly aware of American anxiety about the dangers of military involvement and aggressive action to counter student protest. There were, of course, disagreements and misunderstandings between us. Throughout the period the Korean authorities asserted or implied a degree of North Korean involvement that they could not document and we could not detect. At one point, moreover, this resulted in rumors, allegedly from Japan and China, that a North Korean invasion was imminent. After a swift, exhaustive investigation, including checks with sources in China and Japan, we first informed the Koreans that we could find no substantiation and a day later confirmed in public that "we see no movement [in North Korea] which would lead us to believe that some sort of attack upon the south is imminent." When the Koreans complained that this publicity caused them to lose face, we defended our procedure as absolutely proper and pointed out that circulation of such rumors undermined the credibility of both our countries.

Another source of friction was my effort to get President Choi to drop the fuzzy haze around his political program. I argued that contingency planning for maintaining law and order should be accompanied by a forthright presidential statement of intent to lift martial law promptly and allow new elections on an accelerated schedule. This would, I said, appeal to moderate protesters, even if the president conditioned his promise on maintenance of public order. For a variety of reasons, including the president's innate conservatism, distrust of politicians, and fear of whetting the appetite of protesters, I failed in this effort. Furthermore, President Choi astounded me by deciding to leave the country for a previously scheduled visit to the Middle East over the four- or five-day period when the crisis seemed likely to peak. The president left for the Middle East on May 10 and returned on May 16, being absent the entire time of the massive student demonstrations in Seoul. Although I was tempted to conclude that this was a cruel plot by others to demonstrate the president's lack of importance, the decision probably reflected more mundane considerations.

The Breaking Point

As I had promised General Chun as well as the Blue House, I met urgently with Kim Dae Jung on May 12 and with Kim Young Sam on May 13, urging them to do their utmost to restrain the students from provoking a clash with the authorities. Both of them were in a sober mood and recognized the gravity of the situation. Although highly critical of the government, they concurred with what I was trying to do and assured me that they had been and would continue to work actively to moderate student behavior.

By this point I suspect none of us was having much effect on student behavior, which had developed powerful momentum under the leadership of a group that wanted a massive clash with the police. By Monday, May 12, 1980, campus protests had become rugged and were beginning to spread into the streets. Students were making extreme demands and burning effigies of Choi, Shin, and Chun. Tension continued to build steadily to the point where Secretary General Choi Kwang Soo, in the absence of President Choi, found it necessary to call me into the Blue House on the morning of May 14. He told me that they expected large student demonstrations downtown that same day. If all students came off campus, the government would probably have to use two brigades of special forces troops already positioned in Seoul to reinforce the combat police. In answer to my question, Choi stressed that these forces were better trained and disciplined than the police and would not use weapons in any circumstances. Having several times warned Choi about the dangers, I commented that the decision about what forces to deploy would have to be Korean. We would interpose no objection. The minister of defense called in General Rosencrans, acting U.S. Forces commander in Wickham's absence, to give him roughly the same information.

Back at the embassy we watched as first hundreds and then thousands of students surged into our vicinity, cleverly using small groups, each with a team leader, arriving through a variety of bus routes to outflank the heavy cordons of police who were protecting a large area just north of us extending to the principal government offices and Blue House. The government was determined to keep protesters out of that area, and even though the largest mass of students was approaching northward along the major road from the train station, the police were particularly concerned about the students who had infiltrated the area around us. Using their shields, staffs, and pepper gas delivered by armored vehicles, they would push one group out only to find others coming in from other directions. Both fleeing students and chasing police jumped the low wall around our property, and it was not long before our building was choking with pepper gas. Having sealed the northern flank by late afternoon, the police decided to let the students, some 20,000 of them, stay in the streets yelling slogans and engaging in group singing with a minimum of violence.

As a precaution, we urged foreigners to remain home or at least avoid downtown areas of confrontation. Late that evening, our marines and security officer wisely decided there was no possibility of my going home by car and instead selected two stalwart Korean guards to accompany me for a walk through this human sea. Although I did not relish a brush with danger, I was relieved to find that the crowd was not hostile and was sometimes friendly toward us when they recognized who we were. Apart from sensing a need to walk quickly and alertly, I was impressed by two features of the situation. One was the youth and apparent innocence of the crowd, mostly cheerful young men and women in their late teens gathered around tougher-looking squad leaders. Few seemed charged up with anger, and I wondered if most had not joined the crowd simply because they did not want to be left behind when their peers were on a heroic mission. The other impression was the almost complete absence of older people cheering them on or watching them, as had been the case in 1960.

The student demonstrations peaked the next day, May 15, 1980. The crowds were far larger, reaching an estimated 80,000 in the afternoon, but the police were able initially to keep them concentrated below Namdaemun (South Gate) near the rail station. Once again, however, the student goal was to push north through the main thoroughfare to the sensitive government sector north of our embassy chancery. The authorities were equally determined to keep them out, using aggressive martial arts assault by unarmed combat police to strengthen massive police lines blocking the way with their shields, staffs, and vast amounts of pepper gas. Moreover, around the perimeter of the sensitive area, combat police were reinforced by special forces soldiers wearing berets and carrying arms. This seemed inconsistent with Choi Kwang Soo's assurances to me the previous day that they would not use weapons, but as far as I am aware no arms were fired.

Compared with the previous day, the demonstration became considerably rougher in the afternoon as the students slowly pushed their way north toward the Kwanghwamun intersection. Students were angered by the police's use of rough tactics and tear gas, while the police were angered by the students' use of rocks and metal pipes. Students trapped and burned several of the armored vehicles that were spraying pepper gas. A number of people were seriously injured. And a policeman was killed when protesters drove a truck into police lines. The atmosphere was ominous.[4]

Together with Bob Brewster, John Monjo, Bill Clark, and other members of the embassy staff, I watched this struggle from the chancery roof. We had a good view of the local vicinity, and Brewster kept us supplied with running intelligence from Korean sources, our military forces, and observers stationed around the demonstration area. At times I had a helpless feeling that events were running out of control. This was one of them. I felt much sympathy for the students. I shared many of their goals, and I was also frustrated by President Choi's performance. Unlike the students, however, I understood why the government was unable or unwilling to act, and I had thought much about the likelihood that Choi would be followed by a less attractive leader if his regime were overthrown. Looking at them in the streets, I had the impression that most students were innocents sucked into a risky challenge by hard-bitten veterans of the anti-Park struggle. The behavior of some of these tough leaders suggested that they were revolutionaries, not reformers. They were contemptuous of the campus liberalization sought by Education Minister Kim. They rejected political compromise, and they worried many people, including me, with their radical pronouncements and communist jargon.[5]

Whatever my speculation and prejudices about student motivation, my overwhelming concern as I watched the mass pushing toward us was that some of the students would break through the police cordons and perhaps be killed by the defending soldiers. Even if the government forces behaved responsibly in such circumstances, this almost surely would have radicalized the situation, bringing out younger brothers and sisters in high school and engaging elements of the Seoul population who had so far remained passive and rather disapproving of their educated youth. To my relief, at least in Seoul, this did not happen. Moderate factions within the student leadership

4. An American in charge of the first Miss Universe contest held in Korea refused my firm advice to suspend the proceedings, which took place in the Seijong Cultural Center opposite the embassy chancery during the height of the demonstration. This stubborn decision by an American put Korean lives at risk. Innocent people coming to the contest were often mistaken as troublemaking students and subjected to rough martial arts treatment by combat police.

5. The core leadership operated in secrecy, although major decisions were sometimes ratified by less secret larger meetings. South Korean authorities generally pointed to North Korea as the source of the communist jargon in their communiqués, but I never saw convincing evidence of this. Curiously, some of the radical language reminded me of communist publications in South Korea during the first years after liberation from Japan.

helped to wind down the demonstration and get agreement to stand down all protests planned for the next day.

Political Crackdown and Bitter U.S. Protest

The streets of Seoul remained quiet on Friday and Saturday, May 17 and 18, 1980, while both the students and the martial law authorities deliberated what to do next. The students were reportedly leaning toward taking a breather until May 22, but they were talking of setting another deadline and issuing sweeping demands: the government would have to lift martial law by May 20, complete the political transition by the end of 1980, publicly schedule the resignation of Prime Minister Shin and General Chun, and release all prisoners of conscience. On the other side of the confrontation, the minister of defense convened a large conference of senior military commanders and other officers to consider recommendations to President Choi, who was back from his trip. For me personally, Saturday, May 17, was particularly grim. In addition to what happened later that night in Seoul, it was the day my wife and youngest son left Korea for the United States, beginning a family separation that ended in divorce.

Knowing the president and his advisers were in the midst of a crucial policy review, I arranged to see Secretary General Choi Kwang Soo after he had lunched with President Choi. During our rather long session, I urged that President Choi use the apparent interlude of the next few days to make whatever concessions he could on martial law and the political schedule and to do so with maximum clarity. Choi Kwang Soo talked of a number of useful concessions the president might be willing to put before the people in a few days, although he ruled out setting an early date to lift martial law. He added prophetically that the president would be influenced by the military leadership, which was very critical of the government's tolerant approach to the students. I warned against letting military leaders determine how the government was going to cope with political problems. If the military leaders forced the government into a hard-line political clampdown with the arrest of Kim Dae Jung and others, I said, "the results could prove disastrous for Korea's relations with the United States."

Neither the secretary general nor I realized at the time how ironic our conversation would appear within a few hours. I went back to my office to dictate my report. In late afternoon, just as I was getting ready to send it to Washington, Bill Clark called me from home to tell me that large numbers of riot police had moved onto the Ewha University campus, where they broke up a meeting of student leaders and arrested at least seventeen. I went back to the residence, where I convened a small meeting of senior officers, including Monjo, Clark, Brewster, and (as I recall) General Rosencrans in the absence of General Wickham.

Within a few hours we had the outlines of a sweeping, disastrous political crackdown by the public security forces. After repeated delays, Blue House Secretary General Choi returned my calls to confirm the student arrests, the closing of schools, and the declaration of "emergency martial law." Technically, this status broadened the scope of martial law to include the island province of Cheju, which had been deliberately excluded on October 27, 1979, after Park's assassination. Practically, it meant the president had lost effective control of the process. More worrisome to me, Choi all but admitted that these decisions were made by the military leadership, who bullied the president and cabinet into approving them on grounds that the students, while quiet for a few days, had issued an ultimatum of unacceptable demands and could not be further appeased. Later that evening we heard rumors of Kim Dae Jung's arrest, and overnight the net was extended to Kim Young Sam and Kim Jong Pil, the military effectively thumbing its collective nose at Korea's most prominent political leaders. By morning, campuses were loaded with military vehicles and soldiers. For the first time in my experience, Seoul looked like it was under martial law. By phone and telegrams that night I informed Washington that

> The Korean military leadership, with Chun Doo Hwan presumably playing a central but not necessarily decisive role, has ignored legitimate authority in the Korean government to institute a tough crackdown on students and probably the entire political spectrum. An all but formal military takeover may be in process. A helpless president and cabinet have sanctioned the decision.

As immediate steps I recommended that General Wickham return to Seoul immediately (he arrived back on May 19), that we make a critical public statement, and that I be instructed "on highest authority" to protest the actions to President Choi and the military leadership. To expedite my instructions, I suggested language for the public statement and proposed protest.

The night of May 17 washed away any prospect that President Choi would ever be able to fend off challenges from the left or right to lead Korea to a more democratic constitutional government. President Choi had warned me about a month earlier that if student and labor unrest were radicalized and pushed too far, it might bring on a backlash from the right that would blight all prospects for political liberalization. These were prophetic remarks, but I think he himself helped to trigger the process by allowing Chun to take over control of the Korean CIA.

Washington responded swiftly to the crackdown, instructing me to seek appointments on Sunday, May 18, 1980, with President Choi as well as Martial Law Commander Lee Hui Song and to have the senior intelligence representative convey the substance of these talks to General Chun. More or less simultaneously, Holbrooke called in Korean Ambassador Kim Young Shik to express the U.S. government's dismay and to inform him about my instructions from President Carter as well as our urgent need to make a critical public statement. (To underscore the gravity of the occasion, Holbrooke asked five senior colleagues from the state and defense departments, National Security Council, and CIA to join him for the discussion.)

Shortly thereafter, I carried out my instructions in Seoul, meeting first with Martial Law Commander Lee and then the president. (Acting United Nations Commander Rosencrans and Bill Clark were with me when I saw General Lee. John Monjo accompanied me for the call on President Choi.) Emphasizing that I was under instruction from President Carter, I told them both that the actions of May 17 undermined the credibility of the legally constituted government, frustrated people's hopes for democratic evolution, raised the threat of civil strife, and increased the danger of North Korean intervention. Making clear that we would try not to inflame the situation or undermine the defense of Korea, I pointed out that we were, nevertheless, entering an "extraordinarily difficult period" in our relationship. As evidence, I asked them to read the text of a sharply critical statement we were about to release in Washington. The text issued by the State Department on May 18, 1980, read:

> We are deeply disturbed by the extension of martial law throughout the Republic of Korea, the closing of universities, and the arrest of a number of political and student leaders. We recognize that progress toward political liberalization must be accompanied by respect for the law. However, we are concerned that the actions which the government has now taken will exacerbate rather than alleviate problems in the Republic of Korea. We have made clear the seriousness of our concern to Korean leaders, and we have reiterated our earnest hope that progress toward constitutional reform and the election of a broadly based civilian government, as earlier outlined by

President Choi, will be resumed promptly. We urge all elements in Korean society to act with restraint at this difficult time. As we affirmed on October 26, 1979, the U.S. government will react strongly in accordance with its treaty obligations to any external attempt to exploit the situation in the Republic of Korea.

I commented that we were not only deeply disturbed by what had taken place but also astounded and shocked by the complete lack of consultation. The mutuality so necessary in our relationship had been completely lacking the previous evening. Furthermore, actions such as the arrest of senior political leaders did not square with the president's own political program or with our understanding of what the majority of the Korean people desired. In my conversation with President Choi I urged prompt and public action to signal resumption of movement toward the election of a broadly based civilian government, and I heavily underscored the importance of both freeing the three Kims from detention and allowing the National Assembly to convene as scheduled on May 20.

General Lee justified the political crackdown as unavoidable, given the mushrooming size and threatening course of the student movement. The increasingly radical demands and rampant growth of "communist thinking" among the students posed the threat of massive disorder that the government could not control without undermining the country's external security. He brushed aside my strong complaints about failure of the government to keep its American ally informed, and he asserted that "as an American" I failed to appreciate that the Korean people would understand and accept strong measures to discipline the students.

President Choi was equally defensive and more emotional. Drawing a parallel to the chaos that accompanied President Rhee's downfall and Park Chung Hee's coup, he declared repeatedly that he would not allow the students to overthrow his government. Although I returned to it several times, he did not address our view that the Korean government had jeopardized public support for firm action against students by its unwarranted arrest of respected political leaders and other actions totally inconsistent with his own political program. Instead, he excoriated Kim Jong Pil, Kim Dae Jung, and Kim Young Sam for "pernicious influence" on the students. He asserted unconvincingly that he would proceed with his political program, that the Kims had been "detained," not arrested, and that the National Assembly was free to convene so long as it "refrained from political activity."

Not surprisingly, Brewster received a similar response when, under instructions from me, he conveyed our message to General Chun Doo Hwan.

The views reflected in these conversations depressed me almost as much as the government's actions. Conceivably, the student movement had developed so much momentum by mid-May that only martial law measures could control it. Granting this possibility, I could not understand the logic of compounding the harshness of emergency martial law by simultaneously undertaking repressive measures, such as the arbitrary arrest of the country's senior political leaders.

However, our three Korean interlocutors on May 18 lacked my underlying faith in the democratic process. General Lee was the most straightforward about his beliefs. This veteran soldier and quintessential member of Park's control apparatus was uneasy about democratic development in general. He felt that students and politicians had broken the law and should be punished and that, after order was restored, cautious political development could eventually resume. While President Choi, a Confucian conservative, also had reservations about "western-style" democracy, I think he may have silently shared my view about the error of arresting politicians. Even if he did, however, he did not have the strength to restrain the soldiers. General Chun's view seemed close to General Lee's, but in his case defensiveness about the crackdown was intensified by his determination to use the crisis to advance himself.

During the remainder of the weekend and on Monday, we assessed the damage resulting from the student demonstrations and political crackdown. General Lee was right that the Korean people would "accept" the government's heavy-handed measures. They had no alternative in face of the intimidating display of police and military firepower deployed all around them, particularly on university campuses, street intersections, and public buildings. With the critical exception of Kwangju, the country was quiet. Universities were closed. Kim Dae Jung, Kim Jong Pil, and Kim Young Sam were "detained" on various charges. The National Assembly was still in existence but closed. The media were under heavy censorship and given guidance about what to cover. Vague rumors were circulating about impending purges to clean up politics, business, and the professions. The general mood was sullen, as people carefully sorted out how their lives were going to be affected.

On May 21, I sent Washington a hasty assessment I had drafted before I had an accurate picture of the violence in Kwangju. I said:

The Korean military have all but formally taken over the government—
even though President Choi will probably continue to rubber stamp their
decisions and the new cabinet will carry on routine business more or less
as before . . . I am fairly certain their strategy will be to select political
leaders acceptable to them, neutralize conservative alternatives, hobble the
opposition as much as they legally can, and then implement new political
arrangements which, even if garnished with democratic terminology, will
be rather reminiscent of the previous *Yushin* system.

I coupled this cynical prognostication with a recommendation that "unhappy as we may be, we have now reached a point where we are going to
have to readjust our posture toward greater accommodation to these men
while trying to hold down the damage to other forces." In an addendum,
written after I had a better grasp of events in Kwangju, I made clear that I
did not have in mind a hasty accommodation and that we should work hard
for the most liberal regime possible in Korea.

Although this late-night comment was an accurate prophecy both of
what would eventually happen and what we would eventually find ourselves
forced to do, the change was made tortuous for us by the brutality that kindled
the uprising in Kwangju. The shocking misbehavior of the Korean military
forced us once again to confront the shadow rulers of Korea.

9

The Kwangju Uprising

DESPITE THE REPRESSIVE "order" that the military imposed again through-out the rest of Korea on May 17, 1980, their martial law edicts failed to stop student protest in Kwangju City, the historic center of the Cholla provinces. The immediate cause for continuing demonstrations in Kwangju was the arrest of the region's native son and hero, Kim Dae Jung, and charges that he was responsible for the violence in Seoul. The underlying condition, how-ever, was long-standing regional antagonism. Rulers in Seoul as well as many other Koreans had for centuries discriminated against the Cholla people, treating them as second-class citizens or even outcasts. Antagonism was most pronounced between Cholla and the neighboring provinces of Kyongsang. In contemporary times, Cholla people accused President Park, a native of Taegu in Kyongsang, not only of staffing the civilian and military leader-ship with his fellow provincials but also of leaving Cholla a rural backwater while heaping development assistance on Kyongsang. Although these were exaggerations, there was much truth to them. Kyongsang people were often openly condescending in their attitude, and Cholla people were often deeply resentful.

If these circumstances help to explain the risky, provocative decision of Kwangju students to continue their demonstrations in the face of severe warnings not to do so, they certainly do not justify the barbarity of the regime's response, which triggered the most serious peacetime crisis in Korea's history after the Korean War, leaving a permanent scar on the nation. I have never discovered exactly who was ultimately responsible for such a mind-boggling exercise of bad judgment. There is, nevertheless, no question that the military hierarchy was in charge, and even though the initial decisions may have been made locally, leaders in Seoul issued the mandates and exercised supervision throughout the crisis.

Although the United States only played a limited role in this tragic affair, the crisis in Kwangju sharpened the policy dilemma facing the United States as a consequence of Chun Doo Hwan's seizure of power within the Korean army. In the highly charged atmosphere of 1980, moreover, some of our alleged actions and behavior provoked bitter criticism and controversy. Most people in Kwangju as well as many other Koreans and foreigners concluded that we were at least "guilty by association" with the offending security forces if not directly responsible for their cruel behavior. This was a grossly unfair charge against the United States. Yet it was understandable, given widespread ignorance of our military command relationship with the Korean armed forces and the vicious exercise of "disinformation" that was conducted by elements of the Korean army who wanted to deflect anger away from themselves and onto us.

My account of what happened in that unfortunate city is largely secondhand, a synthesis of information received through military and intelligence channels as well as from foreign journalists, missionaries, and Peace Corps volunteers in Kwangju. No U.S. embassy officers or military units were stationed in the city. The only resident American official was the director of the American Cultural Center, and he was withdrawn on May 22 out of fear for his safety.

Kwangju Rebels against Military Brutality

Although preoccupied with events in Seoul, the embassy was aware that students in Kwangju were engaged in a robust protest movement, and we assumed that events in Kwangju would roughly parallel the pattern in the capital. As in Seoul, students in Kwangju were demanding prompt political change. They, too, were using protest marches to attract public support. Substantial numbers of riot police were deployed to contain them, and troops from both the seventh and eleventh brigades of the Special Warfare Command as well as the Thirty-First Infantry Division based in Kwangju were in reserve nearby. Unlike Seoul, however, when students from Chonnam University and Chosun University in Kwangju resumed large-scale but essentially peaceful protests on May 18, authorities responded with a deliberate

pattern of escalating violence and brutality that eventually goaded the population into a massive uprising.

Beginning after noon on May 18, with the police playing a largely passive role, troops of the Special Warfare Forces sought out young people—
male and female—who looked like students and beat them up as though
they were North Korean agents. The victims were clubbed and rifle butted
(reportedly bayoneted in a few instances). The general population was
stunned by the brutal exercise. On May 19 and 20 the violence increased,
with many killed and wounded. By the night of May 20 the reality and rumors about military brutality had spread throughout the city, drawing huge
crowds into what was to become a citywide insurrection. The trouble peaked
on May 21 when a large mass of students, workers, and outraged citizens
(inevitably including some hooligan elements) attacked government buildings, set fires, seized thousands of weapons and ammunition, and took control of the city. Large numbers of government vehicles were burned, as were
some buildings. Virtually the entire population of Kwangju united against
the army. Military sources alleged that the city was in the hands of radicals
and hooligans. More objective observers were impressed by the discipline
and coherence of people warding off cruel attackers. Finally showing some
common sense, the authorities withdrew the army units to the city perimeter, where they maintained a rather porous blockade of traffic.

News of this uprising was slow to reach Seoul. The embassy initially
learned of trouble on the night of May 18 by way of our cultural center, and
although we received progressively worse news the next day from journalists and missionaries, we did not get a real sense of the seriousness until May
20 and 21. By then, we had the government's story about "rioting and hoo-
liganism" in Kwangju, disturbing reports of brutality by the special forces, as
well as the crudest kind of reminder that the people in other parts of Korea
were going to be kept under control despite trouble in Kwangju. Beginning
on the afternoon of May 21, large convoys of trucks carrying almost a thou-
sand armed soldiers drove slowly through downtown Seoul in a menacing
display of force. The message was underscored by drawn bayonets and wail-
ing sirens.

The vehemence of events on May 21 helped to bring people to their
senses. Kwangju was relatively quiet on May 22 as tension eased with an
informal cease-fire. Talks began toward a peaceful resolution of the conflict
through the offices of a citizens' committee, including prominent church
leaders. The committee was seeking a deal that would allow the government
to resume control and repossess seized weapons in return for an apology,

indemnification for loss of life and property, and amnesty. The newly designated prime minister ("acting" in the absence of assembly confirmation) went to Kwangju and offered to talk to students. Although he was not able to enter the city, he taped remarks for broadcast, which he, but not the people of Kwangju, considered conciliatory.

In contrast to these modestly encouraging developments, the martial law authorities chose that same day to issue a long public statement accusing Kim Dae Jung of masterminding the insurrection in Kwangju. We were dismayed by the mentality of authorities who would not only accuse a man, jailed since May 17, of organizing the irate citizens of Kwangju for events beginning May 18 but also make their far-fetched charge the very day negotiations were begun toward a peaceful settlement. We tried our best to spread word of our outrage to as many politicians and media representatives as we could reach.

Over the next three days, we were buffeted by alternating optimism and pessimism about the negotiations, information on the government side coming to us primarily from Wickham's senior Korean colleagues and on the other side mostly by phone from missionaries and journalists in Kwangju. At one point, Wickham and I felt a breakthrough might be possible, but we were soon disappointed. Both sides were handicapped by hard-line factions whose muscle gave them undue influence. Within the martial law group, the special forces were unrepentant and played on the conservative instincts of the others. General Chun's close schoolmate and fellow native of Taegu City, General Chung Ho Yung, commander of the Special Warfare Forces, was unquestionably one of the hard-liners. Reportedly, this bright but rugged officer, who received his combat experience in Vietnam, wanted his colleagues to let him go in and "clean up" the Kwangju "hooligans." I suspect that Chun himself felt the same way, but he was restrained by broader considerations. Civilians such as Foreign Minister Park, Blue House Secretary General Choi, the prime minister, and possibly the president may have had some sympathy for conciliatory moves, including some kind of apology to the people of Kwangju, but they were cautious in the face of soldiers eager and waiting to overpower "hooligans."

Among the insurgents, the most intransigent element was a relatively small yet influential group of hard-line radicals, including a few who apparently opposed any compromise and wanted to establish a revolutionary government. Militant and armed, they used students and others to advance unrealistic demands and block conciliatory steps. In particular, they prevented the citizens committee's good-faith effort to return the substantial (but far from complete) number of weapons seized during the first days of struggle.

By May 25 the talks were deadlocked and the atmosphere grim. President Choi visited Kwangju that evening, meeting with local leaders and making a fairly conciliatory local broadcast. However, his trip was too late, and he failed to offer enough to check the momentum of a military resolution. The next day the government moved all willing foreigners out of Kwangju, and we learned through Wickham's channel and from the Blue House secretary general that the local commander in Kwangju had been given discretionary authority to reoccupy the city. Later that day, General Lew Byong Hion, chairman of the Joint Chiefs of Staff, officially told General Wickham that the army would reenter Kwangju in force within hours, moving swiftly and by surprise with about 6,000 troops from the twentieth division and special forces soldiers dressed in civilian clothes to conduct paramilitary operations.

At 3:30 a.m. on May 27 martial law forces entered Kwangju and secured the city about two hours later. Very few casualties occurred during reentry (as I recall, only two people were killed), but about thirty heavily armed diehards tried to hold the provincial headquarters building, where they were killed in a powerful assault by a special forces team. The uprising in Kwangju was over, and its people joined the rest of Koreans in sullen submission to the military. We were at least relieved that the Twentieth Infantry Division, supplying most of the reentry force, had performed skillfully, as had units of the special forces (some of them disguised in twentieth division uniforms).

Based on available sources of information, our estimate at the time was that between 200 (the government's claim) and 1,000 people lost their lives. Although many citizens of Kwangju were convinced that the figure was ten times higher, the passage of time and repeated studies suggest that the number of deaths was not much over 200. Of course, hundreds or thousands of others were wounded, and almost everyone in Kwangju was scarred for life by the behavior of the special forces. No one in the Korean government apologized for this outrage. The president eventually made a speech in June, expressing "regret" and declaring his intention to resume political progress. Despite being urged to do so by a variety of people, including me, he did not offer an apology.

U.S. Military Decisions

The basic source of controversy about the U.S. role in Kwangju was the widespread public assumption that General Wickham in his capacity as head of the Combined Forces Command must have known about the deployment of Korean army troops in the Kwangju region and approved their role. In fact, none of the Korean forces involved in the mayhem on May 18–21 were under Wickham's operational control. Nor did he or I have any knowledge of what these forces would be ordered to do.

We did know that special forces brigades had been deployed for possible use in reinforcing police in Seoul and Kwangju and that the marines were ready for the same purpose in Pusan. We were uneasy about this, and, well before the peak of demonstrations in Seoul or the outbreak of violence in Kwangju, Wickham spoke among others to the minister of defense, the chairman of the Joint Chiefs of Staff, and General Chun about the dangers of using the army and the incendiary possibilities if anyone were killed. I talked in equally forceful terms to Blue House Secretary General Choi Kwang Soo as well as to General Chun, making the same points.

The Korean leaders seemed to appreciate our concern about employing soldiers, and they stressed that the use of troops would be a last resort. Secretary General Choi made a point of telling me, moreover, that the special forces had been selected to back up the police because they had been trained for the task. They would not, he assured me, employ weapons. To be sure, I remained uncomfortable about the role of the special forces, because I feared that units trained to be remorseless against North Korean invaders would prove too rough for domestic police duty. Nevertheless, no intelligence available to us at the time nor any aspect of these conversations gave Wickham or me reason to worry that reserve forces would be *ordered* by their commanders to savage unarmed students and innocent bystanders.

General Wickham returned from a trip to Washington on May 19 and resumed his command. This coincided with our first news of serious trouble in Kwangju. As we became aware of the barbarity of the special forces in Kwangju, Wickham and I used all our contacts to express distress and amazement. Given his own record as a combat commander, Wickham's criticism obviously had more impact on his Korean military interlocutors than mine. We were relieved when the troops were withdrawn to the city perimeter the night of May 21, and we urged patience in seeking a negotiated settlement. I was particularly impressed by Wickham's telling his Korean counterparts that military action was unlikely to solve what was basically a political problem. Above all, we were determined to see that any reentry of the military— if it had to happen—would be conducted with a minimum of force.

In this context we did not object to the reinforcement of Korean units in Kwangju with troops from the Twentieth Division, which had demonstrated considerable skill in implementing martial law in Seoul. Some months earlier on October 27, 1979, the Combined Forces Command accepted the withdrawal of two regiments of this division from its operational control so they could be used for martial law duty, and on May 16, 1980, the Korean army notified the Combined Forces Command that it was taking back operational control of the Third Regiment. In Wickham's absence, his Korean deputy acknowledged the shift, requesting only that other forces be made available to replace Twentieth Division soldiers. At least some of the Twentieth Division forces were already deployed around Kwangju by May 20.

When Wickham was informed that the Koreans were considering possible use of the Twentieth Division in Kwangju, and why, he had a generally favorable reaction. While wanting to sustain pressure on the army for a dialogue with the insurgents, he agreed with senior Korean planners who felt that the Twentieth Division troops, among the relatively few trained in riot control, would be far better than the special forces for reestablishing control in Kwangju should negotiations fail. Wickham consulted me. I wanted to discourage a military reentry, but I also recognized the need for sensible plans if the talks failed. I could think of nothing worse than using the special forces for this purpose. I concurred with Wickham's thinking about the Twentieth Division but asked for time to consult my colleagues in Washington, which I did promptly by secure phone. They agreed, and I passed the word back to Wickham. In talking to Koreans, we both agreed to stress negotiations, not reentry.[1] At the time I thought we (Wickham and I as well as the defense and state departments) had "approved" or "agreed" to a Korean request concerning the Twentieth Division, and I later talked in these terms when explaining to Koreans and Americans what we had and had not done during the Kwangju crisis. The connotation of my words did not cause any problem in Korea at the time, but when I first wrote publicly about the issue in 1986, Pentagon lawyers straightened me out. The Koreans were not required to seek Wickham's "approval" for these deployments, only to notify him and to carry out any compensating measures he might require. Whatever the precise provisions of our command arrangements, I believe that both the Koreans and we understood that, in order to sustain our operational cooperation, the Koreans needed a positive American reaction when making significant deployments of forces affecting national defense.

1. The pertinent rules are summarized in "United States Government Statement on the Events in Kwangju, Republic of Korea, in May 1980" (Washington, D.C.: U.S. Department of State, June 19, 1989), par. 1, p. 5, and par. 51, p. 16. See appendix.

In conversations with Koreans and inquiring foreigners, I tried to be as frank as possible about Kwangju. For example, during my backgounder with foreign journalists on May 21, when I sharply criticized Korean behavior and completely disassociated the United States from the brutality in Kwangju, I also acknowledged that the Korean government could not allow chaos to develop in Korea and that the United States could not properly oppose the use of military forces, if necessary as a last resort, to maintain public order. On subsequent occasions, I explained that our approval (technically, our "nonobjection") to the contingent use of the Twentieth Division in Kwangju stemmed from our humanitarian wish to minimize further use of the special forces. After the crisis subsided and misinformation continued to spread like weeds, I stepped up our educational effort, trying to distinguish two phases of military action in Kwangju: (a) the brutal actions of the special forces that triggered the uprising and (b) the military reentry on May 27 that was conducted with little loss of life. We knew nothing of the former and were appalled by it, while the latter was discussed with us in advance. In Seoul I sensed a fair understanding of our behavior and motivation. Unfortunately, people in Kwangju did not hear the truth. Many of them turned part of their wrath onto the United States, and during Chun's years in power this misunderstanding spread even to other areas of Korea.

U.S. Government's Assessment of Kwangju

Without doubt the first four days of the Kwangju crisis were the most dangerous for U.S. policymakers during the troubled months of crisis in Korea. Viewing the problem as an entirely domestic matter, Korean generals authorized their troops to undertake an extraordinary police action in Kwangju—in the process bitterly alienating the city's population and risking North Korean exploitation of the resulting chaos. The United States was not notified in advance, did not receive even a semi-objective account from its Korean ally for several days, and was deliberately obstructed in communicating its views to the Korean people. Combined with chaos in Kwangju, this treatment caught prompt, high-level attention in Washington. Preoccupied with limiting political fallout from the Iran crisis in an election year, the administration was more than usually concerned about the danger of spreading turmoil in Korea.

Wickham, Brewster, and I, of course, kept our Washington colleagues immediately informed of everything we knew, and we also provided jointly and separately a running assessment of the situation by telegrams and phone. A Policy Review Committee meeting of the National Security Council was urgently scheduled in Washington for May 22, 1980. I had already sent in a hasty assessment written before we became fully aware of conditions in Kwangju, but we supplemented it with further reports and secure phone conversations. From his perch at the State Department, Dick Holbrooke orchestrated an excellent paper for the meeting (which was sent to me for comment), and the night before the meeting he called me by secure phone to get my feel for the situation.

Understandably, from the distance of Washington, the potential for serious trouble loomed larger than it did in Seoul. I had also unintentionally set nerves on edge by telling Holbrooke on May 21, "The massive insurrection in Kwangju is still out of control and poses an alarming situation for the Korean military, who have not faced a similar internal threat for at least two decades" (see appendix, item 6). Employing his normal, rather provocative manner, Holbrooke asked me basic questions:

—Would the Kwangju chaos spread and tear the fabric of South Korea?
—Were our military forces in danger?
—Should we withdraw them?
—Would North Korea try something dangerous?

I remember my answers quite clearly. Chaos in Kwangju would not spread to the rest of Korea. Although sullen in their acquiescence to martial law, Koreans were deeply worried by Kwangju and wanted to contain the violence. Our forces were safe. The Korean people wanted their presence to help fend off North Korea. In the highly unlikely event that chaos spread and people turned on our forces, we would have to be ready to withdraw them. With less assurance, I predicted that North Korea would probably play a cautious role. Holbrooke seemed satisfied.

The meeting at the White House (chaired by the new secretary of state, Edmund Muskie, and attended by Defense Secretary Brown, National Security Adviser Brzezinski, Chairman Jones of the Joint Chiefs of Staff, Director Turner of CIA, Holbrooke, and others) reached sensible conclusions from our point of view. As recorded in the National Security Council summary, "There was general agreement that the first priority is the restoration of order in Kwangju by the Korean authorities with the minimum use of force necessary without laying the seeds for wide disorders later. Once order is restored, it was agreed that we must press the Korean government, and the military in particular, to allow a greater degree of political freedom to evolve." With little thought about future researchers going through documents to find villains, Brzezinski summarized this as "in the short term *support*, in the longer term *pressure* for political evolution."[2]

U.S. Official Statements

U.S. public and private actions reflected this Washington consensus. Secretary Muskie expressed deep concern about Korea during a press conference on May 20, and the next day the State Department's spokesman, Hodding Carter, focusing on our worries about Kwangju, stressed the need for restraint and a conciliatory dialogue. Given the hunger for news and potential for misunderstanding the American role, I held a not-for-attribution press briefing for foreign correspondents on May 21 in which I explained that:

—The United States was not informed about the military repression of students conducted in Kwangju;

—The forces involved were not, and never had been, under General Wickham's command;

—We were appalled by the government's actions in Seoul on May 17 and by growing reports of brutal military behavior in Kwangju;

—While accepting the government's need to maintain public order in Korea, we had protested its repressive actions; and

—We were using all channels available to us to urge moderation and press both sides to negotiate a peaceful resolution.

On May 22 at my request, the U.S. government issued yet a further public statement: (a) urging all parties involved in the Kwangju uprising to exercise maximum restraint and undertake a dialogue in search of a negotiated settlement and (b) warning against any external attempt to exploit the situation in Korea. Specifically, at a noon press briefing, the State Department spokesman read the following statement:

2. Tim Shorrock, writing for the *Journal of Commerce* in 1996, obtained the National Security Council summary through freedom of information procedures and confronted me a few years ago with Brzezinski's use of the word "support" as evidence that the U.S. government and I were disingenuous in our public explanations to the contrary. I defended Brzezinski from the charge. Although his use of the word "support" was injudicious, the National Security Council summary made clear that this referred to restoration of order with the minimum use of force necessary. Shorrock dropped the charge in his final version of his story, but his title twisted the facts, and many of his comments were skewed. Tim Shorrock, "U.S. Knew of South Korea Crackdown," *Journal of Commerce*, February 27, 1996.

We are deeply concerned by the civil strife in the southern city of Kwangju. We urge all parties involved to exercise maximum restraint and undertake a dialogue in search of a peaceful settlement. Continued unrest and an escalation of violence would risk dangerous miscalculation by external forces. When calm has been restored, we will urge all parties to seek means to resume a program of political development as outlined by President Choi. We reiterate that the U.S. government "will react strongly in accordance with its treaty obligations to any external attempt to exploit the situation in the Republic of Korea."

To reinforce this message, Assistant Secretary Holbrooke called in Chinese Ambassador Chai the same day to request that China encourage caution in Pyongyang.

This statement (largely drafted by me in Seoul and broadcast by the Voice of America as well as by our military stations in Korea) reflected a complex of considerations. Genuinely worried about possible North Korean exploitation of the Kwangju chaos, South Korean military authorities urged us, as in every other phase of the 1979–80 crisis, to warn Pyongyang against intervention. Although Wickham and I were less alarmed about the north, we had some real concern and thought it best to be prudent. Thus Wickham informally instituted some measures associated with a higher status of alert (DEFCON 3) and recommended the use of more airborne warning and control system surveillance aircraft as well as deployment of a carrier task force to Korea.

At the same time, we wanted to lean hard on the Korean army to conduct a serious dialogue with the citizens committee in Kwangju as well as to find ways to publicize our own position to people in Kwangju. Working with General Lew of the Joint Chiefs of Staff (primarily through Wickham but sometimes directly) as well as with Blue House Secretary General Choi and Foreign Minister Park, I agreed to recommend a further U.S. warning to North Korea, but only if it were accompanied by an explicit call on *both* sides in Kwangju to act with restraint and seek a peaceful resolution.

This equality of treatment in our proposed statement did not sit well with government authorities, but they eventually accepted it. Moreover, I extracted an explicit oral commitment from them that if we issued the statement in Washington, the martial law authorities would undertake to broadcast it throughout Korea and also distribute it in Kwangju through air-dropped leaflets. Underlying all the agreements was an understanding that Korean military forces would refrain from attempting a military solution for a reasonable period (at least two days) during which they would seek a negotiated settlement.

We Americans kept our part of the bargain, and the Korean side appeared to make a genuine effort to reach a settlement with the insurgents, holding off military activity for four days until the night of May 26–27. Nevertheless, in one of the nastiest actions against us during my entire time in Korea, someone in the martial law structure decided not to broadcast or publicize our May 22 statement anywhere in Korea (some Koreans heard the statement from Voice of America or our military networks). Nor were any leaflets dropped in Kwangju. Instead radio and television listeners in Kwangju were told that General Wickham had released troops for use in Kwangju and had *encouraged* deployment of military forces to maintain public order. Whatever the exact words of the Kwangju broadcast, which we did not hear, it was widely interpreted as evidence that the United States supported the actions of the special forces.

On learning of this, Wickham complained sharply to the minister of defense, Chairman Lew, the martial law commander, and others. They claimed that the broadcast was a "one-time action by local authorities without proper authorization." I warned Blue House Secretary General Choi that continuation of these crude efforts to shift blame onto us would force a very firm, very embarrassing denial, and I mentioned that Secretary Muskie was personally concerned. With prophetic accuracy, I emphasized that nothing could be worse for both our countries than to have a sizable anti-American movement on top of all the other problems in Cholla provinces. Although Choi promised a prompt resolution, we never received a proper explanation.

The full damage caused by this treachery became apparent later. In the folklore that grew in Kwangju after the crisis, General Wickham was demonized—and to a lesser extent I also—for sins never committed. It was not until after Chun's ignominious departure from the presidency that the people of Cholla finally began to realize that the military actions of the United States during the crisis had been sensible and honorable.

U.S. Efforts to Seek Peaceful Settlement

The United States was handicapped in efforts to facilitate a peaceful outcome in Kwangju. Not only were we unable to communicate freely with the people, but our views were frequently distorted and, in one key instance, deliberately blocked by the Korean security apparatus. Moreover, we lacked effective official representation in Kwangju, leaving us ill-informed and dependent on untested sources. This combination of circumstances was extremely frustrating and sometimes infuriating. We knew that Korea was going through a momentously important event, yet for the most part we were held to the sidelines.

Despite this, we did about as well as we could. We made a major effort to urge patience and moderation, to encourage a negotiated settlement, and to minimize bloodshed if talks failed and troops had to reenter the city. The latter was probably our most effective accomplishment. John Wickham and Bob Brewster were the main channel for firm American advice to Korean counterparts. In conversations with General Lew (mostly by phone) and miscellaneous meetings with other military officials, I reinforced this message, pointing out that our advice reflected high-level views in Washington. In addition, I worked desperately to prod civilian officials into taking a stand with their military colleagues. When Foreign Minister Park called me in on May 21 to urge us to issue a warning to North Korea, I bitterly criticized the government's actions in Seoul and Kwangju, telling him that as a result I was more worried about internal miscalculations by the generals than about an imminent attack from North Korea. He agreed but lamented the lack of anyone with the stature to talk to the generals.

Perhaps because I discounted his influence after the events of May 17, I made no special effort to see the president during these few days. However, I talked candidly with his secretary general, Choi Kwang Soo, who was well informed, intelligent, and skillful in passing messages to the military leaders. With the same thought in mind, I pressed hard for an early meeting with the new prime minister, Park Choong Hoon, hoping he might have a semblance of the influence exercised by his gutsy predecessor. John Monjo and I saw him alone on May 23, the day after his not very successful trip to Kwangju, and we reviewed with him frankly what we were trying to do. Although we found him sympathetic, we concluded from this meeting and a subsequent one, during which I pushed hard for a formal government apology to the people of Kwangju, that he was not going to confront the soldiers.

This reticence of civilian officials compounded my worry about the outcome of negotiations dominated on the government side by the military and on the other side by militants in Kwangju. I was extremely concerned when the citizens committee failed to reach a compromise, and I was on edge until I learned that the military reentry into Kwangju had been relatively humane. I doubt we Americans could have brokered a better outcome in such a bitter domestic struggle, but in retrospect I recognize clearly that we would have been better informed, and certainly less frustrated, if we had had an authoritative presence in Kwangju, someone who knew the local leaders and could keep us accurately informed on a timely basis, and not had to depend on secondhand reports from miscellaneous sources. We had a strong, Korean-speaking officer in the political section, Spence Richardson, who visited Kwangju after the crisis and prepared a solid report. I now fault myself for not sending him or someone else to Kwangju as soon as I learned about the severity of the crisis. Instead, we struggled to exercise our influence largely by remote control, targeting our efforts on military and civilian leaders in Seoul, certain missionaries in Kwangju, and Protestant as well as Catholic church leaders, particularly Cardinal Kim who was in close communication with Archbishop Yun in Kwangju.

While the negotiators were still active in Kwangju, no member of the citizens committee nor anyone on either side of the confrontation ever suggested that it would be useful to have direct American intervention. That would not necessarily have stopped us from intervening if we had thought we could have been effective. But working from the distance of Seoul, we felt it best to continue with our indirect, though vigorous, efforts to support the committee. We also believed it made more sense to focus on general matters, such as an apology for excesses of the special forces, rather than on the details of contention.

Just before the Korean army reentered Kwangju, we received a last-minute request on May 26 from unnamed student leaders in Kwangju that Washington "instruct" me to mediate a truce. The students made their request to the *New York Times* correspondent, Henry Scott-Stokes, that afternoon. Rather than try to contact me, he passed it indirectly through the copy he was filing to New York. The story surfaced the same evening in a newscast from our own armed forces station about 10 p.m., and I first heard of it around 11 p.m. after I had been officially informed that Korean forces would reenter Kwangju within two or three hours. I was unable to discover essential details or the context of the request; I was certain I could not succeed because Korean troops were already authorized and poised to move into Kwangju. So I declined the request when it was forwarded to me from a journalist by way of the embassy press attaché. At the time, the decision tugged at my conscience, since I obviously did not want to blight any serious peace initiative. Later, when the request was linked to one of the militant holdouts in the provincial capital building, I was reassured that I had made the right decision. The individual who made the request was identified as Yun Sang Won, an apparently dedicated antigovernment activist and theoretician who had hardened under Park Chung Hee's regime to the point where he opposed compromise.[3]

Malicious Distortions of U.S. Policy

Although the lives of people in Kwangju and the security of Korea were far more important matters, I was particularly angered by the deliberate distortions of U.S. policy by General Chun and his underlings in the army. The strain caused by "disinformation" about the May 22 statement was only the beginning of a nasty confrontation that lasted several months.

Just after my meeting with the prime minister on May 23, Lee Dong Won, chairman of the National Assembly's Foreign Affairs Committee, hosted a luncheon for several of us from the embassy with a balanced group of legislators ranging from the opposition left to the conservative right. I seized the occasion to advertise our views, including why we had issued an unusually critical public statement on May 18 and what we were trying to do in Kwangju. Acknowledging (for the conservatives) that the students had in many ways brought on the military reaction of May 17, I emphasized (for the conservatives and the opposition) that the military needed to understand better the political consequences of their actions. The arrest of political leaders and closing of the National Assembly were unjustified and struck me as an act of "political stupidity." I was pleased when the legislators leaked an accurate account of the meeting that appeared in the English-language press, including references to my comments about the need for dialogue and compromise in Kwangju as well as for moving on with political development once the crisis was resolved.

My pleasure did not last long. A number of Korean-language papers turned my remarks upside down, asserting that I had expressed understanding or approval of the events of May 17. Then I learned about the "disinformation" activities of the Korean authorities in Kwangju, and I exploded when General Chun Doo Hwan, speaking to a representative group of newspaper publishers, alleged that the United States was informed in advance about the events of December 12, his appointment to the Korean CIA, and the actions taken on May 17.

3. Henry Scott-Stokes described him as "a pure-blood Jeffersonian democrat." Bradley Martin of the *Baltimore Sun* also wrote sympathetically about Yun but characterized him in more radical terms. See Amalie M. Weber, ed., *Kwangju in the Eyes of the World* (Seoul: Kwangju Citizens Solidarity, 1997).

I immediately wrote an accurate statement of how we learned about the events of December 12, April 14, and May 17 as well as what I had said to the legislators on May 23, and I asked our embassy press attaché to convey it orally to each of the publishers who had met with Chun. Although I told Washington that I did not want a public squabble with Chun, he obviously discovered what I had done. He did not like my "thumb in your eye" response (see appendix, item 1).

Assessment

Two days after quiet returned to Kwangju, I sent Washington a "very personal message" (that was read but not necessarily approved by my colleagues) entitled "Some Basic Recommendations in Light of May 17 and the Kwangju Rebellion." I am quoting rather extensively from it, because it conveys the essence of views distilled from almost six months of coping with Chun's group and agonizing over what we should do.

> While highly visible military force, in some ways akin to a military occupation, has demonstrably preserved law and order through much of Korea, I believe that longer-term political stability will require a significant easing of controls and return to greater political sophistication than we have seen since December 12. If these do not appear reasonably soon, not necessarily in the form of full-blown democracy, I fear disaffection will grow to dangerous proportions with profound effects for us.
>
> We have been demonstrably unsuccessful in trying to stop the march of these self-appointed leaders [Chun and company] or even to slow them down. . . . Members of the Chun group both underestimate and discount our reactions because they believe we have no options. They can be disconcertingly arrogant. . . . Unfortunately, we have been constrained by our own interests in South Korean security to pull our punches and permit this dangerous arrogance to grow. We have not threatened to modify our security relationship, our basic policy towards North Korea, or our economic support, because we have calculated that the threat to do so would be counterproductive and alarming to the populace in general. I continue to believe this basic premise is correct.
>
> As Chun Doo Hwan and associates settle into their new role, they may be educated to some extent by the large number of sophisticated people working with them, and by the trial and error discovery that the domestic

political climate requires positive actions as well as negative ones and that external relationships—both economic and security—require a degree of mutuality.

Given the essentially unchanged nature of our security interests, *the key variable for us will be the real reaction of the Korean public. If, by a reasonable test, most Koreans seem willing to live fairly comfortably with the newly emerging political structure, I think we should be able to also. If the people manifestly cannot tolerate the new leadership and resort to confrontation, we will be forced, whether we like it or not, either to try to bring about change or to disengage.* [Emphasis added later.] I urge that we not jump too quickly to conclusions, because we are faced with a society which contradictorily wants both law and order and change.

This conclusion provoked me to recommend a way to generate more anxiety for General Chun. In the next chapter, I discuss these recommendations in the context of an extensive dialogue with my superiors in Washington as well as with General Chun in Seoul.

——10——

The Ascension and Presidency
of Chun Doo Hwan

SHORTLY BEFORE THE Korean army reentered Kwangju in force, we learned informally that President Choi would soon announce formation of a Special Committee for National Security Affairs to facilitate "interaction" between the martial law commander and President Choi's cabinet. The committee, to consist of key cabinet members and all senior commanders, would function with a steering committee of about thirty members drawn from the military establishment and civilian ministries. President Choi would be the titular head of the committee, and, as one might have assumed, General Chun Doo Hwan would be in charge of the steering group. With his grasp neatly extended to every aspect of government, Chun was able to relinquish direct control of the Korean CIA, and it was understood that this entire transitional structure would dissolve with the end of martial law.

General Chun and his cohorts presumably decided to "recommend" this supragovernment structure to President Choi in conjunction with the political crackdown of May 17, and the idea must have been conceived considerably earlier. Along with the massive display of military force in downtown Seoul on May 21, this development left no doubt who was in control of the government. When they separately discussed the new arrangements with me, Foreign Minister Park and Secretary General Choi asserted defensively that President Choi had not abandoned his political reform program and was "not without influence," yet both of them were transparently embarrassed by a development that subordinated civilian government so unmistakably to the military.[1] Speaking informally, I predicted that their fellow Koreans would view the new arrangements as clear evidence that the military had moved in to supervise everything in Korea, all but formally signifying that an army coup had taken place. Officially, I said that our reaction would depend on what happened to President Choi's timetable for political reform and that we would judge progress by deeds, not words.

Although it took several weeks for the new structure to unfold, some effects were soon apparent. The president, much of the Blue House staff, and most cabinet members ceased being major players in the making of decisions. Although they were still accorded deference and tried to function, they no longer participated in the inner debate over key decisions. Instead, they learned what they could from subordinates who were members of Chun's steering group as well as from other sources. The bureaucracy, previously responsible to the cabinet, was intimidated and beholden to the new structure. Politicians were in disarray. The media were under the heavy wraps of martial law restrictions. Church groups, students, school faculties, and labor activists, while openly critical of what was going on around them, were not experimenting with protest activity.

In contrast to the sullen mood of these largely urban sectors of society, the military seemed relatively united about the need to enforce law, order, and discipline. Many, but not all, members of the business community were of the same view or at least showed no great concern about the setback to political freedom. In both the cities and countryside, moreover, significant numbers of people seemed to be giving the army the benefit of the doubt, reacting to stories about student excesses and the dangers inherent in the Kwangju crisis. It was difficult for us to estimate the net effect of these opposed tendencies. Clearly, large numbers of people were very angry, but very few seemed prepared to challenge the new authorities. Certainly, the moderate center in Korea had been eroded.

On June 12, 1980, two and a half weeks after the reoccupation of Kwangju, President Choi delivered a nationally televised speech to the nation. While he reiterated some of his own program, the tone and content of his remarks revealed the mind-set and plans of his military monitors. He

---

1. Referring, I believe, to the May 17 discussion between the president and the military leadership, Blue House Secretary General Choi Kwang Soo said that it was President Choi who stayed the hand of military extremists who wanted to suspend much of the constitution and dissolve the National Assembly.

dutifully promised that the government would adhere to its previous schedule for political reform (elections in the first half of 1981) and said that the National Assembly's draft would be "considered" in drawing up the new constitution. Offering no apology for military misbehavior in Kwangju, he at least extended "regrets and consolation" to those who suffered during the "lawless days." In contrast to earlier speeches, however, he heavily stressed the theme of law and order and sidestepped the issue of lifting martial law. Completely out of character, he announced that public discipline would be strictly enforced and vaguely described plans to "purify" politics, academia, and labor-management relations.

Apart from a lingering ceremonial role as the nation's spokesperson and greeter of foreign visitors, President Choi faded rapidly from the public scene. Eyes were fixed on the new leaders, who began to spell out how they would conduct government through the new committee structure. They talked of purging (in the Korean context meaning a ban on political activity, not banishment to the gulag) and taming almost every aspect of public life in Korea. Kim Dae Jung would be tried for serious crimes of subversion against the state; leaders such as Kim Jong Pil and Lee Hu Rak (another, rather notorious, former director of the Korean CIA) would be tried for corruption in office or fined; some businessmen might be punished for past corruption, although nothing would be done to undermine the economy, whose recovery was a top priority; schools would be reopened on an experimental basis beginning with professional institutions, which posed less risk of political confrontation than regular universities; and so on.

The U.S. Response

American officials were pulled in contradictory directions. Identifying ourselves with the forces of political change and constitutional rule in Korea, we were profoundly discouraged by the massive setback to political progress. Yet we needed to communicate with the real holders of power in a closely allied country. This was not a new dilemma for us. We had been wrestling with it since December 12, 1979, but the new leaders had now emerged almost all the way out of the shadows. Given their power, we could no longer remain aloof without real risk of isolation and dangerous surprises. Premature acceptance of their new status, however, could prove costly to our relations with other elements of Korean society and endanger our longer-term interests in stability.

Throughout the remaining months of the Carter administration, we debated at length among ourselves and struggled hard to find a tolerable relationship with Chun's group. Unlike our reaction to the events of December 12, there was little hesitancy this time about establishing high-level contact with the new source of authority. We realized that no effort on our part could possibly sustain the pretense that President Choi was still in charge. My instinct after the traumatic events of Kwangju was to request an early appointment with General Chun Doo Hwan. Washington concurred, and, beginning in June 1980, basic communication between the U.S. and Korean governments took place in meetings with General Chun, not President Choi. I went out of my way, nevertheless, to keep in touch with the Blue House and the foreign minister to exchange information, seek advice, and signify our friendship.

Yet Another Review of U.S. Policy

The excesses of the students in May, the government's political crackdown of May 17, the crisis in Kwangju, and the all but formal assumption of governmental power by Chun and his group in early June forced us to face starkly the consequences of Chun Doo Hwan's actions the night of December 12, 1979. During the intervening six months, we had refrained from drastic action to rectify the situation, not because we were mesmerized by the salami tactics of Chun's group, but because the prospects for achieving success were so poor and the consequences of failure so grave. This continued to be the reality, and we remained cautious. Nevertheless, my worry about the way events were unfolding and my strong conviction that political liberalization was important for long-term stability in Korea led me to recommend a tougher posture than I had at any previous juncture in the crisis.

Accompanying the assessment of May 28, with which I closed the previous chapter, I for the first time recommended that Washington introduce a slight element of uncertainty about our security cooperation with Korea:

> I think it would be prudent for us to indicate to the Koreans now that we are undertaking a fundamental review of our policy. After about a month of policy review, we should inform the Koreans that we have decided we will not be able to continue the "full cooperation" (undefined) of the past unless the Korean authorities proceed with amendment of the constitution and the conduct of free elections to form a broadly based government.

We would deliberately refrain from any other threats or from indicating precisely what political developments would be unacceptable to us. Our goals of political progress would be set in sufficiently rounded terms so that we could adjust our position to accommodate the evolution of Korean public reaction to the new leadership.

If Chun and his associates nevertheless proceed remorselessly down the path of recent months to the point where there is serious unrest and growing concern as to whether there is enough national cohesion to deter North Korean attack, we would have to consider more forceful measures to try to jostle changes in the military leadership.

I cannot overstate the dangers of trying to dump Chun. If we were to move prematurely, I believe Chun could unify the Korean army leadership firmly against us, stir up considerable animus among the Korean populace, and probably succeed in injecting the issue into U.S. domestic politics. While we know he is the most unpopular man in Korea, we do not know that he has really overstepped the bounds for a majority of those who hold various kinds of power. We should also keep in mind that there are no ideal leaders lurking around awaiting our anointing hand.

These recommendations came from much thought and discussion with my senior colleagues (Monjo, Clark, Wickham, and Brewster). I believe that prompt and firm execution of my proposal for a fundamental policy review might have provided us a stronger lever on the new authorities than the somewhat less focused approach we finally adopted. Nonetheless, the U.S. government was unable to engage in such a carefully choreographed exercise for a number of reasons. President Carter had legitimate domestic political concerns to take into account during an election year, and members of Congress held a variety of opinions, as did various parts of the administration.

With republicans and others constantly chiding him for the drawn-out hostage crisis in Iran, the president naturally did not want to be seen as in any way undermining a long-standing American ally. Hence, in his response to Daniel Schorr and George Watson on CNN-Television on May 31, 1980, he commented crisply, "We are urging the military leaders and the elected civilian leaders of South Korea to move as rapidly as possible toward a completely democratic government. In the meantime we are making sure that Korea is kept secure . . . I would like to see every nation on earth democratic . . . But we can't sever our relationships with our allies and friends and trading partners and turn them all over to Soviet influence, and perhaps even subversion, simply because they don't measure up to our standards of human rights." I could hardly fault the president's choice of words (ironically so different from those he used during his confrontation with President Park a year earlier), but in the immediate context they seemed to foreclose the option of threatening some attenuation of our military cooperation with Korea. In fact, Chun mentioned Carter's interview to me approvingly when I saw him a few days later. (I had to remind him that the president had also talked of setbacks to democratic government in Korea.)

The same day the president spoke on television, Assistant Secretary of State Holbrooke chaired an important informal interagency meeting in Washington to review U.S. policy toward Korea. Most participants, he reported, concluded that, while maintaining effective deterrence against North Korean attack, we should bring credible pressures on the Korean power structure to (a) moderate both the repressive aspects of its rule and the politicization of the senior military leadership and (b) achieve a measure of legitimacy through constitutional reform and elections. In addition Holbrooke noted a strong consensus:

—Not to meddle with the essentials of our security relationship, meaning our commitment, troops, and command arrangements;

—Not to try unseating General Chun, but to remain sensitive to the possibility that effective opposition to him might yet arise within the military;

—To develop an effective dialogue with the new structure;

—To push Korean leaders to accommodate popular hopes for resumed political development and elections;

—To eschew punitive actions in the economic field; and

—To adopt a somewhat cool and aloof stance toward the present government in order to retain some credibility and leverage for our interests and to prevent excessive identification in the eyes of either the Korean or American people with repressive actions by the generals.

As part of the cool, reserved stance, the group agreed to continue the indefinite postponement of the security consultative meeting, to postpone policy planning talks, and to defer, delay, or downgrade a number of noncritical economic missions.

These views from Washington were generally consistent with our thinking in Seoul.[2] Since Holbrooke had specifically asked what I thought was a likely scenario, I speculated in my response of June 14 that:

2. Although I had been given the gist by secure phone, I had already had a long meeting with General Chun before I received the written record and sent back my comments, which I cleared with John Wickham and Bob Brewster. They also reflected conversations with Deputy Assistant Secretary of State Evelyn Colbert and Korean Country Director Bob Rich. Holbrooke proposed coming himself to survey the scene and meet the new players. I suggested that it was a bit premature, so he sent Colbert and Rich to provide him a "second opinion."

The people of South Korea, while resigned or repressed now, will probably acquiesce in what is happening to them if the military leaders legitimize themselves by democratic forms, maintain their internal unity, cope successfully with serious economic problems, and demonstrate a capacity to learn their job. A minority will never acquiesce. Over the longer run, continued public tolerance of the regime will require a more liberal evolution than the leaders presently seem to have in mind.

I agreed with Washington's view that we should not tamper with our security commitment, military presence, or economic cooperation. President Carter's comments of May 31 effectively precluded us from introducing the slight note of uncertainty I had recommended a few days previously. Endorsing the "posture of reserve," I also elaborated on the potential utility of refusing to grant the new regime complete legitimacy:

> Even though the new officers have rationalized their actions in terms of the national interest, they nevertheless know they usurped power and recognize their leadership must be legitimized through publicly accepted forms as well as practical success. Their need for legitimacy is intensified in a divided country where both halves are competing for the national mantle. In any event, they are eager to have us accept them, and—to a limited extent—we may be able to exploit their concern.

This concept of "deprival" became a central aspect of our strategy toward Chun.

Within this solid consensus about basic strategy, there were, to be sure, differences of view or interpretation between Seoul and Washington, none of which caused a major dispute. The most potentially serious was the language used in our warning to Chun to underscore our disapproval of recent events without, however, weakening our security commitment and inviting trouble from North Korea. Even after President Carter's conservative public stance on May 31 ruled out my initial recommendation for dealing with these inherently contradictory requirements, we kept searching for a formulation strong enough to generate some real worry in the new crowd in Seoul. The final version we settled on was the talking point I was instructed to use with Chun Doo Hwan:

> We remain faithful to our commitment to Korean security, and this is not an issue. As we have previously stated, we will reexamine in 1981 the question of further troop withdrawals. The actions of the Korean government

between now and then will inevitably shape congressional and public attitudes in the United States toward Korea. If a more broadly based support is not visible, the necessary public and political support in the United States for our presence in Korea could be weakened.

I delivered this warning as firmly as I could to Chun, but I felt this statement of the obvious was, on the one hand, not strong enough and, on the other, regrettable for its reference to troop withdrawals, which were repugnant to most South Koreans, not just the soldiers.

Another difference concerned "playing the North Korean card." Some members of Congress suggested to Dick Holbrooke that we tell Chun Doo Hwan we might in certain circumstances find it necessary to review our long-standing refusal to talk with the North Koreans without the South Koreans being present "in order to protect our interests on the peninsula." Apparently, David Aaron, Brzezinski's deputy in the National Security Council, had the same idea.[3] Fortunately, this dangerous idea withered under criticism from those of us who opposed it in light of repeated U.S. commitments to the contrary as well as the overwhelming objection of the South Korean people to such a move.

The most practical difference between Seoul and Washington was the matter of sanctions designed to give some bite to the relatively passive posture of "coolness and reserve" we were adopting toward the new leaders. To some extent this reflected the punitive instinct of our human rights activists (who by this time seemed to have lost all sense of proportion in dealing with Korea), but it also stemmed from a feeling of others in Washington that a business-as-usual approach in the security relationship might undercut Wickham's and my credibility and deprive us of important leverage. While appreciating the latter point, Wickham and I, nevertheless, firmly opposed almost all of the specific suggestions on grounds that they would harm mutual security interests without having much helpful political effect. In particular we objected to modifying our position on the supply of F-16 aircraft or the reduction of joint exercises with the Korean armed forces. Washington eventually resolved the matter more or less in our favor. Nevertheless, although issues such as the F-16s were never formally shelved, my impression was that "normal bureaucratic delay" in the approval procedure became even longer than "normal" in Washington.

3. See Oberdorfer, *The Two Koreas*, p. 131.

Finally, the Kim Dae Jung issue loomed larger on the Washington horizon than it did in Seoul with the myriad problems we faced. There was no political or moral argument between us, only a question of priorities for expending our limited resources. This will be clearer in the following chapter. Initially the only dispute was a tactical one. Given the potentially powerful controversy likely to surround any trial of Kim, Holbrooke asked me if we should try to pressure the regime to skip the trial and exile him to the United States. Foreshadowing my arguments a few weeks later in Washington, I urged that we "reserve any leverage we have to save his life, not waste it in a vain attempt to get him out of jail."

These were the parameters of the American strategy that was in place before Chun's final move in his quest for the presidency in late August 1980. The United States leaned heavily on the new authorities to moderate their repressive behavior and legitimize the emerging regime by lifting martial law, instituting constitutional reform, and holding free elections. We made a major effort to publicize this policy and in a variety of ways registered our reserve toward the new leaders, particularly by preventing high-level visits in either direction. Although we engaged in a fairly rugged struggle with Chun, including considerable public criticism, we did not risk pulling very hard on the powerful levers of Korea's security and economic dependence to force changes.[4] In short, we did not greatly alter the existing policy—a wise decision, in my opinion, at least as long as the Korean people did not demonstrate greater resistance to the emerging leadership.

Frustrating Dialogue with Chun

Despite the outcome of this policy debate, we expended much energy and demonstrated enormous frustration in the evolution of our policy. The ful-

---

4. The *New York Times*, for example, carried an article on June 13 correctly reflecting Holbrooke's comments, made on the condition of no attribution: "The United States has indefinitely postponed sending a high-level economic delegation to South Korea and has put all aspects of relations except a basic security commitment under active review as a sign of displeasure with the new military-dominated leadership, high-ranking Carter administration officials said today. The officials said they had no doubt that Lieutenant General Chun Doo Hwan was planning either to assume power or to have a man of his choice do so, despite continued private and public American exhortations for a return to the period of liberalization that followed the assassination of President Park Chung Hee . . . The United States ambassador had told General Chun and other leaders that the United States believed the direction they were taking was fundamentally wrong and would cause political instability and weaken the country internally and externally." Bernard Gwertzman, "U.S. Showing Displeasure over the Crisis in Seoul," *New York Times*, June 13, 1980, p. A9.

crum for argument with the Koreans was an extended discussion between General Chun and me, taking place over the course of three long conversations at my residence, June 4, June 26, and July 8, 1980. In each instance I was following personal instructions from Secretary of State Muskie, and for the second and third conversations, Muskie's instructions reflected guidelines approved by the president. In the first session, I politely asked a wide range of questions about Chun's and the government's intentions. In the second, I provided him with Washington's reaction, implicitly acknowledging our practical need to deal with him and identifying the benchmarks by which we would judge his conduct. In the third, I read him a message from Secretary Muskie that, among other things, accused him of "abusing" the American security commitment in his efforts to establish control. This was a systematic, cool, blunt presentation of U.S. worries and complaints, which Chun handled with considerable skill.

For the June 4 meeting, I was accompanied by senior intelligence representative Brewster. Perhaps in part because of Secretary Muskie's injunction to me to "inquire, not lecture," General Chun seemed more relaxed, less (obviously) disingenuous, and more politically sophisticated than I had found him previously. I set the tone with the president's May 31 cable television interview, noting the constancy of our security commitment but also the serious setbacks to democratic development since our last meeting—the student demonstrations in Seoul, the declaration of emergency martial law, events in Kwangju, and the establishment of the new Special Committee for National Security Affairs and steering committee. Since all of these had caused great concern in the United States, Secretary Muskie had asked me to seek Chun's views on a number of questions.

In long responses, Chun talked positively but vaguely of resuming normal political activity. Speaking personally (because, he insisted, President Choi, not he, was responsible for political matters), he suggested that the National Assembly and political parties should play a role in amending the constitution and forming a new government. He would acquiesce in direct election of the next president from among several contending candidates, since that was what the people clearly desired (although he would prefer indirect election through some kind of electoral college). Chun was unwilling, however, to predict when martial law would be lifted and, while acknowledging my strong arguments against doing so, did not rule out conducting a referendum under martial law.

After promising to refrain from an assault on the business community and to ensure fair and humane treatment of prisoners, Chun lashed out at

Kim Dae Jung. Accusing Kim and his cohorts of subversion (planning a virtual coup) against the government, he said emotionally that they would be tried under pertinent laws. The roots of Kim Dae Jung would be "completely eradicated." I limited my comment to a statement that Kim, if deemed guilty, should be brought to trial promptly and given a fair hearing. In the meantime, he should be treated with care.

When Chun complained to me about the spread of misinformation, particularly false stories in religious circles about the bayoneting of pregnant women in Kwangju by the special forces, I suggested that when his committee conducted hearings in Kwangju, it might be wise to talk to everyone about these stories and then to issue a statement based on an objective investigation of the facts. I seized the opportunity to complain about the behavior of the special forces, stating that soldiers trained for special combat against North Korean invaders should never have been used for crowd control in South Korea. I urged that this aspect of the Kwangju affair be properly acknowledged. Although Chun agreed that they had been rough and regretted their use, his general defensiveness made it clear that no senior official was about to apologize.

At the end of our talk, Chun more or less acknowledged my point that he and the army had become very involved in politics, despite his earlier assurances to us that they would not. The army would still, he said, eventually return to its military responsibilities. In my report to Washington, I commented that Chun "probably intends to play a very prominent political role in the future, perhaps beginning with the job of shogun to an elected emperor and then moving in as emperor."

About two weeks after this encounter, Secretary Muskie sent President Carter a comprehensive analysis of events in Korea along with policy recommendations, including talking points he wished me to use in my next meeting with Chun. To keep friends informed and signal what was coming, I spoke frankly in advance to both Foreign Minister Park and Blue House Secretary General Choi about what I was going to say to Chun.[5] They were candid about the regrettable cockiness of the new crowd, agreed on the dangers of a nationalistic confrontation, and indirectly urged me to keep up the good work of trying to moderate extremism and liberalize the thinking of the new leaders.

---

5. I was also instructed to inform the foreign minister that the United States would abstain from approving an Asia Development Bank loan to Korea and would explain the vote as a response to events in Korea. Minister Park was unhappy, but not surprised.

I met General Chun on June 26. Explaining that I had been instructed to reiterate and amplify U.S. views in light of comments he had made during our previous session, I carefully read him my talking points. In summary, these said that we believed:

—Real stability in Korea could not be achieved through repressive measures and required discernible progress toward an effective, constitutional, and elected government;

—Failure to move in this direction could weaken necessary public and congressional support for our military presence in Korea as well as jeopardize the confidence of the international economic community;

—A constitutional referendum conducted under martial law would be gravely flawed in both international and domestic terms;

—Manipulating anti-American sentiment against us was highly dangerous; and

—Kim Dae Jung's trial would be viewed with great concern; his torture or execution would have a "grave and crippling impact" on our relations (see appendix, item 8).

I emphasized that we were not trying to impose an American blueprint on Korea, because we knew that political change could only take place through a Korean formula. Our key concern was that the formula be acceptable to the majority of the Korean people.

Chun listened with particular attention to my complaints about anti-Americanism, showing his only signs of unease during the entire meeting. He stated flatly, albeit unconvincingly, that there would be "no problem." Although anti-American sentiment did exist, it was exaggerated on the left and posed no serious problem on the right, including the army. Admittedly, five or six months earlier some officers (including, I am sure, Chun himself) had characterized me as a "governor general," but that was "incorrect" and diminishing.

With some prodding from me, Chun reaffirmed the objective of "democratizing" Korea so long as order could be preserved. Although he did not rule out lifting martial law before the constitutional referendum, he urged us not to make this a condition of our support. As before, his most emotional comments concerned political detainees. He dismissed my comments about how foreigners would view any kind of trial for Kim Dae Jung, firmly announcing that Kim would soon be brought to public trial for attempting to overthrow the constitutional government. Americans, he complained, did not understand the seriousness of Kim's crime or the extent to which he was distrusted by most Koreans. Chun was less wrought about Kim Jong Pil.

The only matter that was resolved to our complete satisfaction was Chun's ready agreement to resolve a conflict of interest by relieving General Wickham's Korean deputy on the Combined Forces Command from his recent assignment to Chun's steering group.

This second talk certainly served to clarify and sharpen Chun's understanding of our position. On the issues of martial law, political prisoners, and anti-Americanism, I felt that Chun might possibly try to accommodate us within narrow limits. Despite some agreement on clichés, such as "democratization," however, it was obvious that we remained a gulf apart on the central question of political liberalization and the highly charged matter of Kim Dae Jung. I commented to my superiors in Washington that Chun struck me as a tough, authoritarian figure motivated by ambition and narrow beliefs: "He clearly underestimates the complexity of the people and the world around him. I sense he has a long way to go before he has enough knowledge to run the Republic of Korea successfully."

I had let the Blue House, foreign minister, and General Chun know that I would be seeing Secretary Muskie shortly after the June 26 meeting. Not having returned to Washington for almost a year and working for a new secretary of state whom I had never met, I felt out of touch and handicapped compared with earlier years. While I was serving as his deputy in Washington, Dick Holbrooke had allowed—even encouraged—me to work closely with Secretary Vance. Knowing them both quite well was enormously reassuring when I had to make decisions without guidance from headquarters. Since I wanted to meet the new secretary to get a sense of his appreciation of the Korean problem, Holbrooke arranged for me to go down to Kuala Lumpur, where Muskie was attending a meeting of foreign ministers from the Association of Southeast Asian Nations, and ride back with him on his plane as far as Japan.

My weekend trip was extremely useful. Secretary Muskie had cleared his calendar so that we were able to talk without interruption for three hours on the plane and a bit more at Yokota airbase in Japan, where General Wickham joined us. After listening to my fairly systematic review and replies to his questions, Muskie commented that he felt Chun Doo Hwan was abusing the American security commitment to Korea. I thought this was an apt characterization, and we agreed that I should tell this to Chun under instruction. I drafted my instructions on the plane, the secretary made a few changes, and I sent them back to Washington for concurrence from the Defense Department and National Security Council (see appendix, item 9).

Armed with these instructions, I met General Chun for the third round of our discussion on July 8. (Since my deputy, John Monjo, would be carrying on for me during my home leave and consultations in Washington, I had him join me in addition to Bob Brewster.) I made clear to General Chun that what I was about to say was Secretary Muskie's personal reaction to what I had told him during our talk on the plane. Apart from the secretary's unmistakable imprint and unusually blunt language, the statement that I then read to him hewed closely to the substance of the one I used at our previous session. It began by explaining that the United States had vigorously fulfilled its deterrent role and defense commitment only to find that the authorities in Korea "have abused this American commitment." On the issue of the regime's legitimacy, it stated, "We lack confidence that what the Korean authorities are currently doing to establish a government will have the support of the Korean people." And on the matter of countering the misrepresentation of our views to the Korean people, it said we looked forward to "more progress than we have experienced in the recent past."

While expressing appreciation for our determination to maintain our basic security relationship, Chun denied abusing our security commitment, except possibly on December 12, 1979, for which he apologized. Since his rationalization for this behavior demonstrated his failure to understand Muskie's point, I commented that we were referring to an ongoing situation in which Korean authorities were not giving adequate weight to our views. Even though our government had reiterated our security commitment to Korea, we would not be able to maintain the necessary support in our country for this commitment unless the Korean government had the legitimacy of being supported by the Korean people. Chun assured me rather mechanically that he "fully understood" my point.

Chun minimized the issue of anti-Americanism, paraphrasing the arguments he used during our previous session, and he foresaw a gradual easing of censorship, making clear, however, that it would be a long time before Korea enjoyed American-style freedom of the press.

Once again our sharpest exchanges were over Kim Dae Jung. I reminded him that I had previously cautioned him that actions against Kim would draw strong reactions from the American and Japanese governments, even though we would try to avoid inflammatory language in our public statements. With this introduction, I provided him a copy of the strong statement issued in Washington on July 7, 1980, commenting critically on the Martial Law Command's investigative report of July 4, which, among other things, alleged that Kim was a confirmed communist, was directly responsible for events in Kwangju, and sought to overthrow the Korean government. With some emotion, Chun told me to tell Washington that Kim was being tried for violating the laws of the land; there was no political intent or motive involved. He warned that we should not act as though we believed "Kim Dae Jung should be the president of Korea."

At the end of our meeting, I told Chun that, despite his denials, many people in the United States looked on the trial as a political one and that much would depend on the nature of the trial and the sentence Kim received. Expressing concern at having heard a number of Korean military officers dismiss the dangers of killing Kim, I bluntly told Chun, "Before you execute Kim, you had better turn him over to me, and I will get him out of here." He urged that we not jump to the conclusion that Kim would be executed, and, to my pleasant surprise, he agreed to permit foreign observers from respected international organizations at the trial "so long as there are only one or two, and they do not become another cheering section for Kim Dae Jung."

So ended my portion of the dialogue with Chun Doo Hwan during the summer months of 1980. We had managed to be blunt with each other without arousing anger. I had delivered a clear message to Chun, including the benchmarks by which we were going to judge him. Chun seemed ready to accommodate us on the margins of our disagreement, and he was beginning to play with us on the issue of Kim Dae Jung. Although he did not dispute the concept of political legitimacy, we remained far apart on what was necessary to achieve it.

Censorship and Distortion of U.S. Views

Throughout the transition of Chun's nine-month ascension from major general to president of the Republic of Korea, we were plagued by censorship and deliberate distortion of U.S. views by the Korean authorities. Chun Doo Hwan and members of his core group seemed oblivious of or indifferent to the consequences of treating a critically important ally with the same loose standards of integrity they had learned to employ in psychological warfare against the North Koreans. As I have recounted in previous chapters, Chun privately and semi-publicly insinuated U.S. complicity in President Park's assassination, and despite the lack of any evidence and my firm denial, he continued to allude to the issue for several months. In circumstances where ignorance of the facts generated conspiracy theories, this dishonesty damaged our standing among important groups of Koreans, including members of the senior military community. During and immediately after the Kwangju crisis, his martial law cohorts led the people of Kwangju to believe that the United States approved the use of the special forces, helping to sow the seeds of a misunderstanding that damaged the American image among Koreans generally, not just among the victims in Kwangju.

Together with the more innocent effects of severe censorship, this deliberate effort to manipulate the truth reached a point in mid-June where I informed Washington that not only the Korean people but even American citizens in Korea had little knowledge, or only distorted knowledge, of the U.S. government's position on key developments and policy. President Carter's May 31 cable television statement, for example, was stripped of references to setbacks to democracy; Secretary Muskie's comments on Korea were euphemized into expressions of general support; and critical U.S. government commentary was totally ignored. In addition, I complained that some elements of the new regime were working to portray General Wickham and me as out of line with our government's policy—both by creating or encouraging local misinformation and by trying to reach over our heads to Americans who would, they hoped, be more understanding. More than one American correspondent, I said, had played their game.

Although there was no way we could override the Martial Law Command's control over what appeared in the Korean media, we ensured that our armed forces radio and television networks sustained full coverage of U.S. statements and opinion, knowing that large numbers of foreigners and considerable numbers of Koreans would be kept informed in addition to the American community. As a further measure, we packaged important U.S. statements in the form of English- and Korean-language press releases, sending more than 3,000 copies to the broadest possible target audience. We realized that many Korean recipients would not receive the material, while others, including some military officers, would profess their unwillingness to read it. I also proposed to the State Department that Holbrooke, Armacost, or Rich seek to testify before subcommittees of the House and Senate in hopes that the testimony would seep back into Korea via the grapevine. Armacost promptly did so.

Most of our citizens, many other foreigners, and members of the Korean elite welcomed this service, which we kept going for several months, but it was insufficient to repair the damage done by the earlier distortions and led to considerable friction with the Korean Ministry of Defense, which objected from the start to having military officers among the recipients.

Minister Choo nagged me steadily and sought reinforcement from his new colleague at the Foreign Ministry. We eventually yielded, and our media effort withered away as both censorship and the sense of crisis eased. For the first few weeks, it was energy well spent, and I enjoyed tangling with Minister Choo over his stubborn effort to keep his troops ignorant.

Chun Doo Hwan Replaces Choi Kyu Ha

Since I thought that General Chun and his colleagues would keep events under firm control at least through the end of the summer, I returned home for leave and consultations from mid-July until late August 1980. I knew that there might well be surprises while I was away, but surprises seemed to be a permanent condition in Korea, and I had complete confidence in the ability of my deputy, John Monjo, to deal with whatever came along. I planned, moreover, to spend quite a bit of time in Washington and always to remain within phone contact of Seoul.

Both the Koreans and the State Department kept Monjo very busy while I was away. Most of his effort with the Foreign Ministry, Blue House, and General Chun centered on the impending trial of Kim Dae Jung, where we wanted Kim to have a fair chance to defend himself and to do so under international observation. I cover these efforts in the next chapter. But the summer "surprise" was Chun's unexpectedly early vault into the Blue House and an internal American problem along the way. Monjo handled both skillfully.

When I left Seoul on July 15, I did not have a clear picture of what was to become of President Choi. The assaults on his rule, first from the left and then from the right, seemed to have fatally damaged his presidency. His resignation immediately after the Kwangju tragedy would not have surprised me, yet in his diminishing appearances, he still maintained a posture of continuing resolve. Were Choi finally to quit, there was absolutely no doubt in my mind that Steering Committee Chairman Chun Doo Hwan would be his effective successor. To this day I have no special knowledge of what changed this situation. In the absence of better explanations, I speculate that the relative ease with which Chun assumed real political control in the months of May, June, and July caused him to be more and more overbearing with Choi Kyu Ha, finally triggering Choi's decision to resign. More certainly, I believe the rumor mill was lubricated and filled to hasten the process. In any event, about two months after his June address to the nation, a severely weakened Choi Kyu Ha resigned as president on August 16, 1980. The only candidate to replace him was Korea's new strongman. Having had himself promoted to full general and then retiring from the army, Chun Doo Hwan was elected president of the Republic of Korea on August 27, 1980, by the Council on Unification in accordance with the provisions of the *Yushin* Constitution. The council, an electoral college, consisted of 2,500 members selected and elected under the guidance of officials who, in turn, were appointed by the central government.

The policies and behavior of the U.S. government obviously played some part in this accelerated transition. Viewed objectively, we added to the weight bearing down on President Choi while complicating but not stopping the plans of Chun. For many Koreans, however, this honorable, if marginal, American role was distorted by Chun's apparatus into allegations that the United States backed Chun. As I have explained in the previous chapter about Kwangju, we tried hard to stop this damaging manipulation of reality, but the process of distortion continued. To make matters worse, we inadvertently provided Chun with a tool that he employed shamelessly to his tactical advantage.

For more than six months, John Wickham had been meeting periodically with Chun Doo Hwan in the latter's military capacity as head of the Defense Security Command. Wickham used these sessions, which were always carefully coordinated with me, to review military matters, and, when I thought it would be useful, to reinforce points I was making to Chun and other leaders about general policy. With Monjo's concurrence, Wickham continued this practice while I was away. Seeing Chun on August 8, 1980, he not only covered military matters but also reviewed in faultless fashion the issues I had addressed in my long dialogue with Chun. Toward the end of the conversation, Wickham mentioned a rumor that President Choi would resign in the near future and expressed his hope that this would not occur for reasons of stability. Chun responded, "Well, that's a rumor." He did not complete the sentence. The negative twist in Wickham's question and his comment about the U.S. reaction were precisely correct.

In my absence Wickham's profile was higher than normal among U.S. officials in Seoul, and this quite natural phenomenon would not have raised eyebrows if Chun had not been in the midst of his endgame for taking over the presidency and if several American correspondents had not been in town hungry for a story. Poorly advised, I believe, by his public affairs officer, Wickham agreed to see two of these journalists, Terry Anderson of the Associated Press and Sam Jameson of the *Los Angeles Times*, on a not-for-attribution basis on August 7. On the subject of how the United States would react if General Chun were indirectly elected to succeed President Choi Kyu

Ha, they quoted a "highly placed U.S. military official" as saying, "Provided that he comes to power legitimately and demonstrates over time a broad base of support from the Korean people, and does not jeopardize the security of the situation here, we will support him because that, of course, is what we think the Korean people want." Given what Wickham and I had been saying to each other privately for several months and reporting back to Washington, this commonsensical comment was not far out of line with American thinking, but it was, nevertheless, an untimely, premature public statement.[6] It should have been left unsaid or at least accompanied by an explanation of what was meant by the words "support" and "comes to power legitimately." Wickham should also have been more circumspect in his other comments.

Anderson and Jameson, both well known for being responsible journalists, were more impressed by Wickham's talk of "support" for Chun than by the way he qualified his remarks. Naturally, they filed attention-grabbing stories. Compounding the problem, Chun, in an interview with *New York Times* correspondent Henry Scott-Stokes on August 8, identified the "highly placed U.S. military official" as Wickham, thus obviating the nonattribution constraints of Wickham's remarks. The stories from Seoul led to heavy coverage in the American media. Korean regurgitations, which were shamelessly censored and twisted to suggest unqualified U.S. government support for Chun, added to the sensation. Chun was delighted. While angered by what he felt to be misrepresentation of his views, Wickham was, of course, most embarrassed by the effect in Washington as well as in Seoul. When queried, the State Department spokesman was in the awkward position of having to declare that the comments attributed to Wickham did not represent U.S. policy and that the question of who should be president of Korea was a matter to be decided by the Korean people.

I first read versions of Wickham's remarks while vacationing in New York, and I got some rather confusing additional detail by phone from Bob Rich in Washington. I interrupted my leave to attend an informal interagency meeting convened in Washington by Deputy Assistant Secretary of State Armacost on August 14 to discuss President Choi's impending resignation and the Wickham flap. We agreed to ask Wickham, who was visiting the commander in chief, Pacific, in Hawaii to stay away from Korea at least until

---

6. Ironically, Wickham, who had reacted even more negatively than I to Chun beginning with the insubordination of December 12, had by this time apparently become somewhat more resigned than I to Chun's final move to the top. The difference between us, however, was minor.

Choi resigned. We also agreed on the nature of talking points and public statements that we should use in Washington and Seoul to set the record straight—the United States had never endorsed Chun as president and expected him to seek validation from the Korean people through the political reforms promised by Choi. Most important, we recommended that President Carter send Chun a letter setting forth the facts and our expectations of the Chun presidency. Monjo favored sending such a letter as well as publicizing its general character. I strongly endorsed the idea, arguing that, apart from clarifying our policy, a firm letter from Carter, if delivered by me on instruction, would help to restore U.S. lines of authority in Korea.

Although Wickham was criticized for what he did, I never heard anyone blame him for causing major damage to our position in Korea. When the storm struck, Dick Holbrooke called Wickham in Honolulu, told him he had made a mistake, and then defended him before angry superiors who feared a repetition of the Singlaub affair. When I arrived in Washington, I quickly made clear to the leadership of the state and defense departments that I considered Wickham an outstanding officer whose unfortunate interview should be viewed in the context of the good judgment and exemplary cooperation he had provided us beginning with the events of December 12. No one in the State Department disagreed with me, nor did the chairman of the Joint Chiefs of Staff when he asked me privately if I was still satisfied with Wickham. We promptly informed the Koreans that Wickham continued to enjoy his government's confidence as military commander, and I felt very comfortable knowing that he would be a colleague for the remainder of my tour in Korea.

The brouhaha over Wickham's comments more or less coincided with conclusive intelligence that Chun's move to replace Choi was imminent. Monjo sent in a well-reasoned recommendation about how we should deal with this, pointing out the technical legality of Chun Doo Hwan's impending election, the likelihood that the vast majority of the Korean people would accept the change fatalistically, and the prospect that we would have to live with Chun, perhaps for a long time. Monjo recommended that we:

—Accept Chun as president, extending at least the minimum normal courtesies;

—Use a presidential letter to make clear our expectations about political reform, including a popularly elected president, as well as lenient treatment of the regime's opponents; and

—In various ways publicize this position, making clear that we had never endorsed Chun's election and would judge him by his deeds.

As I recall, no one in Washington dissented from this sensible advice. American officials were quick to register anger and dismay over the way Korean authorities had twisted reality to imply U.S. support for various actions, with misconstruing Wickham's remarks being only the most recent and egregious. Mike Armacost began the process on August 11 during a session with the Korean CIA station chief. Holbrooke and Acting Secretary of State Christopher underscored our concern in their meetings with Blue House Secretary General Choi Kwang Soo, who was visiting Washington as an emissary from Chun. I was with Holbrooke on August 20 when he forcefully described Chun's action as an example of Chun's abuse of the security relationship. Choi clearly understood the danger of continuing the practice and promised to explain it carefully to Chun. When Monjo, as chargé, made the same points to Chun under instruction from Washington, Chun simply ducked comment, going on to discuss another matter. In my capacity as ambassador, I might have been able to extract a response from Chun, but I could not have reversed the course of events.

U.S. Policy toward the New Regime

To register coolness and reserve toward his regime, the United States decided not to send any special representatives to President Chun Doo Hwan's inauguration. I returned to Seoul from Washington on August 28, and in my ambassadorial capacity I alone represented the United States at the ceremony held September 1, 1980. Two days later, I met with President Chun to deliver President Carter's letter of congratulation. This letter, which we had translated into Korean, began with a reaffirmation of our desire to maintain security and economic relationships and ended with a courteous offer of cooperation. In between, it broke from the mold of congratulatory messages to convey three substantive points:

—We were greatly troubled by recent events in Korea;

—Chun needed to ensure stability in Korea through development of popularly supported political institutions and greater personal freedom; and

—Kim Dae Jung's execution or even death sentence could have serious repercussions.

Sorting out roles, Carter also mentioned pointedly that I was responsible for contact with Chun and his cabinet while Wickham enjoyed his full confidence to carry out our defense commitment.

President Chun read the letter carefully and invited me to give an account of my discussions in Washington. Noting the realism of our decision not to tamper with our security or economic relations, I emphasized that almost everyone with whom I talked (including representatives and senators, Republicans as well as Democrats, some of whom I named) was unhappy over recent developments in Korea. They were skeptical that the Chun government would do enough to enlist popular support, and they were angry over the misrepresentation of U.S. government views. They were particularly disturbed over the Kim Dae Jung trial, which would weigh heavily in their calculations. Outside the government, I was disturbed by the number of people—some quite conservative—who asked me whether there was any significant difference between North and South Korea. I cautioned Chun that he should be aware that his emphasis on law, order, discipline, and efficiency had left Americans with an image of regimentation, which was damaging to South Korea. This could be corrected if the government carried through with its political agenda in ways that generated popular support.

I concluded my rehearsed remarks by saying that we accepted the Chun government as a political reality and were prepared to work with it. The criteria by which we would judge it would be the nature of the new constitution, the degree of freedom with which the Korean people were able to consider that constitution, the conduct of new elections, and the disposition of the Kim Dae Jung case. I complimented the president on his new cabinet, especially his selection of Prime Minister Nam Duk Woo, a highly regarded figure.

Chun thanked me both for the speed with which President Carter had communicated his private concerns and the frankness of my own review. He assured me that he would work vigorously to sustain and improve ties with the United States and urged that we be "patient" before judging his government.

I was surprised by the brevity of Chun's response, but I thought it was far more skillful than his past practice of tangling with me over almost everything I said. In my report to Washington, I limited my comment to saying that Chun struck me as a fast learner who seemed comfortable, and very pleased, to be sitting in the chair of his former Blue House mentor, Park Chung Hee.

Following is the full text of President Carter's letter to President-elect Chun, dated August 27, 1980:

Dear President-elect Chun:

As you assume your responsibilities as President of the Republic of Korea, I want personally to assure you of our desire to maintain the basic economic and security relationships that are so important to the interests of both of our nations.

At this time, I want you to know that recent events in Korea have troubled us greatly. We have noted your reaffirmation of the commitment by former President Choi to submit a new constitution soon to a public referendum and to hold popular elections under that constitution by early next year, but the conditions under which these developments take place will be critical in determining the future of your country and its international standing. We regard free political institutions as essential to sustaining a sound relationship between our two countries.

The trial of Mr. Kim Dae Jung has attracted wide international attention. I do not raise this delicate matter with any wish to interfere in your internal judicial processes. Nevertheless, I urge you privately to take whatever steps are necessary to avoid having the issue of fair treatment erode your nation's relations with the United States and other countries. Mr. Kim's execution, or even a sentence of death, could have serious repercussions. I have authorized Ambassador Gleysteen to discuss this matter further with you under conditions of total confidentiality.

Ambassador Gleysteen will also maintain close contact with you and your new cabinet in the months ahead as you seek to resolve the other pressing issues facing your nation.

We remain firm in our determination to honor our security commitment to the Republic of Korea against external aggression. General Wickham has my full confidence in this commitment.

I recognize the difficulty of the issues you face. Nevertheless, I urge you to take the earliest possible action to ensure the stability of the government through the development of popularly supported political institutions and greater personal freedom for your citizens.

In closing, Mr. President, let me repeat that I look forward to enhancing the cooperation between our two nations in support of our common interests in the months ahead.

Sincerely,

Jimmy Carter

Chun replied to Carter on September 8, promising, among other things, to lift martial law before elections under the new constitution. In dealings with the media, our two governments described this presidential exchange quite differently, the United States stressing the need for political liberalization and Korea inevitably focusing on Carter's reaffirmation of the security commitment. Chun and his aides declined our suggestion to publicize portions of the letters.

The Marginal Effect of U.S. Policy

Although the regime's censors routinely warped news about American policy, many members of the educated elite in Korea had a reasonably good understanding of our policy derived from a variety of sources, particularly our armed forces radio and television network and the materials the embassy was energetically disseminating in Korea. Whatever the gaps or distortions in public understanding, moreover, President Chun Doo Hwan and his close colleagues were quite clear about U.S. policy. Under instruction, I made frequent representations to the president and his associates urging that the new constitution accommodate a broad spectrum of opinion and allow a popular election among several candidates; that the National Assembly be convened to allow resumption of normal political activity; that martial law be lifted before the popular referendum as well as the presidential election; that censorship be eased; that Kim Dae Jung's life be saved; and that political detainees and prisoners be rehabilitated. These representations were systematically reinforced during many other high-level contacts with Korean military as well as civilian officials in Washington and Seoul.

Nevertheless, judging by results and substance rather than form, this steady pressure from the United States seems to have played an even more marginal role than our earlier effort to contain the effects of the December 12 army coup. There were some obvious reasons.

First, Chun Doo Hwan was not really worried about our commitment to Korea's security and economic survival. This bold and aggressive risktaker had not agonized about American reactions the night of December 12, and since that time not only had he survived the Kwangju crisis but his regime had been assured, both publicly and privately, that the United States would not tamper with basic security and economic relations. Perhaps my abortive recommendation after Kwangju that we threaten him with a "fundamental review" of our policy would have given him pause, but I suspect that he still would have bullied his way into the presidency.

Second, despite my effort to keep some balance in our approach to Chun, it quickly became clear to him that the Carter administration placed the highest priority on saving Kim Dae Jung's life. So long as he kept us anxious but hopeful about Kim's fate, he was able to go his own way on the issues of governance without generating severe strain in the U.S. relationship.

Third, Carter lost the November 1980 presidential election to Ronald Reagan, and Chun knew that at least some of Reagan's advisers were less concerned than Carter about the domestic policies of the Korean government. Although hindsight has sharpened the picture, I was quite conscious in 1980 that each of these factors undermined our negotiating strength.

Depriving Chun of the U.S. Seal of Approval

Although we were handicapped by being unable or unwilling to reinforce our policy with powerful military or economic leverage, we had some success in consciously exploiting the new regime's eagerness to be accepted as a fully legitimate government. With a seal of approval from Korea's ally, Chun knew that he would find it easier to enlist domestic support, engage the international community, and compete with North Korea. Without it, he could survive but would suffer considerable frustration and indignity. For Chun himself, the ideal symbol of success would be a successful summit meeting with the president of the United States, but he and his cohorts were also eager to resume the normal exchanges of cabinet-level officials. For most military officers, the acid test was U.S. willingness to conduct the high-profile, long-postponed security consultative meeting.

The Carter administration withheld these signs of approval. The security consultative meeting with its attendant session of defense ministers was indefinitely postponed. No cabinet-level meetings took place. Only a few friendly Korean official visitors were received in Washington, where they were subjected to firm American "advice," and no major American official came to Korea except a few persons on economic missions, the U.S. army chief of staff, and, after the U.S. elections, the secretary of defense on a special mission.[7] Perhaps most annoying to Chun, the U.S. government minimized its ceremonial association with his regime. At the beginning, this symbolic stance was sometimes spiced with displays of anger, particularly after Chun's insubordination the night of December 12, but by mid-1980 normal behavior had resumed for the most part, and considerable tolerance had developed on both sides. Along with my colleagues, I maintained friendly contact with a wide range of Korean officials. My relationship with Chun,

7. We welcomed General Meyer's visit in June 1980, because he was prepared to speak forcefully on command discipline, military professionalism, and the importance of civilian leadership. Secretary Brown came briefly in December with a final message from Carter for Chun Doo Hwan regarding Kim Dae Jung.

while reserved, was not hostile. Despite my real anger over the way he ma-nipulated Korean popular understanding of American policy, we had both learned to discuss highly charged subjects in a civil manner.

Granting my subjectivity as one of the principal architects and implementers of it, I think this policy of reserve toward Chun was more successful than mounting heavy rhetorical assaults without the backing of major sanctions that we deemed (correctly, I believe) too dangerous. Our stance probably contributed to some of the constitutional improvements. It helped to prevent the holding of the new presidential election under martial law. And, as I explain in the following chapter, it was a critical aspect of our effort to spare the life of Kim Dae Jung. To be sure, the longer Chun was in power without revolt from the Korean people, the harder it was for us to hold the line against normalized relations. Moreover, once bargaining be-gan over the Kim issue, willingness to normalize our behavior was inherent to a successful resolution.

The Nature of Chun's Regime

What this policy of reserve did not accomplish was meaningful progress toward our fundamental goal of a new, broadly based Korean regime se-lected by a democratic process. As we used to say in the embassy, Chun Doo Hwan was a "son of *Yushin*," so it was hardly surprising that his new regime blended the need for "democracy" and "order" with a heavy stress on the latter. In form if not substance, there were some improvements over Park Chung Hee's *Yushin* Constitution. While still providing for indirect election of the president, the new constitution established a larger and semi-demo-cratic electoral college and limited the president to one term. More impor-tant, it eliminated the provision for appointed members of the National Assembly. The cabinet that Chun selected to work within this framework included many highly competent figures, including economic technocrats. With the help of a bureaucracy that had been pruned and disciplined, they made rapid progress in improving economic conditions—an important rea-son the Korean public was not more restive under harsh rule. Chun, who was a hands-on leader, worked closely with his cabinet, proving to be an eager learner willing to listen and sometimes to acknowledge error.

These virtues did not disguise the fundamentally repressive nature of the new era. Despite our dire warnings, the popular referendum on the con-stitution was held under martial law (reduced from "emergency" to "normal" five days before the vote), and martial law was only lifted on January 24, 1981, nine days before Chun arrived at the White House and about a month before the presidential election, on February 25, which Chun won thanks both to the absence of any significant competition and to conservative electors kept in line by the incumbent government's patronage and manipulation. Although the National Assembly was reconstituted to include many respectable politicians, including some opposition figures, it was enfeebled by the effects of massive purges that removed thousands of politicians, journalists, academics, and labor leaders from the active scene without jailing them.

In short, the regime created by Chun was as authoritarian as that of Park Chung Hee's final years. Although the mailed fist employed in the massive crackdown of May 17 had been retracted, the new regime maintained control through arbitrary rules and shameless intimidation of opposition from any quarter. Compared with Park's worst years, the only distinct improvement was a leader who was younger, more flexible, and sometimes more willing to back down when he overstepped the bounds.

——11——

The American Effort to Save Kim Dae Jung's Life

DURING MY FINAL consultations in Washington before returning to Seoul, Dick Holbrooke asked Acting Secretary of State Christopher to convene key officials concerned with the Kim Dae Jung issue. All of us at this meeting in late August 1980 readily agreed that the United States needed to make an extraordinary effort to save Kim's life, but I was surprised when someone asked if this should not be our supreme objective over the next few months. I pointed out that we needed to deal with other people in Korea who were also under detention and that we were heavily committed to bringing about a broad agenda of political reforms. Being overly preoccupied with Kim Dae Jung might play into the hands of Chun and his cohorts. Although I found some sympathy for my arguments, there was overwhelming sentiment to concentrate on Kim Dae Jung. I knew from a stormy, argumentative session I had had with Secretary Muskie a few days earlier that he was part of this consensus. When Holbrooke took me into his office for a chat, I found Muskie grumbling about generals, and, not familiar with his style, I annoyed him with some unintentionally provocative comments. Although Holbrooke tried to rein me in, he did not move fast enough to stop the secretary from grabbing the papers in front of him and flinging them in the air in anger. After he vented with a round of senatorial rhetoric, he calmed down, and we had a reasonable conversation. The experience reinforced my decision to ride along with the tide, since I was as eager as any to save Kim Dae Jung and would do my best to do so. Nothing decided at this meeting in any way restricted my activity, but once back in Seoul I found that this powerful preoccupation would complicate my work and sometimes generate considerable friction.

Several months before this August meeting, the U.S. government had already begun a vigorous campaign to save Kim Dae Jung. Immediately after his arrest on May 17, 1980, we protested bitterly to the Korean ambassador in Washington as well as to the martial law commander and President Choi in Seoul. Thereafter, Kim was a major, or the only, topic of my (or Chargé Monjo's) ten or more meetings in 1980 with Chun Doo Hwan, the last occurring during the final weeks of the Carter administration in December. I also met twice on the subject with General Roh Tae-Woo, the defense security commander, who was probably President Chun's closest confidant and a key member of the leadership's inner core, as well as many times with Lho Shin Yong, the capable new foreign minister, who was considerably closer to the new military hierarchy than his predecessor.

Equally important, our contacts at high levels in Seoul were mirrored in Washington, where U.S. officials inserted the Kim Dae Jung issue into virtually every conversation with a Korean of any significance. With the help of General Wickham, Bob Brewster, and my senior embassy colleagues, we spread the net to many other Korean officials as well as to military officers, many of whom were reported to favor Kim's execution. While trying to discourage Congress from threatening sanctions, we welcomed reinforcing actions by our senators and representatives, and, to an unprecedented degree, we invited members of our business community to register their views with the Korean authorities. In my foreign service career, I can recall few other examples of such a concentrated effort by the U.S. government on behalf of a single individual. Fortunately, most knowledgeable Americans were impressively united behind this campaign, including many anticommunist conservatives who, despite their reservations about Kim Dae Jung as a leader, believed that his execution would dangerously impair American support for Korea.

Our efforts passed through a number of phases. The first was the protest and the unsuccessful effort to get Kim released from arrest, followed by representations against harsh treatment and demands for a modicum of fairness in trial procedures. In the process we told Chun that any trial of Kim would be viewed with great concern by Americans, while his execution would have a "grave and crippling impact" on our relations. Although undefined, this threat of dire consequences was the strongest language we had ever used with Chun Doo Hwan, and before my return to Washington in July Chun agreed to allow international observers at the trial. Despite our efforts, he refused, however, to allow Amnesty International and the International Council of Jurists to be included, limiting foreign observation to the U.S., Japanese, and a few other embassies along with press coverage through a pool arrangement.

The second phase, during the trial, concerned what we should say about the verdict and whether we should intensify our pressure on Chun. For me, this was by far the most excruciating period. From my Seoul vantage point as the senior American representative and interlocutor with Chun Doo Hwan, I was rationally convinced that self-restraint by the United States was the only way we could succeed, in essence giving Chun a long tether to deal with the powerful opposition within his ranks as well as his own contradictory feelings. Yet I also realized that I was walking on thin ice, with no guarantees of success, and that failure would be enormously damaging to the administration in the heat of the 1980 elections. Without much anguish, I decided to be guided by my "rational" conclusions. In general, I found that Washington ultimately supported me, although sometimes only after berating me as if I were a surrogate for Chun.

Shortly after my September 3 conversation with Chun, I sent a message that I knew would cause heartburn in some quarters of the State Department and White House. Acknowledging domestic political pressure to make a very strong, very strident statement when the trial reached a verdict of death for Kim Dae Jung, I urged restraint. To do otherwise might jeopardize our efforts to save Kim's life, violate President Carter's statement to President Chun that we did not intend to interfere with Korea's judicial process, and single out Korea for treatment we did not accord other friendly nations. In keeping with this, I provided the department with a draft statement, which was very restrained yet contained some critical content.

A few days later, I learned by phone from my State Department colleagues that President Carter and Secretary Muskie (for reasons never revealed to me but probably stemming from the human rights community) remained gravely concerned about the almost inevitable prospect that Kim Dae Jung would receive a death sentence. Despite my cautious prognosis that the sentence would be commuted by Chun, they were considering various ways to underscore their view to President Chun, including the threat of sanctions and dispatch of an emissary to Seoul, probably a senior military figure. I sent a long message to Secretary Muskie and Deputy Secretary Christopher, cautiously reiterating my assumption that Kim would receive a death sentence that I hoped—but could not guarantee—Chun would eventually commute. Despite my certainty that Chun understood the tough message we had already sent him, I said that I was prepared to try once more to get advance assurance from Chun that a death sentence would be commuted and to underscore that "even the issuance of a death sentence would be a most serious matter between our countries."

I strongly opposed going beyond this to demand a prearranged outcome of the trial. I warned rather huffily that if such an effort were coupled with the threat of sanctions, I would find my position as ambassador "untenable," because I had, on the basis of written and oral instructions, made clear to Korean authorities that we would not undertake such sanctions. I recommended making the representation myself on instruction from President Carter, commenting that "using a military officer to convey a purely political message is, as we have seen from this past summer's experience, a dangerous procedure, damaging to the proper role of our military officers here and easily manipulated by the Koreans."

Dick Holbrooke, who was in Australia, entered the fray with a message that, while loyally identifying him with Carter's and Muskie's concerns, effectively supported me. Even though concurring with my view on a military emissary, Holbrooke suggested that an emissary, possibly Ambassador Mansfield from Tokyo or preferably himself, might be appropriate at some point. I would have accepted Holbrooke, but Mansfield, even if willing, would have been inappropriate. Although he was a legendary political figure for whom I had the greatest respect, he was at the time serving as ambassador to a country that Chun and many other Koreans resented deeply. I was told later that he would have declined the role, as he did in the case of the Philippines. Very quickly, I received instructions to see Chun more or less as I had proposed.

I met with Chun privately on September 16 to convey the gravity with which President Carter would view the execution of Kim Dae Jung or even his being sentenced to death. In response to his point-blank inquiry as to what we were asking of him, I said that we hoped for something less than a death sentence, but since we could not ask him to manipulate the Korean judicial process, we were most concerned that, when the case came to him as president, he would commute Kim's sentence in a statesmanlike gesture.

Chun refused to give me the flat assurances I was seeking but left me confident that he intended to do what we wanted. Clearly relishing the irony of lecturing the American ambassador about the problem he would face if he were seen as violating judicial procedures, he warned me that public knowledge of our meeting could backfire because the Korean people were highly sensitive to foreign intervention. He also bridled at my mention of possible pressure on the administration to cut PL-480 grain sales and foreign military sales credits. In conclusion, he said that he had to take many considerations into account. Even though our pressures on him had reduced his ability to accommodate President Carter's desires, he would bear in mind political as well as legal issues when the case came to him from the Supreme Court. His overriding concern would be political stability in Korea. He acknowledged (but only by a nod) my request that he assure us he would take into account human rights concerns and his own statement to me that he did not view Kim Dae Jung as his personal enemy but as the antagonist of deceased Park Chung Hee.

In my urgent report back to the State Department I commented that:

> I am not sure whether our latest representation has helped or hindered matters, but I am convinced that we will rapidly undermine our position if we put any more pressure on Chun until a later stage in the process. I have in mind no further pressures from me, from the Washington end, or from any emissary. Our need to make a strident public comment on the issue will be at the expense of Chun's willingness to take into account what we want him to do.

I also provided the department with the suggested text of an even more restrained statement than the one I had previously recommended. To my great relief, Washington concurred. With a minor amount of editing, the State Department issued the following statement after the verdict on September 17, 1980 (see appendix, item 10):

> As is well known, we have followed the Court Martial trial of Kim Dae Jung with intense interest and deep concern. The government of the Republic of Korea is fully aware of our views. We obviously have strong feelings about the extreme verdict which has been handed down. Nevertheless, since the case is subject to judicial review, we have no additional comment on the matter at this time.

A week later John Monjo, Bob Brewster, and I had a long luncheon conversation with Defense Security Commander Roh Tae-Woo. During this rather friendly occasion, Roh philosophized over the cultural factors that affect the U.S.-Korean relationship and defended the series of events that led his friend Chun to the presidency, justifying it as a process forced on the military by the ambition of self-serving politicians. When we got to the subject of Kim Dae Jung and I reiterated our position, Roh excoriated Kim as a communist-leaning, unscrupulous politician, citing his 1971 campaign against Park and role among students the past spring. Roh reminded us, however, that Koreans valued life highly; Park may have been a dictator, but he never killed anyone. He urged that we be patient. Since Roh was close to Chun and known for being a tough, no-nonsense soldier, I was somewhat encouraged by the message he was conveying.

With the remarkable exercise of self-restraint manifested by our public statement of September 17, the U.S. government ceased further public comment on the Kim Dae Jung issue for the duration of the Carter administration. We also refrained from exerting direct pressure on President Chun for quite some time. In discreet contacts with other officials we, of course, continued our campaign, and, as I discuss below, we continued to agonize among ourselves and with the Japanese about what to do.

Contingency Planning

In late September and early October 1980, Dick Holbrooke and I exchanged frank messages, probing each other's thinking about strategy on the Kim Dae Jung issue. Although these were noncommittal, private communications about a contingency that, to our relief, did not occur, they are an important part of the historical record, revealing the boundaries of our thoughts at the time as well as highlighting the quite different pressures at work in Washington and Seoul. In Washington, the human rights community tended to favor exerting maximum possible pressure on Chun, having little knowledge of or sympathy for my arguments about the need for restraint. Working through Congress and the human rights machinery of the government bureaucracy, they found considerable resonance at high levels of the Carter administration for some of their well-intentioned, but ill-considered, proposals. Holbrooke and Rich had the unenviable task of coping with them. In Seoul I felt that we had shot all the ammunition we were willing to use and that the prospects of success were fair. I was convinced that further pressure or public criticism by our government would lead to a destructive backlash.

Prompted by his questions in late September, I sent Dick Holbrooke an assessment and a carefully reasoned proposed course of action. I said that I thought the Korean authorities understood quite clearly that the consequences of executing Kim would be very serious, specifically that they would sour the tone of Korean relations with the United States and Japan as well as jeopardize congressionally approved military credits at a time when Korea could ill afford such sanctions. Although I realized that Chun and his co-horts probably calculated that they could survive our wrath, I remained cautiously confident that they wanted to avoid severe strain in the relationship. To encourage them toward moderation, I urged that we continue our own posture of public restraint and reserve any further direct pressure on Chun until November or December, when Kim's case came before him on completion of judicial review. At that time, I agreed that we needed to send a strong message probably by a presidential emissary. In the meantime, even before our elections, I argued in favor of hinting to Chun that we would reward a favorable outcome by warming up our relationship with his regime through a friendly high-level visit and rescheduling the security consultative meeting in December.

In his response Holbrooke chastised me—with good reason—for some impractical and ill-tempered comments I had included in my message about Congress, and he also resisted my suggestion that we try to enlist help from the Reagan forces, explaining that Reagan was firmly determined to avoid any association with administration policy.[1] But the burden of his response was a warning to me that if Kim were killed, the fury of the Carter administration would overpower my objection to adopting major sanctions. Given this political fact of life, he wondered whether we should privately warn Chun in advance, perhaps coupling the warning with the promise of warmer relations if he commuted Kim's sentence. The sanction Holbrooke had in mind was to tell Chun that if he executed Kim we would "reexamine our policy of not talking to the North Koreans without full South Korean participation." Making clear that he was not committed to such a drastic step, Holbrooke asked for my reaction before making any recommendation to Secretary Muskie.

I doubt that Holbrooke was surprised by my swift negative reaction. I argued that:

—Given my understanding with Chun, any further threats from us would be dangerously counterproductive;

—In view of congressional reactions to Carter's 1977 troop withdrawal plan, it was unlikely that any U.S. administration would be able to carry out such a radical departure in policy. Surely, if the Republicans won the election, they would refuse to carry out the threat;

1. Richard Allen, Reagan's principal foreign affairs adviser, recently confirmed this judgment, but at the time I felt that we should try harder to solicit an "independent" message from Reagan to Chun before the election. See Richard V. Allen, "On the Korean Tightrope, 1980," *New York Times,* January 21, 1998.

—The proposed action would punish the entire Korean people for our unhappiness with the behavior of one segment and severely shake South Korean confidence in the constancy and common sense of the United States; and

—Our proper policy toward North Korea should not be adopted in the spirit of retaliation against the leaders of the south. Effectively, we would be rewarding North Korea for its intransigence.

Although these ideas continued to roil debates in Washington, Holbrooke did not recommend a drastic departure in our policy, and the proposal dropped out of our long-distance conversations. Armacost, who had been sent once again by Holbrooke to check up on me, also helped to smooth out any differences.[2] Although I never received formal, written authorization to explore a warmer relation with Chun if he commuted Kim Dae Jung's sentence, I nevertheless began informal conversations with Blue House Secretary General Kim Kyung Won in which I "speculated on a personal basis" about how our respective governments might interact if there were a favorable resolution of the Kim Dae Jung issue. I kept Holbrooke informed, mostly by secure phone.

Complications

Before discussing this process and the denouement of our confrontation with Chun over Kim Dae Jung, I should mention one minor and one major complication in our efforts to save Kim's life. Unlike their surprisingly muted reaction to Park Chung Hee's assassination and Chun Doo Hwan's seizure of power, some governments and parliaments of Western Europe, Australia, Canada, New Zealand, and Scandinavia suddenly adopted a high—almost theatrical—posture of sharp public criticism of Kim Dae Jung's trial and death sentence. This angered Korean officials but never led to any retaliatory actions. In the case of Japan, however, the Korean authorities were less tolerant. They denounced Japanese criticism and on several occasions organized "spontaneous" anti-Japanese demonstrations around the Japanese embassy. At one point in late November, I feared that the protests might slip out of control and greatly complicate the issue. When I spoke bluntly to

---

2. Although objecting so strongly to threatening Chun with a change in policy toward North Korea, I myself sometimes used the threat indirectly to make South Koreans think hard about the costs of alienating Americans.

President Chun about my concerns on December 6, he seemed to have reached the same conclusion.

Korea's discriminatory treatment of Japan was quite unfair, because Japan's policy was, in fact, closely parallel to U.S. policy, reflecting similar interests and frequent consultation. Of all my diplomatic colleagues in Seoul, Japanese Ambassador Ryozo Sunobe was by far the best informed, and at each juncture of the chaotic events following Park's assassination, I found that we independently reached more or less the same conclusions. After Kim Dae Jung's arrest on May 17, the Japanese government sought his release. After failing to deflect Kim's receipt of a death sentence, the Japanese government also made a variety of discreet approaches to Chun Doo Hwan requesting that he be prepared to commute the sentence. Throughout the period, moreover, the Japanese government resisted domestic pressure to engage in a public confrontation with the Koreans.

There were, nevertheless, understandable reasons why the Koreans chose to vent their annoyance with "foreign intervention" onto the Japanese. One was resentment about getting advice on a domestic issue from a country that had subjected Korea to harsh colonial rule and the heavy costs of World War II. The other was the relatively favorable image that Kim Dae Jung enjoyed among Japanese, resulting from his friendly attitude as well as Japan's severe embarrassment that he had been forcibly abducted and almost killed while in Tokyo. These ties led Japanese newspapers and commentators to protest Kim's treatment in harsh terms, as did members of the Socialist party (which enjoyed close ties with the North Koreans and had refused to recognize the legitimacy of any government in South Korea). To protect their flank, some members of the ruling Liberal Democratic party joined the ranks of those pressuring the Japanese government to adopt a tougher posture.

At several points before and after our elections in November 1980, the Japanese government seemed on the verge of engaging in public criticism of the Korean government, but it was ultimately deterred by Ambassador Sunobe's views and Prime Minister Suzuki's reluctance to break ranks with us on a Korean issue. Although the high-level consultative process between our governments was time-consuming and added another element of strain for us in Seoul, the net effect of private and government actions in Japan probably helped Kim Dae Jung's cause, as did the same combination in the United States.

The far more serious complication was President Carter's defeat by Ronald Reagan in the November 1980 election. While republican campaigners often cited Carter's troop withdrawal policy in Korea as an example of the Democrats' failure to consolidate the strength of our alliances against the communist threat, Korea was not a major election issue, and a number of prominent republicans, including Senator Robert Dole, and supporters of the Republican party such as the *Wall Street Journal*, publicly warned Chun against killing Kim Dae Jung. Six weeks before the election, I was still sufficiently confident to tell Holbrooke that it was my impression that Republican contacts with Chun had not undercut the administration's position. Whatever my inner doubts, I also told inquiring Koreans that a Republican victory would not change U.S. policy on the issue. I was, nevertheless, uneasy about the situation, since Koreans tended to assume that a Republican administration would have or display less concern about the fate of Kim Dae Jung. Hence my proposal to Holbrooke that we try to enlist Reagan and his staff into positive support for Kim, an effort that was thwarted by Reagan's unwillingness to be associated with Carter's policies.

As the election approached, I became more concerned because of what certain Americans were reportedly telling Koreans. In particular, we heard from Korean intelligence sources that a prominent American who had served in previous Republican administrations (identified recently to be Alexander Haig) had allegedly told representatives of the Chun government that Korea should deal with Kim Dae Jung as it saw fit from a domestic point of view without worrying excessively about international ramifications.[3] This alarmed me and my colleagues in Washington, and it provoked Mike Armacost, in his politically neutral capacity as a deputy assistant secretary of state, to mention the report to Richard Allen, who was then serving as Reagan's key foreign affairs adviser. According to his own account, Allen commented that the individual in question "had no connection with Reagan's campaign and certainly did not speak for us." I remained very concerned, however, and—most fortunately for Kim Dae Jung and the United States— so did Allen who, in his own words, believed that "saving Mr. Kim's life was a worthy priority on humanitarian and political grounds."[4]

Naturally, when it actually occurred, the Reagan election victory intensified my anxiety about how Koreans would read the mixed signals they had been receiving from Republican figures regarding Kim Dae Jung. Underestimating the political obstacles left by a bitter campaign, my thoughts focused on enlisting help from sympathetic people associated with Reagan. I wanted Holbrooke and Armacost to renew their efforts with Richard Allen,

3. Oberdorfer, *The Two Koreas.*
4. Allen, "On the Korean Tightrope."

which they would have done without prompting, and I hoped to reinforce the process by meeting Allen myself. More quixotically, I decided to contact the vice president–elect, whom I had gotten to know during the Ford administration when he was our representative in Beijing and I was dealing with China affairs in the State Department. I promptly wrote George Bush a relatively brief but comprehensive letter, urging an authoritative Republican statement to Chun about sparing Kim's life. To my bitter disappointment and great annoyance, the State Department did not deliver the letter for more than two weeks, thereby dissipating whatever good it might have done. It was agreed, however, that I should return to Washington around Thanksgiving time to meet with administration officials and, I hoped, Richard Allen.

Intensifying my worry about how Koreans would interpret our election results, we detected a more or less coincident surge in anti-Kim sentiment among young Korean army officers, including some of Chun's closest confidants. A surprisingly large number of well-placed individuals were demanding obstreperously that Kim Dae Jung be executed. Some were quite brazen in their chest-thumping campaign against Kim, asserting that if he were not killed, he would once again return to haunt their "nation-saving" efforts and that foreign distress over his death would dissipate over time. The apparent growth of this sentiment energized John Wickham, John Monjo, a few other senior officers, and me to step up our own systematic campaign against simplistic views by talking to virtually every influential officer or official known to us, including some of the younger colonels themselves.

One of my most pointed conversations in this counter-campaign was with Foreign Minister Lho Shin Yong who asked me to lunch on November 13 to discuss Kim's case in light of the Republican victory. I told him I thought that the Reagan administration's position would not differ much from the Carter administration's. The president-elect could not be indifferent to Kim's fate. If Kim were executed, Korea could count on being treated as an international pariah. Editorial writers and members of Congress would keep up a drumbeat of criticism. More serious from the foreign minister's point of view, there could very well be a shift in U.S. attitudes toward North Korea. I reminded Lho that, although this might seem illogical, there were Americans who wanted to be associated with a "breakthrough" in U.S.–North Korean relations. They might well seize on Kim's execution to justify indulging their long-standing temptation.

Lho, who voiced his general agreement, told me later the same day that he had seen fit to report some parts of our conversation to President Chun and Secretary General Kim Kyung Won (presumably including my references to North Korean policy). Promising to be helpful with the president when the Kim Dae Jung issue came before him, Lho urged that we resume the security consultative meeting and normal contacts. When I questioned the merit of holding the security consultative meeting with an outgoing administration, Lho urged that Secretary Brown at least visit Korea during his scheduled meetings in Tokyo. I asked if it would help our cause with the president. He assured me it would. This seed, planted by Lho, bore fruit. Brown's brief visit to Seoul in December was an important part of the bargain on Kim Dae Jung.

Although I found the conversation with Lho somewhat reassuring, my anxieties were beginning to overwhelm me. About a week after the talk with Lho, I sent Washington a cable that for the first time wobbled away from the semi-confidence I had steadily conveyed since the summer months.[5] I jolted Washington by declaring, "On the basis of all information available to me, including personal contacts with senior officials, I fear President Chun will uphold the death sentence verdict against Kim Dae Jung." In this message, sent on November 20, 1980, with Wickham's and Brewster's endorsement before my return to Washington, I urged that we maintain a restrained public posture all the way until the end. I recommended, however, that we promptly convey "highest-level messages from the administration and administration-elect," delivered by separate emissaries.

Groping toward a Bargain

I always realized that if and when President Chun agreed to commute Kim Dae Jung's sentence, he would want something in return and that his obvious target would be American "approval." Initially his senior officials, particularly the minister of defense and senior Korean commanders, sought this by trying to reschedule the long-postponed security consultative meeting. We consistently refused to do so without progress toward political development and resolution of the Kim Dae Jung issue.

In the early fall, some weeks before our election, we began to hear indirectly through a variety of channels that President Chun wanted to be invited to Washington. Although it may have been discussed earlier with

5. Neither my memory nor records illuminate exactly why I wobbled at this critical point. Since my recommendations were unchanged, I presume I decided to "play it safe" rather than be proudly consistent. My choice of words was also influenced by my need to grab attention at high levels in Washington.

republican contacts, for me the idea first surfaced during a number of informal conversations I had with Blue House Secretary General Kim Kyung Won, beginning in October and lasting though December. As I recall, he introduced the thought rather elliptically, asking speculatively how we would respond if President Chun were to brave the wrath of his young colonels and commute Kim's sentence. I mentioned rescheduling the security consultative meeting and holding cabinet-level visits. After the secretary general suggested that there would need to be more, perhaps a Washington visit by Chun, I acknowledged that this would be a reasonable expectation, pointing out, however, that I could not commit the United States, particularly on the eve of our presidential elections. Without saying so, I thought a visit could not be scheduled until Chun had completed the political reforms which he had pledged.

Even before Reagan's victory, I realized that my conversations with President Chun and his cohorts were only one strand in the Korean government's increasingly diffuse contacts with the United States. I was quite aware that the Blue House was in touch with various Republican individuals and was considering all my comments about U.S. policy against this new horizon. Kim Kyong Won told me that he himself was contemplating a visit to the United States, although he delayed it until after the election when he, General Lew, and other emissaries went off to Washington for meetings—some with administration officials, but others about which we were not informed. This of course complicated my life, but I sensed that President Chun still valued my opinion and influence within the existing establishment on Korean matters.

Before leaving Seoul for my Washington visit, I met with President Chun on November 21 following a most interesting session the same day with Defense Security Commander Roh Tae-Woo. Both men had asked to see me, presumably to ensure that I conveyed their views on the Kim Dae Jung affair accurately when I met with members of the administration, Reagan's transition team, and Congress. Nothing really new was said to me, but I was encouraged that they wanted to see me and that they carefully left the door open for a favorable decision on Kim Dae Jung. I stressed that with new administrations in Seoul and Washington, the United States and Korea had an unusual opportunity to overcome strains and restore the rapport absent since the 1970s. If Kim were executed, Korea would find the American relationship once again soured, with great damage to our mutual interests.

Both men acknowledged this, but pointed out that they were faced with strong hostility toward Kim Dae Jung not only within the army but also in the general population. General Roh, to whom I had added my warning about possible changes in the climate of American thinking about policy toward North Korea, identified himself as a moderate and implied that it would be wise to commute the sentence. President Chun, who was very cordial, urged that we ease his problem by continuing our public position of restraint. He said that he would be guided in his decision by what he thought would be best for Korea's stability. I acknowledged that he should act in Korea's national interest but pointed out that Korea's relations with the outer world were an important aspect of those interests. Chun seemed to agree.

These conversations left me less glum as I headed off for a difficult time in Washington. The city seemed gray and cheerless to me, not only because of my preoccupation with Kim Dae Jung's fate but also because it was the second time in four years that I, a career foreign service officer, was identified with a defeated administration (President Ford's in 1976 and President Carter's in 1980). I went about my consultations as efficiently as I could, and I accomplished my main objective, albeit in a rather feckless way. With some difficulty, I was able to see Richard Allen in his transition team office for a few minutes on November 28. Since he had made clear to me that he was incredibly busy, I had to truncate my remarks to a bare minimum, stressing the urgency of conveying authoritatively to Chun that president-elect Reagan strongly opposed Kim's execution. Allen told me rather brusquely that he was already aware of the problem, presumably from Holbrooke and Armacost who had called on him a few days earlier.[6] Although he declined to tell me what he intended to do about it, he seemed to recognize the need for action.

I also had a memorable meeting with Secretary Muskie and Deputy Secretary Christopher. I think Dick Holbrooke may have been present part of the time, but no one else. Muskie had asked to see me, and I was expecting a comradely pat on the back for the brief time we had been in the trenches together. Instead, in his best senatorial style, I was given a tongue lashing for all of Chun Doo Hwan's sins and asked once again why we should not publicly denounce Kim Dae Jung's death sentence. I told him rather angrily why I thought a statement would be disastrous. Since we had successfully restrained ourselves for so long, it made no sense to issue a strident statement at the critical stage when Chun wanted us to keep quiet. Belated public criticism from the outgoing administration might appease the human rights community, but it would jeopardize the incoming administration's efforts

6. See Michael Armacost and Richard Holbrooke, "A Future Leader's Moment of Truth," *New York Times*, December 24, 1997.

to save Kim's life. The innuendo of this comment provoked Christopher, and we wrangled for almost two hours. After venting his frustration, the secretary finally resumed his normally friendly manner and thanked me for my efforts.

I was a bit stunned by this episode, which left me wondering what had happened to all the carefully reasoned messages I had sent the secretary. Perhaps I should blame myself for having used a scary headline for the assessment I made just before returning to Washington. In any event, I was relieved that no statement was ever issued. Until recently I gave myself credit for having again persuaded Muskie on the wisdom of this restraint. Thus I was surprised to learn from Richard Allen's article that not long after my conversation with Muskie, in December 1980, he invited Allen to his home. Telling Allen that he was convinced the Koreans were intent upon killing Kim, he asked that Allen join him in a public denunciation. Allen declined after consulting the president-elect.[7]

The Denouement

Back in Seoul after these conversations, I was faced with uncertainty in three directions, primarily from President Chun but also from the United States, where authority was bifurcated between outgoing and incoming administrations. Although uneasy about all that could go wrong, I was resigned to uncertainty and concentrated my efforts where I thought they might still be useful. Specifically, I tried to facilitate the Carter administration's final appeal to Chun and continue fighting against persistent pressures in Tokyo as well as Washington to publicly denounce Kim Dae Jung's death sentence. I was painfully aware that there was not much I could do from Seoul to ensure that the president-elect would register strong opposition to Kim's execution.

President Chun had more than a lingering interest in the final actions of the Carter administration. A public salvo from President Carter or Secretary Muskie on Kim Dae Jung certainly would have complicated his decision because of the potential effect both within the Korean army and general public. Chun was quite explicit about this in his conversations with me, and he genuinely appreciated my role in restraining impulses in Washington. Moreover, granting that he was looking primarily to President-elect Reagan to bestow the U.S. seal of approval he so coveted for his regime, the impact

---

7. See Allen, "On the Korean Tightrope."

within Korea would be greater if it were preceded by some last-minute softening of the Carter administration's policy.

Building on this, I had recommended to my superiors in Washington that Defense Secretary Harold Brown be the emissary to make President Carter's final pitch for clemency for Kim Dae Jung. While in Washington, I had pursued the idea vigorously, enlisting Brown's support, and on return to Seoul I made a formal recommendation and received prompt authorization to tell President Chun. Publicly, the meeting was to be characterized as a consultation on bilateral security matters, not a session of the security consultative meeting. Privately, the Koreans knew the secretary would be speaking in light of conversations with Carter and Muskie (see appendix, item 11).

I had a rather relaxed meeting with President Chun on December 6, 1980, during which I informed him that Harold Brown was prepared to visit Korea briefly on December 13 and handed him a letter from President Carter, dated December 1, 1980, politely urging clemency for Kim Dae Jung. I also gave Chun an account of my talks in Washington, including those with members of Congress and individuals associated with the next government. I said that President Carter's letter reflected the preoccupation of informed Americans with the Kim Dae Jung issue. I had found little difference between Republicans and Democrats. All were deeply worried that an execution would severely damage Korea's image and handicap all our dealings with the Republic of Korea. When I explained to these Americans the dilemma Chun faced and the domestic factors he had to take into account, they in turn asked that he give proper weight to the potential international damage.

Chun was delighted with the news about Secretary Brown, did not object to my having delivered Carter's letter before the Supreme Court rendered its decision, did not lecture me on the evils of Kim Dae Jung, and thanked me for "such a clear exposition of American opinion." On the way out, Secretary General Kim Kyung Won, who had accompanied us, patted me on the back and said that the meeting had been a "most productive" session.[8]

The Carter administration's last pitch for Kim Dae Jung was made by Secretary Brown, who in a brief visit skillfully combined personal warmth toward his Korean counterparts with the stern message he was carrying from President Carter. In his lengthy talk with President Chun on December 13, Brown explained the severe consequences an execution would have for the

8. The second portion of this meeting regarded our mutual concern about a flare-up between Japan and Korea, and I explained how we were encouraging the Japanese to maintain their policy of restraint.

future of our security and economic relationship. Chun responded with a hard line, telling him, "The decision of the court must be respected. If the court confirms the death sentence, that sentence should be carried out." This was the most restrictive statement ever made to us. Yet Chun went out of his way to stress the deep historical debt Korea owed the United States, the importance of economic and security ties, and his willingness to consider our advice carefully. The tone of the meeting, moreover, was cordial.

In his report to the president, the secretary commented that he could not strike the balance between discouraging and encouraging remarks: "We have taken our best shot; I hope it is enough." I was slightly more upbeat in my report: "I sensed a degree of hard-line posturing . . . but the theme that came through most clearly to me was Chun's emphasis on Korea's debt to us and his willingness to take our views into account."

Only Chun Doo Hwan or his close associates at the time are in a position to assess the importance of the Carter administration's extraordinary efforts on behalf of Kim Dae Jung. I believe they were important, critically so before the U.S. presidential elections. Granting that others conducted the assault and took the casualties in a battle from May until December 1980, I have little doubt, however, that after the elections the president-elect and his adviser Richard Allen deserve credit for making the clinching move.

Allen's account of this is consistent with what I sensed to be going on. After being approached by Carter administration officials and having himself heard the hard line from visiting chairman of the Korean Joint Chiefs of Staff, General Lew Byong Hion, in late November, Allen talked to the president-elect, who agreed that the execution of Kim Dae Jung would be a "moral disaster." With Reagan's authorization, Allen spread the word that if harm came to Kim, Korea would encounter great difficulties with the new administration. A few weeks later, Major General Chung Ho Yung (the smart but tough commander of the special forces and, in my opinion, a most unhelpful player during the Kwangju crisis) arrived to see Allen as Chun's emissary. He too began with the hard line that Kim should be killed. After the nastiness had almost broken the dialogue, Allen commented that killing Kim Dae Jung would result in an American reaction "like a lightning bolt from heaven striking you." The next day Chung started bargaining. He tried to get President Chun invited to Reagan's inauguration, which would have been highly irregular. Allen countered successfully with the offer of a Chun visit after the inauguration, but only if Kim Dae Jung's sentence were drastically reduced.[9]

9. See Allen, "On the Korean Tightrope."

This deal, which appears to have taken place shortly after Secretary Brown's visit to Seoul, ended the confrontation between the U.S. and Korean governments. Given my own conversations in the Blue House, it did not surprise me, and it was a great relief after the months of anxiety about the fate of Kim Dae Jung. Incidentally, I first learned of it when my Korean tennis partner told me early in the morning that he had heard on the radio that President Chun would be visiting President Reagan. He was incredulous that I was not informed. Later that same day, Bob Rich called from Washington with the official news and asked me to return promptly to help prepare for and participate in the summit session.

President Reagan's invitation to President Chun was announced on January 21, 1981. On January 23, the Korean Supreme Court upheld Kim Dae Jung's death sentence, and one day later President Chun commuted the sentence to life imprisonment and lifted martial law. President Chun Doo Hwan arrived at the White House on February 3, 1981, as President Reagan's second foreign guest.

I approved of the deal, although I think the visit should have been scheduled for a few months later. I bridled, moreover, during the toast at the White House luncheon. The president, who had not done much homework on the complex issues discussed before lunch, seemed in his element for the toast. Having tossed out the carefully crafted suggestions we had made, he instead welcomed Chun with a flourish of rhetoric from General MacArthur. Without even a hint of the political agenda we had struggled so hard to advance in Korea, he spoke only of our common struggle to advance freedom and defend against communism.

Although some years later President Reagan redeemed himself in my estimation by taking a stand against Chun's excesses, in 1981 I felt he was wrong—very wrong—to adopt such an uncritical stance during his first meeting with a man who had seized power in a coup, presided over a brutal suppression of Kwangju citizens, and usurped the presidency of Korea. The words and the pictures flashed back to Korea tarnished the image of the United States in Korea, and to the people of Kwangju they reinforced a widespread misperception that we had colluded with Chun's forces. Obviously, this was not President Reagan's intent, but it was an unfortunate by-product of his not wanting to be associated with the outgoing administration. I would have recommended a slightly slower schedule and less warmth in Reagan's embrace.

Did Chun Doo Hwan really intend to execute Kim Dae Jung? I am not sure.

Did we make a mistake by placing extraordinary stress on the Kim Dae Jung issue? Not necessarily, but the display of our eagerness weakened our negotiating position. With the advantage of hindsight, I believe it would have been better to warn Chun privately at the very beginning that, if he allowed Kim to be killed, he would destroy the basis of our friendly relationship and that we would publicly condemn the action and recall our ambassador indefinitely. We would then have been more comfortable with our consciences while we waited for him to act. In self-criticism, I would say that my genuine fear of undermining Korea's security and prosperity inhibited me from proposing this course.

Would we have been better served if candidate Reagan or later President-elect Reagan had swiftly sent Chun a tough private message about sparing Kim Dae Jung's life? Absolutely yes. There were no valid grounds for his refusal to do so.

Did Chun manipulate us? In a sense, yes, but our eyes were open, and the deal we struck was an honorable one.

Epilogue

PRESIDENT CARTER was defeated in his zealous effort to withdraw all U.S. ground combat forces from Korea, and when President Reagan publicly criticized the attempt as misguided, a majority of informed Americans and most South Koreans probably agreed with him. In a less personal endeavor, Carter also presided over an essentially unsuccessful American effort to push Korea toward political liberalization. In contrast to their position on the troop issue, many Americans (including me) and large numbers of Koreans supported this activist policy. Although this effort may have contributed to later progress in Korea, there was a widespread sense of failure when Carter left office in 1980.

In the brief interlude between President Park's assassination and General Chun Doo Hwan's seizure of power, the United States tried hard but was unable to convince the politically weak interim leader of Korea to take bold measures that would have matched public expectations. Along with almost everyone else in Korea, U.S. officials were then caught by surprise and pushed to the sidelines during Chun's well-executed coup on December 12. Unwilling to risk major sanctions, we were unable to prevent Chun's encroachment into the political realm. In the absence of strong alternative leadership to Chun or sustained popular resistance, we, along with the Korean people, eventually accepted the reality of his rule, the final act being President Reagan's invitation to President Chun as his first significant foreign visitor at the White House. There was little evidence in 1980 that vigorous U.S. efforts advanced the cause of democratic governance in Korea, while it was apparent in the case of the Kwangju crisis that actions taken without our knowledge or approval seriously damaged our reputation among important segments of the population.

Nevertheless, the tumultuous events discussed in this book were the dark side of what can now be seen as a very positive evolution in Korea. Koreans survived seven years of President Chun Doo Hwan's highly unpopular though relatively competent rule. His government was authoritarian, lacked legitimacy, was widely opposed for hobbling potential opposition forces with a web of repressive measures, and disappointed those who thought it would at least break the chain of corrupt practices in Park's era. Yet, despite periodic resort to harsh measures, Chun's government was administratively effective. He selected relatively good people to work for him, and his penchant for crude experiments in political regimentation was softened by his willingness in some instances to back down from clearly unpopular actions. Conduct of foreign policy and north-south issues became noticeably more global-minded and flexible. Renewal of vigorous economic growth moderated widespread unhappiness with the political climate.

U.S. relations with Chun were reminiscent of those with President Park during the first half of the 1970s; the United States was distressed over political developments in Korea but registered complaints through diplomatic channels rather than public criticism. Under American pressure, Chun permitted Kim Dae Jung to leave the country in December 1982 for a period of exile in the United States, and in 1985 he (reluctantly) did not prevent Kim's high-profile return on the eve of National Assembly elections. Partly in response to international opinion, newly important because of the impending Olympics, Chun also allowed a modest expansion of press and political freedoms after 1985. Nevertheless, much of this progress seemed wiped away with the approach of the next presidential election in 1987. Chun resorted to a hard-line stance, stubbornly refusing opposition demands for a direct popular contest and insisting that his designated successor, Roh Tae-Woo, be elected indirectly under the same protected constitutional arrangements by which he himself had come to power.

The year 1987 was a watershed for democratic politics in Korea. Public unrest over Chun's tough stance spread beyond perennial demonstrations of students and extremists to become a potentially massive threat. The regime in turn threatened to use whatever force was necessary to maintain order. Both rulers and ruled were conditioned by memories of the eruption that traumatized Korea in 1980. This time, however, there was less question about popular impatience with the military's long domination of the political scene. Unlike 1980, protesting students often appeared to enjoy the support of their parents and other members of the greatly expanded middle class in Seoul and other urban areas. Koreans in 1987 were very conscious of the recent Philippine experience where "people power" had brought down the Marcos regime. Moreover, the U.S. government had broken its silence with well-timed public statements reinforcing its strong private pressure on Chun to accept democratic reform, including a polite but clear letter from President Reagan urging patience and compromise to achieve a fair election.

At the peak of tension on June 29, 1987, presidential candidate Roh Tae-Woo surprised everybody with a dazzling display of statesmanship and daring. In a dramatic public statement, he abruptly accepted the opposition's demand for direct election of the next president. Despite the liability of his close association with Chun, he also agreed to election arrangements that were universally seen as fair. Roh's bold intervention defused the crisis and paved the way for three successive presidential elections that demonstrated the successful rooting of democratic government in the Republic of Korea.

Toward the end of 1987, with his two rivals, Kim Young Sam and Kim Dae Jung, splitting the opposition vote, Roh was able to capitalize on his newly achieved stature (and the advantages of an incumbent administration) to win the election by a plurality. As the first freely elected president since the 1960s, this former general and close collaborator with Chun in the December 12 incident impressed his fellow countrymen by his steady, temperate leadership, which significantly relaxed political tensions and served as a transition to complete civilian rule. With his connections in the military and security apparatus, he was able to keep his former colleagues in line while he gradually accommodated pressures for further democratic change, including the National Assembly's investigations and hearings on the December 12 coup and the Kwangju incident. The economy continued to surge; Roh was quite successful with his sophisticated policies toward Korea's communist neighbors; and the burst of international recognition during the 1988 Olympics in Seoul gave Korea a big psychological boost.

Five years after his own election, President Roh's coalition with former oppositionist Kim Young Sam provided the latter with the margin of votes to defeat Kim Dae Jung in the 1992 election. As Korea's first civilian president in almost three decades, President Kim Young Sam swiftly launched a series of reforms. He replaced a military hierarchy beholden to others with a good slate of new officers, implemented new legislation for local election of governors and mayors, and stole the opposition's thunder by introducing long-delayed financial reforms ostensibly designed to clean up corruption in business and political circles. Unfortunately, these widely praised, but mostly ill-prepared, moves did not prevent collusion of his own administration in stunningly corrupt business deals. These, and the misfortune of the 1997 financial collapse, severely damaged his legacy.

Ex post facto, President Kim's reforms exposed large political slush funds maintained by Roh and Chun. For several years President Kim Young Sam had firmly resisted opposition demands to prosecute the former presidents for their role in the December 12, 1979, seizure of power and the subsequent use of troops to suppress demonstrators in Kwangju. Having first decided that the issue should be "left to history," President Kim changed his mind under the new wave of pressure unleashed by the slush fund scandal. In a humiliating reversal of fortunes, former presidents Chun Doo Hwan and Roh Tae-Woo were detained for investigation, tried, sentenced, and jailed in 1996—Chun for life and Roh for seventeen years—for their roles in the events of 1979–80 as well as for the illegal fund-raising during their presidencies. I had reservations about the constitutional precedent of prosecuting and jailing former presidents. I also would have favored less severe punishment for corrupt fund-raising practices that were rampant throughout Korea's political culture. In any event, I would have felt more comfortable if the trials had been pursued earlier, if the sentences had been less severe, and if President Kim Young Sam had seen fit to commute the sentences, particularly Roh's, almost immediately. Apart from his competent administration of the nation at a time of great change, President Roh Tae-Woo deserved special credit for his crucial contribution to the evolution of Korea's democratic politics.

Even though the main candidates in the 1997 presidential election all favored clemency for the former presidents, President Kim Young Sam, more beleaguered than most lame duck leaders because of the corruption scandal and financial crisis, deferred the decision to his successor. In an extraordinary twist of fate, Chun's and Roh's sentences were commuted by Kim Dae Jung, the man they had victimized in 1980 and now the newly elected president of the Republic of Korea.

Kim Dae Jung's election in 1997, for the first time giving control of Korea's administration to an opposition leader, symbolized stunning changes. A man many, if not most, Koreans had thought would never become president was finally elected to lead the nation at the time of a devastating crisis. This could never have happened without the remarkable transformation of Korea's political structure or the mellowing effects of events on Kim Dae Jung himself. Korea had evolved into a democracy politically strong enough to withstand a massive economic blow. Although elected by a narrow plurality, Kim Dae Jung had moved toward the center of Korean politics so that people seemed prepared to accept, rather than worry about, his vision and strong leadership qualities.

Functioning democracy has taken hold in Korea faster than I thought possible, bringing forth the political stability that was so elusive in earlier years. Nevertheless, as we have seen from this account, the process was often painful for the Korean people as well as a strain on the U.S.-Korean relationship.

Reflecting today on events twenty years ago, I would underscore several aspects of this experience. The first and most important is that we were deeply "entangled" in Korea, yet only marginally effective in influencing the course of the country's domestic development. Although there were times when we were tempted to think otherwise, this limitation of our power was an inescapable circumstance of our relationship with Korea. Stated simplistically, since we judged our military presence and cooperation in Korea to be critically important aspects of our national interest in sustaining East Asia's stability and security, it was logical we would shy away from actions that would jeopardize this interest, even at the cost of temporarily "accepting" adverse domestic developments within Korea. This ultimate concern about our self-interest in the region's strategic equilibrium kept us both engaged in Korea as well as inhibited from applying major sanctions in 1979–80. And it would shape our decisions if there were a Korean crisis today.

Going beyond abstraction, moreover, the pattern of our responses in 1979–80 demonstrated in almost textbook-like fashion how our security commitment and military presence in South Korea inevitably became overriding concerns in times of upheaval, largely because of the potential threat we perceived from North Korea. On the night of December 12, 1979, these anxieties deterred us from employing powerful sanctions against Chun Doo Hwan's group, and the immediate focus of Washington officials during the Kwangju uprising in May 1980 was once again the effect on our forces and security commitment.

Although we were constrained from using our security cooperation as leverage against the new leaders, we did not really have the opposite choice of standing "idly by" during a period of struggle and contention in Korea. No American administration, not even President Reagan's, could have remained on the sidelines in such circumstances. At a minimum, we needed to protect ourselves, and it would have gone against the grain of American opinion if we had not used obvious opportunities to nudge events in a favorable direction: opposing repression and supporting democracy.

The Carter administration's mix of advice and pressure toward these objectives constituted overt intervention in Korean domestic affairs. As a superpower and protector of Korea's security, we were able to do and say things in Korea that would have created an enormous political storm in China, Japan, or even the Korea of today. Koreans at the time were divided in their reaction, some wanting even more intervention, others deeply resenting it, while most were indifferent or ambivalent. In any event, we rarely hesitated before doing what came to us almost naturally. As the protecting power, we felt we had a right to be concerned about popular demands and other matters affecting political stability.

Some of this effort failed completely, and none of it played more than a marginal role. The reasons are obvious, at least in retrospect. Inhibited from adopting major sanctions, such as threats to reduce our security cooperation or alter our policy toward North Korea, we had to do our best with rather weak and sometimes counterproductive measures, including private exhortation, public criticism, and some relatively modest sanctions. In these conditions, our most effective tool seems to have been refusal to bestow an American seal of legitimacy on upstart leaders who wanted it and needed it. Our influence was further constrained by lack of critical intelligence, by the conservative, cautious character of President Choi Kyu Ha, whose constitutional authority we were trying to uphold, and, above all, by the lack of major opposition from the Korean people who, despite the students, the disaffected, and the angry citizens of Kwangju, were not generally in a revolutionary mood.

Partly offsetting these handicaps, U.S. conduct in Korea benefited from an unusual degree of internal efficiency and a minimum of the friction, posturing, or ego-driven behavior that often complicate crisis management. Especially during the crisis years of 1979–80, Washington provided exceptional support to us in Seoul, and we in turn performed in a cooperative style. This internal coherence made the best use of our limited leverage. It protected our flanks from cunning upstarts and allowed us to draw on the friendship of many key Korean soldiers and civilians.

Even so, the demonstrable result of American efforts to foster democratic and representative government was discouraging. Although in constitutional terms Chun's new government was an improvement on Park Chung Hee's *Yushin* regime, it was no less repressive in practice. Generally, our influence was most effective when we encouraged moderation of harsh behavior, focused sharply on limited goals, such as saving the life of Kim Dae Jung, and linked our limited objectives to developments desired by the

Korean leaders. With the passage of time and better understanding of our actions, more and more Koreans may look favorably on what we tried to do. At least we were leaning in the direction the Korean people wanted to go.

Could the United States have been more effective? Perhaps, but I can think of no measures that would have altered the basic character of a contest between domestic forces over which we had little if any real control. To be more specific, could we have employed stronger sanctions against the new army leadership, such as dropping plans to supply F-16 fighter aircraft to South Korea, without risking real danger from North Korea? Conceivably, North Korea might have remained cautious while we "disciplined" our ally in this manner, but in 1979–80 the clear consensus among us was that the danger of hostile North Korean action was too high.

Could we have jostled Chun Doo Hwan out of his leadership role? I doubt we could have. Chun's initial actions as a "young turk" were quite popular in the army, and he moved swiftly to place reliable people throughout the army and security structure. If we had openly challenged him, large numbers of officers would have rallied around him. There would have been the grave danger of a nationalistic backlash and fighting within the Korean army. If Chun had been a slower learner and a less competent leader, he would have been more vulnerable. My own sense of caution was strongly reinforced by concern that our track record for such manipulative actions was poor and by my fear that we might end up with another military strongman even less attractive than Chun.

Why did U.S. intervention in the 1987 crisis help to push Chun Doo Hwan to accept a free democratic election of his successor while more strenuous efforts in 1979–80 failed? This is a fair question that will have to be answered by future historians with access to all relevant materials. My tentative thought is that the difference lies in the issues of contention, the role of the Korean middle class, and changes in the international climate. In 1979–80 the issues before the people were rather diffuse and confused. The Korean people were divided, and even middle-class parents generally refrained from supporting student protest. In 1987 the issue was sharply focused on the popular election of Chun's successor versus continuing "military rule." People had been wearied by seven additional years of authoritarian rule; Koreans were aware that Marcos had fallen; and Korean values were changing with the rapid growth of a middle class. In 1987 this group overwhelmingly backed its children and joined them in the streets of Seoul. Although U.S. actions were helpful, they were still marginal.

Despite its limited effectiveness, I am convinced that the energetic American effort in 1979–80 to improve the process of governance in Korea was far sounder and better implemented than President Carter's campaign at the beginning of his administration to withdraw U.S. ground forces and advance the cause of human rights in Korea. To a disturbing degree, those policies were conceived in ignorance of real conditions and attitudes in Korea. Both were pursued with ideological zeal. One was completely thwarted, and the other accomplished little that was not later reversed. The high priority given both created inner conflicts between them. Even the effort to extract a human rights gain from abandonment of the ill-considered troop withdrawal effort was almost botched. Both policies had unintended consequences.

Decisions to extract the United States from direct engagement in Vietnam and to restructure the balance of power through a rapprochement with China had an unsettling effect in Korea. Combined with the final collapse of South Vietnam and Korea bashing in some American circles, these American actions reinforced Park Chung Hee's authoritarian tendencies and left Koreans, including Park's bitterest opponents, feeling extremely insecure. Given this uncertainty about America's commitment—a malaise that had spread through much of East Asia in 1975—President Carter's troop withdrawal policy was ill-conceived and ill-timed. His decision to implement it as a priority of his new administration was taken without prior study of the policy's potential impact on the Korean peninsula or elsewhere in Asia, without consulting Congress, and against the advice of his most senior and experienced cabinet members as well as military leaders.

I think I have not been unfair in describing President Carter's action as rubbing salt into Korean wounds. Not only did the effort fail, but by unifying disparate elements within the military, bureaucracy, and Congress into a united front of opposition, Carter probably generated more support for U.S. ground force deployments in Korea than there would have been if he had chosen to ignore his campaign promise. Roughly 37,000 American soldiers and airmen remain in Korea today.

President Carter's parallel decision to select Korea as a target country for his new administration's focus on human rights was more understandable in terms of the American tradition, but the abrasive, confrontational manner in which human rights were pursued added appreciably to the sense of insecurity and strain over the troop issue. Carter was not noticeably more successful than his predecessors, who in quieter ways also opposed political repression, urged moderation, and where possible blunted crude moves, such as the kidnapping of Kim Dae Jung. Arguably, moreover, the high-profile pressure on the Park regime added to internal strains by encouraging Park's opponents. Certainly, Park's hard-line response to this activity helped bring on the demise of his regime.

My final reflection is a very personal one—provoked by the Carter administration's policies toward Korea but reinforced by my experience with China and Taiwan. From the way I have cast my final paragraphs, it is quite apparent that I am critical of America's tendency to be impatient, ethnocentric (if not imperial), and ignorant of local conditions as we pressure certain countries for greater progress toward our ideals of political governance and human rights. To an inexcusable extent, we underestimate the complexity of the metamorphosis required for relatively poor countries to go from authoritarian or even totalitarian rule to democratic systems, and too often we brush aside the progress some of these countries have achieved during the transformation. In 1977, for example, we rarely acknowledged the extent to which Korea had already achieved the human rights goals of economic security, fair distribution of wealth, social mobility, and educational opportunity. We treated Taiwan much the same way, and today we often fail to give China credit for important advances in human rights, despite the leadership's struggle to avoid the central features of democracy.

Success of the kind Korea achieved politically in 1987, and Taiwan shortly thereafter, requires a change in values and priorities among large numbers of people, which in turn requires a substantial period of vigorous development and foreign exposure. Even though contacts with the outer world are very much involved in this process, the changes are generated from within these countries, not from outside. Our criticism and exhortation may sometimes help on the fringes of this process, but they play a relatively small, sometimes even negative, role.

It is appropriate and necessary for us to state clearly where we stand on the issues of human rights and political governance in countries where we have undertaken far-reaching commitments. There may be times when a more assertive role by our government is warranted. Korea in 1979–80 may have been such an instance. When we adopt an interventionist posture, however, we should keep in mind both moral and practical requirements that we:

—Focus on improvements that are in fact the highest priority of those we wish to help;

—Acknowledge progress that has been made; and

—Refrain from parallel pressures that antagonize both rulers and ruled in the target countries.

The Carter administration got it mostly wrong in 1977. Its political goals were set too high. It did not give credit to the Park regime for the extent to which it had satisfied the principal concerns of its citizens at the time, even though the accomplishments would not be enough for Koreans today. To make matters worse, the administration antagonized both the government and the people of Korea by seeking to pull out U.S. ground forces.

There are at least overtones of the same error in our treatment of China today. Too many Americans, including responsible officials, focus on currently impractical goals (such as organizing political opposition in China's Leninist political structure), disregard significant improvements in China's human rights environment over the past twenty years, and indulge those who challenge Chinese sovereignty over Tibet. This kind of behavior by outsiders does not improve the environment for democracy and human rights in China. It does complicate our government's ability to manage inescapable problems we have with China (for example, Taiwan), and it strains one of the most strategically important relationships we have in Asia.

In short, whether dealing with Korea or China on these issues, we need to restrain ourselves.

Appendix:

Selected Telegrams on Korea in Crisis

THIS APPENDIX CONTAINS the full text of some messages between the U.S. Embassy in Seoul and Department of State that I quote or paraphrase at various points in the book. My selection was constrained by space considerations and difficulties in obtaining declassification of certain documents. Nevertheless, I believe that reading a few of these original texts will give readers some feel for how the Embassy and State Department reacted to important events during the crisis years in Korea. All the messages have been declassified and "decaptioned." However some captions, such as EXDIS and NODIS, still appear. These restrictive captions were used to limit distribution of sensitive material within the bureaucracy.

1. April 9, 1979   From U.S. Embassy Seoul to Department of State
     Carter/Park Summit

Declassified 7/19/99

O 090943Z APR 79
FM AMEMBASSY SEOUL
TO SECSTATE WASHDC IMMEDIATE 7494
SEOUL 05187
NODIS
FOR EA HOLBROOKE ONLY FROM GLEYSTEEN
SUBJECT: CARTER/PARK SUMMIT
REF: A. STATE 86093. B. SEOUL 4902

1. (S-Entire text).

2. I know there is a strong desire at the highest level that there be some helpful human rights development prior to a presidential visit to Korea. I recommend against explicit linkage in our formal proposal to the Koreans—both because I do not think it is necessary and because President Park might be offended to the point of setting back our cause. The best course would be for us, in proposing the visit, to emphasize President Carter's belief that the major aim of a visit must be to consolidate the US/ROK relationship and his hope that internal developments in Korea as well as bilateral developments between us will contribute a constructive atmosphere. Having delivered these euphemisms to the Blue House directly or through the foreign minister, I would propose more direct conversations with the KCIA director, the secretary general of the Blue House, the foreign minister and any other official who could help. I have been doing this for some time, and you also did it very effectively while you were here.

3. In these discussions I have in mind specifying ROKG actions that we would find helpful but not going so far as to threaten last minute cancellation of the summit, adverse decisions on troop withdrawals or things of that kind. Your statement that "the details of the visit will be calibrated to reflect the situation at the time, as it is understood here (in Washington)" is of course an important element of reality which we may be able to employ to some benefit. At the same time it is a knife that could cut our hands. We must avoid appearing overbearing and discriminatory in the way we treat Korea as opposed to many other countries. We must be especially careful not to insult the Koreans and keep in mind Park's concern not to make it easier for his opposition to take actions which might cast a pall over the summit.

4. You know from my most recent assessment (REFTEL B) that I am unhappy and uneasy about the human rights situation here. I am hopeful that the ROK's perceived need for stage setting events will enhance the prospect for some modest step. I am convinced, however, that our greatest leverage within the foreseeable future will be through a direct discussion of the issue between the two presidents. As I have said before, I do not expect even this to result in very significant progress. I see no real prospect of a genuine liberalization of Park's rather authoritarian regime.

5. Despite my caution, which I trust you will convey fully to the secretary, I think the ROKG "recognizes" the desirability of some positive development either before or in association with the summit. We can be quite certain such a development will be less significant than we would

like. A release of political detainees is certainly possible. I tend to agree with my colleagues who rule out release of Kim Chi Ha as too much to expect, but at least I will make this suggestion to an appropriate official. The odds for lifting EM-9 seem poor at present. Park is being advised against this step by key officials who argue that it would convey an excessively positive signal at a time when the political dissidents are on the offensive and would result in opposition action damaging to the summit. I must remind you that I cannot guarantee even a minimal degree of progress before the summit. And I also see a real risk that if we press the ROKG too hard we may simply push them into superficial gestures.

6. Other events may affect the human rights situation, especially the discussion of it at the summit if not in the pre-summit period. I wish I could but I do not dare assert that even full satisfaction of the ROK's security and economic needs could be translated into meaningful human rights progress. But I am sure that Park's unwillingness to run internal risks will increase if he senses that we are not going to make any further changes in troop withdrawal schedule or that the executive branch is going to change its opposition to economic protectionism.

7. In short, I favor a vigorous indirect attempt to obtain some progress on human rights in connection with, if not before, a Carter/Park summit. Some modest move is possible, but a dramatic one such as lifting EM-9 seems highly unlikely. We should keep our inner expectations modest while pushing for as much as we can get.

GLEYSTEEN

2. October 28, 1979   U.S. Embassy Seoul to Department of State
   Initial Reflections on Post–Park Chung Hee Situation in Korea

Declassified 7/19/99

O 280919Z OCT 79
FM AMEMBASSY SEOUL
TO SECSTATE WASHDC IMMEDIATE 1857
BT
S E C R E T SEOUL 16370
NODIS
SUBJECT: INITIAL REFLECTIONS ON POST–PARK CHUNG HEE SITUATION IN KOREA

1. (S) Entire text.
2. BEGIN SUMMARY: We still do not know whether the stunning events of October 26/27 were a well planned military coup, a more limited

"elimination" of a leader feared by some members of the establishment to have lost his touch, or simply a bizarre incident. But the result is to create a situation of uncertainty. The key players are still the previous establishment forces prone to an authoritarian political structure. The unnatural quiet prevailing is almost sure to give way to rising tensions as various elements of the political scene probe the measure of their power.

3. It is hazardous to make far-reaching judgments at this point but I think the ROK structure will hold together short of chaos, in part because of the unifying effect of the North Korean threat and the existence of bureaucratic structures which now provide considerable continuity. A modestly liberalized Yushin structure would be welcomed by a majority of Koreans, but I am not optimistic that it can be realized now. We can identify some possible successors to Park, such as Kim Chong P'il and Chung Il Kwan, but who will succeed Park is the hardest guess of all. A popular contest in which Kim Tae Jung and Kim Yong Sam could at least enter the competition seems unlikely.

4. We are off to an excellent start in our own dealings with the new circumstances here—thanks to Washington's swift reaction. In the future we will be faced with more difficult problems than those of the past few days. We can expect many elements in Korea to ask our help in pursuing their own ends. I urge that we resist the temptation to suggest architectural designs to the Koreans in favor of :(A) providing reassurance against the threat from the north, (B) urging the observance of "constitutional processes" and (C) gently working through all channels toward political liberalization. We should avoid critical public comment or punishing actions unless and until the new regime has blotted its copybook, and we should keep in mind that the new authorities of Korea do not enjoy the same economic cushion that helped President Park so decisively during recent years. Finally, we should remember that we could easily provoke a very unhealthy anti-American reaction if we press too hard, too crassly, and too soon for structural change in the ROK. END SUMMARY.

5. The stunning events of October 26/27 were not revolutionary but they have created circumstances where we cannot comfortably go on making some of the basic assumptions of the past. We are faced with new uncertainty and the need for care in the way we comport ourselves.

6. In the few days between my return from Washington and Park's death, I was struck by the pervasiveness within the establishment of worry about where the government's hardline policies were leading Korea. People in almost all sectors and all levels told us of their anxiety and were

becoming increasingly bold in identifying President Park as the man making the wrong decisions, listening to advisors who were telling him what they thought he wanted to hear. In our last conversation with him (October 18), even Park himself seemed to question the wisdom of his hardline decisions.

7. Combined with the mystery in most accounts of Park's death, this sense of malaise in the Blue House prompted many people to assume Park was killed in a military coup. This was my own initial conclusion which I have since revised in the absence of corroborating signs. A more plausible possibility is that some individuals around the president, perhaps led by KCIA director Kim Chae Kyu, may have decided to eliminate the president while leaving the government structure intact on the assumption they could arrange an acceptable successor. Some accounts of the killing do suggest conspiracy, and Kim Chae Kyu may have been one of those who felt Park's hardline actions were endangering the republic. Even this more limited explanation is not very convincing because of the risks involved.

8. Whether the killing was a well planned military coup, a more limited "elimination," or simply a bizarre incident, we are faced with a new situation in Korea whose hallmark will be uncertainty. The key players are still the previous establishment forces—above all the military who, even if we can encourage them toward more liberal directions, have not changed their spots and comfort in working within an authoritarian political structure. Before long the unnatural quiet which prevails will give way to rising tension as the various elements of the political scene sort out their positions and probe the measure of their power. Would-be successors to the president must already be hard at work on their plans of campaign. The political opposition will almost surely seek more reform than they are likely to achieve, and if they push too hard too soon we may see a rapid return to political polarization. Confusion and uncertainty are quite possible. It is unlikely that some leader with the right combination of firmness and subtlety will move in smoothly to take over. While the jockeying of less suitable leaders is going on, we will not be able to assume, as we have during the past many years, that there is a tough, capable, commonsensical—if authoritarian—leader who is thoroughly in charge.

9. At this point, I think it hazardous to make far-reaching judgments. I am reasonably comfortable in stating that I expect the situation to hold together short of chaos. Fear of weakening themselves in the face of a North Korean threat and worries about alienating other elements of Korean society may help keep the military relatively unified. Certainly so

far the constitutional process has worked smoothly. The Cabinet has performed as it should and the military have gone out of their way to do the right thing. But competition and confusion may develop to the point of triggering a more classic form of coup. In any event, I cannot predict how long it will take for a new equilibrium to develop. Although a modestly liberalized Yushin structure would be welcomed by a majority of Koreans, it is hard to see how it would be realized among a people who are so fractious, blunt and aggressive with the result that hardliners tend to rise to the top. We may be faced with an attempt to preserve the status quo with a less effective leader.

10. Above all, it is hard to predict who will come out on top. The constitution calls for an indirect election of a new president within 90 days. If one occurs, the person selected may not be the permanent leader. Kim Chong P'il is one obvious contender as is Chung il Kwan. The former would be likely to take charge; the latter would be more likely to preside over a more diverse power structure. Yi Hu Rak will be hard at work trying to pull strings even though he is probably too hated to be chosen as the leader. The military may prefer temporarily to allow the acting president to preside beyond the 90 day limit and retain power in a military collective leadership. A popular contest where people such as Kim Tae Jung and Kim Yong Sam could at least enter the competition seems highly unlikely at this time.

11. Given this large degree of unpredictability, we will have to exercise extra care in our own approach to the ROK. We are off to an excellent start, having swiftly made statements and taken actions to emphasize the continuity of our protector role. As we move on, however, we may be faced with far more difficult problems. First, there will be elements in Korea who wish to borrow our influence. I have already been approached by some and I expect to be approached by many more generals, dissidents, political oppositionists who want our help to pursue their own ends. Even without these supplicants, I would urge most strongly that we de-emphasize our proclivity to suggest architectural designs in favor of a quieter role in providing reassurance against the threat from North Korea, urging observance of the "constitutional process" (we should avoid embracing the Yushin constitution), and gently working through all channels toward political liberalization. We will have to be careful about the channels we use. We must avoid conveying the impression that we would be happy with a military takeover, but we must also work with the military who will be a very influential factor—even toward liberalization. Strong statements

of support such as we made yesterday provide an excellent basis for this relationship.

12. We should also not treat the new regime as an inheritor of the sins of the Park regime. Until the new crowd have blotted their copybook, we should go out of our way to avoid critical public comment or to take symbolic punishing action, such as abstentions in the IFIS. While we intend to continue to press for liberal treatment for political activists, we must avoid early pressures for any dramatic steps of liberalization. We should be as generous as possible in dealing with economic issues since the current ROKG does not enjoy the same economic cushion that helped Park Chung Hee so decisively during recent years. Finally, we should keep in mind that the Korea of 1979 is not the Korea of the early '60's when we were able to bully the early Park regime into constitutional reforms. I don't think there is any change in the popular desire for a more liberal government, but since the 1960's, U.S. pressures on Korea have accumulated to the point where we could face an extremely unhealthy anti-American reaction should we press too hard and too crassly to bring about structural change.

13. Department please pass Amembassies Tokyo and Kuala Lumpur, Kuala Lumpur for EA Assistant Secretary Holbrooke.

GLEYSTEEN

---

3. November 19, 1979   U.S. Embassy Seoul to Department of State
Charges of U.S. Complicity in President Park's Death

Declassified 7/19/99

O 190559Z NOV 79
FM AMEMBASSY SEOUL
TO SECSTATE WASHDC IMMEDIATE 2434
BT
S E C R E T SEOUL 17592
EXDIS
SUBJECT: CHARGES OF U.S. COMPLICITY IN PRESIDENT PARK'S DEATH

1. (S) Entire text.

2. BEGIN SUMMARY: suspicion of U.S. complicity in the death of President Park persists in Korea, especially on the left and right of the political spectrum, and may complicate our lives for some time. Apart from specific allegations by communist fabricators, Japanese and some U.S. media have contributed to the sense of conspiracy by implying that

U.S. criticism of the Park government was intended as a signal to would-be coup makers and saviors of the nation. Conceivably Kim Chae Kyu may claim he was encouraged by me and my predecessor to strike against Park. He was not, as the message below explains. END SUMMARY.

3. Suspicion of U.S. complicity in the death of President Park persists in Korea, especially on the left and right flanks of the political scene and may complicate our lives for some time. Some dissident and church groups believe—in some cases approvingly—that we were part of Kim Chae Kyu's conspiracy, at least to the point of having given a signal. Students have been reported as sharing this view, and some of the late president's cronies (e.g., General Mun Hyong Tae, DRP chairman of the National Assembly National Defense Committee) worry that we were somehow involved in his killing. Japanese media contributed heavily to this speculation at early stages, and a few journalists for prestigious American papers did their bit. The most malicious were Pyongyang, Moscow, and Beijing propagandists.

4. In this atmosphere I have been vaguely accused of having told individuals or groups that I doubted the Park government would last for more than one more year. Obviously, I never engaged in such subversion, but our public criticism of certain actions by President Park may well have led some Koreans to misconstrue our words and actions to mean that we had concluded that he was nearing the end of his rule and that we would not be unhappy to see him depart the scene. And fondness for conspiracy is sufficiently great in some Korean circles that people might infer this, despite the fact that we repeatedly emphasized our continuing coopera- tion with the Park government and explained our policy of keeping security and economic issues separate from our political disagreements with the ROKG.

5. I do not rule out the possibility that at his trial Kim Chae Kyu may make some reference to what he believed to be evidence of U.S. dissatis- faction with Park, perhaps referring to U.S. ambassadorial conversations with him.

6. I have checked with Dick Sneider and can state flatly that neither of us ever signalled to Kim Chae Kyu or any other Korean that we thought the Park government's days were numbered or that we would condone Park's removal from office. My conversations with Kim Chae Kyu were recorded on both sides. I would never have been so reckless as to touch on the tricky subject of President Park's prospective tenure. The nearest I came to it was in the following answer to a question Kim put to me during our last conversation on September 26.

QUOTE: Nearing the conclusion of the session, the director asked the ambassador for his analysis of the Korean economy and his views on future domestic political developments. On the former point, the ambassador stated that while he was not an economist he did believe that there would be slowing in the Korean economy over the next six to twelve months. During this time there would be continuing press on wages and political pressures because of gradual inflation. Nevertheless, he felt the Korean economy was basically sound and would continue to grow, but probably not at the same pace as in the past. Addressing the political question, the ambassador replied that in looking at the South Korean scene there were two issues which concerned him. The first was the prospect of growing political polarization which could seriously divide the nation and create political instability. The current National Assembly gyrations involving the NDP illustrated this tendency. The second issue which should concern Koreans was that of the peaceful transition of power. On this point the ambassador was still not confident that the current constitution or political institutions were yet able to address this issue and he believed that it is a subject which should concern all Koreans. Finally, the ambassador added that he did not agree with those who tried to compare the Korean situation with Iranian developments. Korea is much stronger domestically and Koreans have common value interests. This was not true in Iran. Therefore, he felt optimistic regarding Korea's future. Director Kim replied that the ambassador's judgments were very accurate. He added that during any transition period or other periods of domestic crisis, like war, the Korean peoples' values will remain constant. The most important foundation for Korean development and security is political stability and this must be protected by the government. UNQUOTE

7. I offered my not-particularly-prescient comment on this exchange in the following excerpt from my cabled report of the conversation:

QUOTE: Kim, who seemed unusually interested in my views on the state of the Korean economy and evolution of Korean politics, left me with the impression that he is not alarmed about the government's ability to maintain basic control but is more concerned than in the past about the accumulation of grievances against the Park government and the relatively depressed economic climate in which such grievances can grow. Clearly he expects the NDP to split and assumes that various opposition elements will continue their tactics of confrontation. Although Kim said he agreed with me, I am not really sure that he favors greater restraint by ROKG security authorities. I suspect he thinks the opposition should exercise restraint while the government takes rough deterrent action against selective targets. UNQUOTE

8. COMMENT:_____, I fear Congressional hearings on recent Korean events, and our prospective policies, might focus on these issues. Should they do so they would assist our enemies at a time and in a way that would deeply distress Koreans and damage basic U.S. national interests.

9. I would have no objection to the department's showing this message to appropriate congressmen and their staffs.

GLEYSTEEN

4. December 13, 1979   U.S. Embassy Seoul to Department of State
Younger ROK Officers Grab Power

Declassified 7/19/99

O 130927Z DEC 79
FM AMEMBASSY SEOUL
TO SECSTATE WASHDC IMMEDIATE 2999
INFO AMEMBASSY TOKYO IMMEDIATE
SEOUL 18811
EXDIS
E.O. 12065:RDS-3 12/13/89 (GLEYSTEEN, W.H.) OR-M
SUBJECT: YOUNGER ROK OFFICERS GRAB POWER POSITIONS

1. (S) Entire text.

2. Following are my groggy conclusions at this still early stage of the December 12 incident in Seoul.

3. We have been through a coup in all but name. The flabby facade of civilian constitutional government remains but almost all signs point to a carefully planned takeover of the military power positions by a group of "Young Turk" officers. Major General Chun Tu-Wan, advantaged by his powers of security and investigation, seems the most important figure of a group of men who were very close to President Park and generally associated with security. Various motivations may have been at work: revenge for President Park's death, concern that the older officers were mishandling political issues and fear that unless these were managed more decisively that social unrest would break out very soon; longstanding rivalries; and, without doubt, the lust for power and cockiness of certain young officers that they know better than their elders. According to a

report given the station chief today, the organizing group planned its actions for at least ten days and drew support throughout the armed forces among younger officers. They have already developed a list of new assignments in the army, and the promotion of the [new] present Vice Minister Kim Yong Hyu to defense minister.

4. According to the same report, the Young Turk officers intend to be all things to all people. They are going to be anti-communist, pro-American, concerned with advancing younger talent to senior positions, and determined to pursue an orderly process of political liberalization. Some of the alleged motives are contradictory, and over time a more distinctive pattern may develop. While I am encouraged to hear they want to avoid social unrest and are unwilling to have their troops "fire on the people," I am not aware of many instances where militancy and cockiness have permitted the degree of tolerance and compromise necessary for successful political activity.

5. The new pattern of authority which we have been groping to identify during the past few weeks has now been further complicated. Civilian authority has been further weakened. Within the military, the divisions I estimated as potential dangers a few months from now have already manifested themselves. And finally just as we were surprised by the speed of this power grab, we should not completely rule out counter-moves or similar action by other discontents if the going gets rough.

6. Unless one swallows the Young Turk rationalizations hook, line and sinker, the December 12 incident is bad news from our point of view. The military of Korea who have remained remarkably united for 18 years under the firm, authoritarian hand of Park Chung Hee have now engaged in actions of insubordination which have not only generated animosities that may take years to work their way out but have also set a precedent for others to follow. In doing so, they totally ignored the Combined Forces Command's responsibilities, either ignoring the impact on the U.S. or coolly calculating that it would not make any difference. By their actions they have also run a serious risk *vis-a-vis* North Korea without giving it much thought. Although we may yet be delightfully surprised to find that they adopt a position on political liberalization that stiffens the back of President Choi and pleases the politicians, the odds are that we will be disappointed. In an emotional popular sense, the similarity in American minds to events of 1961 may reopen all sorts of questions that have been helpfully closed during the past two years in terms of American attitudes toward Korea.

7. Ultimately our real influence is going to stem from Korean awareness that they are significantly dependent on the U.S. in both the military and economic area. As tempers cool and individuals begin to reflect, we may be more effective than we were last night in trying to exercise our influence. Hopefully we may find that some of the officers are more susceptible to reasoning than others, and we may discover better ways to underscore our concern. Last night General Wickham and I delivered a very stern warning to both the old military hierarchy and the new group, telling them that there would be grave consequences if a military falling out undermined the civilian government's program to bring orderly political liberalization to Korea. The strong public statement issued today in Washington, which will hit a wider audience, may prove an even more effective warning. (I have had the statement brought to the attention of General Chun and his colleagues.)

8. I have called on President Choi to express our deep concern about these irresponsible military actions (SEPTEL) and General Wickham and I and others will obviously make opportunities over the next few days to convey to the new military group our concern over the danger of insubordination, particularly in light of the North Korean threat, the importance of sustaining constitutional civilian government, and the danger of disappointing popular expectations of political evolution. Without threatening, we can point out that any one of these issues could mushroom into a serious problem in US/ROK relations with damaging effect on both countries.

9. At the same time, I do not think we should treat the new military hierarchy as so bad that we decide to risk seriously alienating them. We will, therefore, have to couple our blunt talk and warnings with reaffirmation of our common interests, and state that we wish through a process of mutural accommodation to continue our cooperation.

10. General Wickham, Bob Brewster and I will work out a program of people to see and things to say to them. None of us looks forward with relish to this prospect because we all have been associated during the last six weeks with this type of missionary work and so much of it seems washed down the drain.

11. General Wickham is in general agreement with this message.
GLEYSTEEN

5. December 16, 1979   Department of State to U.S. Embassy Seoul
Gleysteen's Dec. 14 discussion with Gen. Chun Doo Hwan

Declassified 5/12/99

O 160301Z DEC 79 ZFF6
FM SECSTATE WASHDC
TO RUEHUL/AMEMBASSY SEOUL IMMEDIATE 9220
INFO RUEADWW/WHITE HOUSE IMMEDIATE 3183
BT
S E C R E T STATE 323609
NODIS
CHEROKEE
SUBJECT: KOREA FOCUS—YOUR DISCUSSION WITH MG CHON TU-HWAN
REF: SEOUL 18885

1. (S) Entire text.

2. We have just received the report of your discussion with Major General Chon (REFTEL) and consider it highly useful that you have had this prompt direct contact with him.

3. We already had in final review in Washington an instruction to you to meet with General Chon and cover exactly the points you have made. That instruction had already been approved in substance at highest levels. We had considered carefully the disadvantages in your personally meeting with Chon, since we do not wish to seem to anoint him. However, we had concluded, as you did, that a direct meeting was essential in order to convey the seriousness of concern of the U.S. government.

4. We approve your tactic not to establish regular direct contact with Chon. That is best handled through General Wickham unless the structural situation should change.

5. Our objectives at this stage are clearly two fold: both to prevent a dangerous disintegration of army unity, and to preserve the momentum toward broadly based democratic government under orderly civilian leadership. The latter will require buttressing the image of President Choi and the Cabinet as much as possible.

6. The American press is interpreting the new Cabinet as having been packed by the younger generals with their own people. We do not now read the Cabinet that way, but it will take rather forthright and visible action by the civilian government to prevent that image from hardening, both here and in Korea, with consequent further negative impact on the interaction of forces in Seoul.

7. Please share this message with General Wickham.

6. **May 21, 1980** **U.S. Embassy Seoul to Department of State**
   The Kwangju Crisis

Declassified 5/12/99

O 210956Z MAY 80
FM AMEMBASSY SEOUL
TO SECSTATE WASHDC IMMEDIATE 6483
BT
S E C R E T SEOUL 06463
EXDIS
SUBJECT: THE KWANGJU CRISIS

1. (S – Entire text)

2. The massive insurrection in Kwangju is still out of control and poses an alarming situation for the ROK military who have not faced a similar internal threat for at least two decades. The immediate cause is obviously the extent to which the political crackdown hit Kim Dae Jung (M–R: Kim Tae-Chung) and other natives of Cholla, but by now almost all elements of the population seem to be engaged in a violent, provincial free for all reflecting deep-seated historical, provincial antagonisms. At least 150,000 people are involved, there has been great destruction, and our most recent information is that the rioters have broken into armories and seized weapons, live ammunition, and demolitions. The Korean army plans to pull its military forces out of the city tonight, maintaining roadblocks and concentrating defense on two military installations and a prison containing 2,000 leftists. The authorities are trying to get a ceasefire so that they can talk to the rioters about their demands for an apology, release of prisoners, and removal of martial law forces. While all these moves seem intelligent, they have not worked so far and the December 12 generals obviously feel threatened by the whole affair.

3. General Wickham has agreed to a high internal alert status against infiltration, and he has informally taken some measures associated with DEFCON 3. He has also urged that Defense consider what force augmentations might be possible if we become increasingly concerned about the potential for North Korean exploitation. He has been careful to avoid any formal actions which might be provocative and lead to an escalation with North Korea.

4. We have discussed, in addition, what we might do. One man who could help if he were willing would be Kim Dae Jung, but he is in jail and

probably would not be willing to be helpful unless he could extract far-reaching concessions. No other heroes are likely to step forward. If the rioting gets even more serious, I suggest the department consider reiteration of the May 18 statement focusing it on a call for all concerned to calm the situation, establish a dialogue with each other, and avoid a fissure which could greatly increase external threats. The statement could conclude by taking note of Pyongyang's protestations of innocence and state that we intend to hold them to their declaration. As of now, I am against any local American statement because it could backfire with charges that we were in collusion with the government. A statement in Washington which balanced the call for moderation to both sides would pose less difficulty. Unfortunately, no American statement in a situation of censorship and rioting is going to be heard by many people.

GLEYSTEEN

7. **May 29, 1980   U.S. Embassy Seoul to Department of State**
Press Distortions of the U.S. Reaction to May 17 and Other Events

Declassified 5/12/99

O 290746Z MAY 80
FM AMEMBASSY SEOUL
TO SECSTATE WASHDC IMMEDIATE 6671
C O N F I D E N T I A L SEOUL 06855
SUBJECT: PRESS DISTORTIONS OF THE U.S. REACTION TO MAY 17 AND OTHER EVENTS

1. (C) Entire text.

2. General Chun Doo Hwan (M–R: Chon Tu-Hwan) recently told a representative group of leading publishers/editors that the U.S. was informed in advance of the events of December 12, his appointment to the KCIA, and the actions taken on May 17. Even though some of his interlocutors could hardly contain themselves, Chun did it with a straight face. In addition, some but not all Korean papers have misconstrued some of my remarks as "understanding" or "approval" of the events of May 17. After deliberating the issue with my staff, I asked our press attache Norman Barnes to convey the following oral message to the same media group addressed by Chun. Because we do not wish to get into a public squabble with Chun or even to go too far in correcting

the record, we made the message oral and did not leave any written record.

3. BEGIN QUOTE: I have been asked to clarify two matters on which there may be some misunderstanding.

4. The first concerns the degree of notification given to the United States government prior to certain events. Both General Wickham and Ambassador Gleysteen learned about the arrest of former Chief of Staff of the Army Chung Seung Hwa after the fact and were unable to establish contact with the arresting authorities for several hours to determine what was going on. The United States government learned of General Chun's appointment to the KCIA by casually acquired rumors about four hours prior to the public announcement: Ambassador Gleysteen was officially informed 30 minutes before the announcement. The United States government had no advance knowledge that the authorities were going to arrest student leaders on the Ewha campus May 17th. We obtained official confirmation about an hour after telephone calls from American eyewitnesses. Roughly 30 to 60 minutes before the Cabinet meeting, the ambassador was informed that there would be a Cabinet meeting to endorse a declaration of emergency martial law. There was no mention of intended arrests of political leaders.

5. The second matter concerns an informal luncheon on Friday, May 23, during which Ambassador Gleysteen made informal remarks to bipartisan members of the National Assembly about the United States government's attitude toward the current situation in Korea. The ambassador's comments were accurately reflected in stories which appeared the next day in the *Korea Herald* and the *Korea Times* English language papers. Some Korean language papers, however, stated that the ambassador expressed "understanding" or "approval" of the events of May 17. This is a serious distortion of what he said. In discussing the events of May 17, the ambassador first said he reserved judgment about the need for emergency martial law and tough measures to deal with the student demonstrations. He then expressed strong disapproval of the arrest of political leaders, the closing of the National Assembly, and general political clampdown that occurred thereafter. He reminded the assemblymen that these views were reflected in comments by the official State Department spokesman in Washington on May 18. END QUOTE.

GLEYSTEEN

8. June 21, 1980   Department of State to U.S. Embassy Seoul
Instruction to Convey U.S. Policy Concerns to Korean Leaders

Declassified 5/12/99

DRAFTED BY EA/K:R G RICH:AG
APPROVED BY D – THE ACTING SECRETARY
EA:R C HOLBROOKE
EA:M H ARMACOST
DOD/ISA: N PLATT
PM: D O'DONOHUE
NSC: D GREGG (SUBSTANCE
S/ : P KREISBERG
S/S :LPBREMER
S/S–O:SSTAPLETON ROY

O 210133Z JUN 80 ZFF6
FM SECSTATE WASHDC
TO AMEMBASSY SEOUL IMMEDIATE
INFO USDEL SECRETARY IMMEDIATE
S E C R E T STATE 163085 TOSEC 040058
NODIS
CHEROKEE
SUBJECT: KOREA FOCUS: INSTRUCTION TO CONVEY U.S. POLICY CONCERNS
TO KOREAN LEADERS

1. (S) Entire text.

2. Prior to your travel to Kuala Lumpur for consultations with the secretary enroute to Tokyo, you should seek to obtain appointments with the foreign minister and with General Chun Doo Hwan (M–R Chon Tu-Hwan) to convey the policy concerns of the U.S. government as outlined below. We need your assessment of Chun updated from your June 4 meeting. This is intended as a reiteration and amplification of existing U.S. policy, and is not intended to break new ground.

FYI: for the secretary: This cable has been coordinated and cleared with the Defense Department and the NSC.

3. Our objectives and strategy:

Having concluded that General Chun Doo Hwan (M–R: Chon Tu-Hwan) and his colleagues have successfully established military control of the Korean government and that the army is presently united behind the measures being taken, we have determined that we must at the present stage focus our influence on moderating the regime's unacceptable behavior and moving it toward constitutional government, a reduction of military involvement in politics and administration, implementation of sensible economic policies, and restraint in dealing with political opponents. Simultaneously, we seek to avoid over-identification with the present Korean regime and its excesses and indicate that we are waiting to see whether its actions will warrant a fully normal US-ROK relationship.

4. Scenario for immediate representations:

A) You should cover all the points cited in the instructions below plus representations regarding the imprisoned political leaders (see SEPTEL) with General Chun. Note that we have carefully considered his comments to you during your meeting June 4 and have reviewed the impact of recent events on the important relationships between our two countries.

B) It will be necessary for you to meet with Foreign Minister Park on Monday, June 23, and thus probably prior to your meeting with General Chun. By SEPTEL you will receive instructions to inform the Korean Government Monday that we will abstain in Manila on Tuesday when the Asian Development Bank brings a Korean loan to a vote.

5. Your meeting with General Chun:

A) The specific objective of this meeting with Chun will be to convey to him our implicit recognition that as a practical matter we must deal with him, while letting him understand that his conduct will determine the nature of the relationship and that we intend to preserve some freedom of action of our own over coming months.

B) You are authorized to make the following points:

—We have listened to Chun's statements about his hopes of establishing an effective, constitutional, elected government. We will judge these intentions by the actions which take place.

—We believe that extended reliance on repressive measures will jeopardize rather than promote stability; extended involvement of the military in politics will distract the armed forces from their defense tasks and risk public disaffection with the ROK army.

—In his meeting with members of the American Chamber of Commerce, we understand Chun said that the next government would be more "liberal" than that of President Park. This is important. In our view, if the Korean people are not able to sense a political progression and growth, the resulting instability would bring dangers which both we and General Chun wish to avoid.

—Korea's long-term economic well-being depends heavily on the confidence of international bankers, investors, and traders. They believe that a healthy economy with stable growth prospects can only be forged with the unified support of the Korean people.

—We remain faithful to our commitment to ROK security and this is not an issue. As we have previously stated, we will reexamine in 1981 the question of further troop withdrawals. The actions of the Korean Government between now and then will inevitably shape congressional and public attitudes in the U.S. toward Korea. If a more broadly based support is not visible, the necessary public and political support in the United States for our presence in Korea could be weakened.

—The forthcoming constitutional referendum scheduled for October can be an important benchmark for restoring constitutional government. However, if the referendum is conducted under martial law the mandate will be viewed as gravely flawed both internationally and domestically.

—Efforts to misrepresent U.S policies or associate us with actions which are purely the decision of the Korean Government create serious problems for us and diminish our ability to cooperate for mutual interests. We are also disturbed by indications that some Korean leaders may be stimulating anti-American sentiments. Such actions are inconsistent with and raise serious questions about the intimate security cooperation which up to now has been exemplified by the US-ROK joint command arrangements.

C) In addition to the above fundamental outline of our position and the dangers we perceive over the mid-term if certain developments should occur or continue, you should then state to General Chun that there are two matters involving immediate issues on which you are instructed to make known the views and requests of your government: the question of the political leaders and others who have been imprisoned since May 17, and the linkage of the Combined Forces Command with domestic political structures. Of these two, the issue of the arrested political leaders is by far the most important, so you should note you will dispose of the CFC issue first:

—We find the appointment of the deputy commander of the Combined Forces Command (CFC) simultaneously to a seat on the Special Committee for National Security Measures a most unfortunate linkage of the ROK-US joint command arrangements with Korean domestic politics. Therefore, we must formally request that CFC Deputy Commander General Paik either be removed from the special committee or relieved of his CFC responsibilities.

—Imprisoned political leaders (see SEPTEL).
CHRISTOPHER

9.   July 2, 1980   Department of State to U.S. Embassy Seoul
     Instructions to See General Chun
_____

Declassified 5/12/99

DRAFTED BY AMBASSADOR GLEYSTEEN
APPROVED BY S – THE SECRETARY
EA: M H ARMACOST
NSC:DR. BRZEZINSKI
EA/K:RGRICH
8/S:LPBREMER
PM:DODONOHUE
S/P:PKREISBERG
DOD:DR. BROWN

O 022318Z JUL 80 ZFF6
FM SECSTATE WASHDC
TO AMEMBASSY SEOUL IMMEDIATE
INFO AMEMBASSY BEIJING IMMEDIATE
S E C R E T STATE 175:46
NODIS
CHEROKEE – FOR THE AMBASSADOR FROM THE SECRETARY
BEIJING FOR ASSISTANT SECRETARY HOLBROOKE
SUBJECT: KOREA FOCUS: INSTRUCTIONS TO SEE GENERAL CHUN

1. S – Entire text.

2. As you know from our discussion on the plane to Yokota, I want you to see General Chun Doo Hwan (M–R: Chon Tu-Hwan) once again to emphasize that while our security commitment to the ROK is firm, Chun and his group are abusing that commitment in ways that will undermine Korea's long-term stability. In talking to Chun you should reaffirm our security commitment forcefully but indicate I lack confidence that what he and his group are doing to establish a government will have the support of the Korean people and thus be consistent with our mutual security interests.

3. I suggest you tell Chun that you had a thorough policy discussion with me during which you gave me an account of your last conversation with him. You should then say I have instructed you to convey the following points:

A. The commitment of the U.S. to the security of the ROK is firm. We have gone out of our way to warn the North Koreans against military adventure. We have on several occasions deployed U.S. military elements to give substance to our warning, and we have tried to make clear to the South Korean people that we are continuing to play this protective role against external danger.

B. Nevertheless, the secretary believes the authorities in Korea have abused this American commitment in their efforts to establish control.

C. We are convinced that long-term Korean stability and the security of the region require that any Korean government achieve legitimacy and the positive support of its own people. We lack confidence that what the authorities are currently doing to establish a government will have the support of the Korean people. We fear that the government's approach will not be consistent with our mutual security interests.

D. How the US-ROK relationship develops in the future will depend on the actions of the Korean authorities. If underlying stability is not achieved through the positive support of the Korean people, the necessary public and congressional support in the United States for our security relationship can be seriously weakened.

E. In previous conversations we have made clear what issues are the subject of our special concerns. Actions, not words, will determine the degree of American confidence and reactions in the weeks to come. If Chun asks, you should remind him that the issues about which you have conveyed our concern are:

—efforts toward resumption of political development and accomodation;

—the establishment of a constitution which will permit broadly based government through free, popular elections;

—the adoption of a new constitution under conditions which allow public discussion and free choice;

—concern for the handling of political prisoners in accordance with humane and internationally accepted standards of due process of law, including family and legal access and verification of their welfare, and with full consideration of the impact of political amnesty on international public opinion; and

—efforts to reduce rather than exploit the resentment and frustration which exist in some Korean circles toward the U.S.

F. We expect the current authorities to help us prevent further misrepresentation of our position. We want to cooperate, where this is possible, with Korean authorities to help protect and foster a secure, prosperous, and free Republic of Korea. We look forward to more progress toward these goals than we have experienced in the recent past.

4. We understand that the public charge and indictment of Kim Dae-Jung is imminent and will probably take place before you see General Chun to carry out these instructions. In that case, we will want urgently to have a synopsis of the charges and your comments thereon in order that

we can authorize you to comment to Chun under instructions on that important development. I believe you should be armed with the fact that you are commenting with full authority from your government.

5. You should seek an appointment with General Chun as soon as feasible to convey these instructions which emanated from your consultations with me. However, I leave to you the exact timing in view of the possible interaction of the Kim indictment.

MUSKIE

10. September 5, 1980 U.S. Embassy Seoul to Department of State
U.S. Public Comment on Kim Dae Jung Verdict

Declassified 5/14/99

O 050904Z SEP 80
FM AMEMBASSY SEOUL
TO SECSTATE WASHDC IMMEDIATE 8933
C O N F I D E N T I A L SEOUL 11646
EA ONLY – FOR HOLBROOKE AND RICH FROM GLEYSTEEN
SUBJECT: U.S. COMMENT ON KIM DAE JUNG VERDICT

1. (C) Entire text.
2. I have talked to Jeffrey Smith and my colleagues here about two aspects of the Kim Dae Jung (M–R: Kim Tae-Chung) case which we will face very soon. The first is our public comment. I realize that there will be pressures to make a very strong, very strident statement but I am firmly convinced that we should control ourselves and focus on our main concern. To do otherwise might jeopardize our efforts to save Kim's life, violate President Carter's statement to President Chun that we do not intend to interfere with the ROK's judicial process, and single Korea out for treatment that we do not accord other friendly nations. Above all, we must not say things publicly about Kim Dae Jung which do no good and simply anger those Korean military officers who will have to be persuaded to accept something less than execution of a death sentence against Kim.
3. With these thoughts in mind, and assuming a death sentence, I recommend we volunteer the following statement:
QUOTE: As we have stated previously, we were deeply disturbed by the arrest, detention and trial of Mr. Kim Dae Jung, whose political rights were fully restored on February 29, 1980. We are, therefore, most concerned that he has been given a death sentence by the court martial

authorities, and we hope this sentence will be reversed or at least moderated in further stages of the judicial review. We have our own views as to the fairness of the court martial proceedings but in accordance with normal practice we believe it inappropriate to make any comment on this aspect of the case at this stage of the judicial proceedings. END QUOTE.

4. The second issue we discussed was Smith's report. I think we would be guilty of officious meddling in another country's internal affairs if Smith were to issue a formal, public observer report on the Kim Dae Jung trial and I hope to God that you can keep us from doing so. At the same time, Smith will have to make some kind of report to his superiors. He is agreeable to a memorandum to Legal Advisor Owen which would state clearly the things the Koreans have done properly as well as those things which are not in keeping with Korean or international practice. The tone would be flat and he would try to avoid catch words and phrases. The report would be classified.

5. I have captioned this message "EA Only" but you should feel free to have it distributed in any way you see fit.

GLEYSTEEN

11. December 4, 1980   U.S. Embassy Seoul to Department of State
Secretary Brown Visit to Korea

Declassified 5/12/99

O 0410037 DEC 80 ZFF4
FM AMEMBASSY SEOUL
TO SECSTATE WASHDC IMMEDIATE 0771
S E C R E T SEOUL 16166
FOR SECRETARIES MUSKIE AND BROWN FROM GLEYSTEEN
SUBJECT: BROWN VISIT TO KOREA

1. (S) Entire text.

2. I would like to renew my recommendation that Secretary Brown make a one-day visit to Seoul at the time of his trip to Japan.

3. There are several reasons I strongly favor a Brown visit. First and by far most important, it now seems unlikely that the Supreme Court will have rendered its verdict on Kim Dae Jung (M–R: Kim Tae-Chung) by that time; hence, Harold Brown could authoritatively convey to President Chun the seriousness of our concern. Second, senior Korean military leaders, particularly those with whom we are in regular contact, would be

genuinely upset if the secretary were to break his normal practice of visiting both Korea and Japan, whereas if he were to come to Korea the display of solidarity would enhance the willingness of these officers to be helpful to us, albeit in ways that are indirect. Third, we could defend the visit on human rights grounds. We would have to absorb immediate complaints about the "business as usual" symbolism, but in the longer run, we could fully defend ourselves. If the Kim Dae Jung verdict were to swing in the right direction, no one would complain. If we were to fail, the record would show that the real purpose of the secretary's visit was a last minute appeal on the Kim issue.

4. I have one caveat, however. The secretary's visit would have to be publicly characterized—both on the record and on background—as associated with security matters, not Kim Dae Jung. If we were to describe his trip as a Kim Dae Jung mission, it would negate the advantages and probably undercut our objectives. I recognize, of course, that some of our media might associate the trip with the Kim affair, but I do not think such speculation would do much harm.

5. If a decision can be reached before I see President Chun December 6, I could tell him that Secretary Brown is prepared to make a brief visit to Korea on December 13, subject of course to a Korean desire that he do so and the absence of unhelpful developments regarding Kim Dae Jung. I am virtually certain Chun would accept the offer.

6. General Wickham concurs.

GLEYSTEEN

Glossary of People, Places, Institutions, and Functions

A NOTE ABOUT KOREAN NAMES. Koreans generally give their surnames first, followed by given names. Since there is no universally accepted way of transliterating Korean names into English, I have simply used the spelling preferred by the individual concerned.

Aaron, David. Deputy national security adviser to President Carter.

Abramowitz, Morton. Career foreign service officer. Deputy assistant secretary of defense for international security affairs under Secretary of Defense Harold Brown.

Acheson, Dean. U.S. secretary of state during the Truman administration before and during the Korean War.

Allen, Richard V. Foreign policy adviser to presidential candidate Ronald Reagan in 1980 and subsequently national security adviser to President Reagan.

Armacost, Michael H. Career foreign service officer. Senior staff member in the National Security Council for East Asia in 1977. Subsequently deputy assistant secretary of defense for international security affairs and then deputy assistant secretary of state for East Asia.

Blue House. The offices and residence of the president of the Republic of Korea. Known to Koreans as *Chong Wa Dae.*

Brewster, Robert G. Senior intelligence representative for the United States in the Republic of Korea, 1978–81.

Brown, George. General. Chairman of the U.S. Joint Chiefs of Staff at the beginning of the Carter administration.

Brown, Harold. Secretary of defense under President Carter.

Brzezinski, Zbigniew. National security adviser to President Carter.

Bush, George. Vice president of the United States under Ronald Reagan.

Capital Security Command. Internal security force of Korean army stationed in Seoul city. By mutual agreement, not under the operational control of the U.S. commander of the Combined Forces Command.

Carter, Jimmy. President of the United States, 1977–81.

Cha Chi Chol. Chief of presidential security in 1979 under President Park Chung Hee. Assassinated along with President Park.

Chang Myon. Prime minister of the Republic of Korea, 1960–61.

Choi Kwang Soo. Secretary to President Park Chung Hee and subsequently secretary general of the Blue House under President Choi Kyu Ha.

Choi Kyu Ha. Interim president of the Republic of Korea, 1979–80.

Cholla. A region in southwestern Korea, embracing two provinces and the city of Kwangju. Birthplace of Kim Dae Jung.

Chong Seung Hua. General. Army chief of staff in 1979 and administrator of martial law after President Park's assassination.

Choo Young Bock. Air force chief of staff in 1979 under President Park Chung Hee and subsequently secretary of defense under presidents Choi Kyu Ha and Chun Doo Hwan.

Christopher, Warren. Deputy secretary of state under President Carter.

Chun Doo Hwan. General. Defense security commander in 1979 under President Park Chung Hee and President Choi Kyu Ha. Acting director of the Korean Central Intelligence Agency and chairman of the steering group of the Committee for National Security Affairs. Succeeded President Choi Kyu Ha in 1980 and elected (indirectly) president of the Republic of Korea in 1981.

Chung Ho Yung. General. Commander of the Special Warfare Forces during the Kwangju crisis.

Command arrangements. The Combined Forces Command was established in 1978 by joint agreement between the governments of the Republic of Korea and the United States to deter external aggression against the Republic of Korea and, if deterrence fails, to defeat the attack. Its sole mission is defense against external attack. The Combined Forces Command, whose commander is an American officer and whose deputy is a Korean officer, is subordinate to a binational Military Committee headed by the chairmen of the Joint Chiefs of Staff of the Republic of Korea and the United States. Each nation places certain selected units under the operational control of the commander in chief, but retains the national right of command, including the right to remove units from the Combined Forces Command operational control upon notification. In the event of notification, the Combined Forces Command commander can neither approve nor disapprove, but can only point out the effect such removal might have on the mission of external defense. Once forces are removed, the commander no longer has authority over them. As described in "United States Government Statement on the Events in Kwangju, Republic of Korea, in May 1980," U.S. Department of State, June 19, 1989.

Clark, William Jr. Counselor for political affairs in the U.S. embassy, Seoul.

Defense Security Command. A powerful military intelligence agency established by Park Chung Hee to monitor and help control all military units. In his capacity as the commander of this organization, Major General Chun Doo Hwan was assigned to investigate Park's assassination, and his investigation provided a pretext to arrest his superior and seize power within the Korean army.

Demilitarized zone. Located along the Korean War armistice line, a two-kilometer strip roughly thirty miles north of Seoul.

Dole, Robert. U.S. senator.

EM-9. Emergency Measure 9 issued by decree under conditions of martial law in 1972 by President Park to enforce the strictures of the *Yushin* Constitution. Its language and interpretation allowed extremely arbitrary arrests of Park's critics and opponents.

Ford, Gerald. President of the United States, 1974–77.

Fraser, Donald. U.S. representative.

Glenn, John. U.S. senator.

Habib, Phillip C. U.S. ambassador to Korea, 1971–74, assistant secretary of state for East Asia 1974–76, and under secretary of state for political affairs 1976–78.

Haig, Alexander. Secretary of state under President Reagan.

Holbrooke, Richard C. Assistant secretary of state for East Asia during the Carter administration.

Humphrey, Hubert. U.S. senator.

Jaworsky, Leon. Attorney of Watergate fame employed by Congress to investigate the Korean bribery scandal in 1977.

Kim Chae Kyu. Director of the Korean Central Intelligence Agency in 1979. President Park's assassin.

Kim Chi Ha. Korean poet jailed by Park Chung Hee. Human rights activists, especially Catholics, focused much energy on seeking his release.

Kim Chong Huan. General. Chairman of the Joint Chiefs of Staff in 1979 prior to Chun Doo Hwan's coup.

Kim Dae Jung. Opposition political leader from the Cholla region. Election rival of President Park, who harassed and jailed him. Arrested and tried for treason in 1980 by Chun Doo Hwan's regime. Survived death sentence. Elected president of the Republic of Korea in 1997.

Kim Il Sung. Chairman of the Communist party and president of the People's Democratic Republic of Korea.

Kim Jong Pil. Park Chung Hee's collaborator in 1961 coup d'état. Founder and director of the Korean Central Intelligence Agency. Prime minister and government party leader.

Kim Kwan Suk. Head of Korean National Council of Churches.

Kim Kye Won. Retired general and ambassador. Secretary general of the Blue House under President Park Chung Hee in 1979. Witness to the assassination.

Kim Kyung Won. Political scientist and government official. Secretary to President Park Chung Hee in 1979. Blue House secretary general under President Chun Doo Hwan in early 1980s.

Kim Ok Gil. Minister of education in President Choi's cabinet. Previously president of Ewha University.

Kim Sang Man. Chairman of the board of *Dong A Ilbo* (liberal newspaper) and Korea University.

Kim Sou Hwan. Cardinal. Leader of the Roman Catholic Church in Korea.

Kim Young Sam. Leader of the main opposition party in 1979–89. Thrown out of the National Assembly by President Park's henchmen in October 1979, restored to leadership after Park's assassination, and detained after student demonstrations in May 1980. Elected president of the Republic of Korea in 1992.

Kim Young Shik. Former foreign minister and Korean ambassador to the United States, 1977–81.

Kissinger, Henry A. U.S. secretary of state under President Ford.

Koreagate. A scandal in which agents of the Korean government tried in the mid-1970s to bribe U.S. officials and members of Congress.

Korean Central Intelligence Agency. Established under Park Chung Hee's rule to monitor and control threats to the regime from North Korea as well as from any domestic source. One of Korea's most ubiquitous and hated agencies.

Kwangju. The biggest city in the Cholla region of southwestern Korea. Kim Dae Jung's home base and site of the major uprising in May 1980.

Lee Dong Won. Former foreign minister and chairman of the National Assembly's Foreign Affairs Committee in 1980.

Lee Hui Sung. General. Army chief of staff and martial law administrator following the coup on December 12, 1979.

Lee Hu Rak. Former director of the Korean Central Intelligence Agency and confidant of President Park. Arrested on corruption charges in May 1980.

Lew Byong Hion. General. Deputy commander of the Combined Forces Command in 1978–79. Chairman of the Joint Chiefs of Staff in 1980–81. Korean ambassador to the United States beginning in 1981.

Lho Shin Yong. Career diplomat. Appointed foreign minister under President Chun in 1980.

Long, Robert. Admiral. Commander in chief, Pacific.

MacArthur, Douglas. General. Commander in chief, United Nations Forces in Korea 1950–51.

Mansfield, Mike. U.S. senator and ambassador to Japan during the Carter and Reagan administrations.

Martin, Bradley. Correspondent for the *Baltimore Sun* during the Kwangju crisis.

Meyer, Edward C. General. Chief of staff, U.S. army, 1980.

Monjo, John C. Deputy chief of mission, U.S. embassy, Seoul, 1979–82.

Muskie, Edmund S. U.S. senator. Secretary of state, 1980–81.

Nam Duk Woo. Veteran economic official and prime minister under President Chun Doo Hwan.

Nixon, Richard. President of the United States, 1969–74.

Oberdorfer, Don. Correspondent for the *Washington Post.*

Panmunjom. Village where the Korean armistice was signed and site for military contacts between the two sides.

Park Choong Hoon. Veteran economic official and acting prime minister in 1980 toward the end of President Choi's regime.

Park Chung Hee. General. Leader of a coup d'état in May 1961. President of the Republic of Korea, 1963–79.

Park Tong Jin. Career diplomat. Foreign minister, 1975–80.

Platt, Nicholas. Career diplomat. Deputy assistant secretary of defense for International Security Affairs and subsequently senior staff member for East Asia at the National Security Council.

Reagan, Ronald. President of the United States, 1981–89.

Rhee, Syngman. First president of the Republic of Korea, 1948–60.

Rich, Robert G. Jr. Career foreign service officer. Country director for Korean Affairs, U.S. Department of State, 1977–82.

Roh Jae Hyun. General. Minister of defense under President Park Chung Hee and President Choi Kyu Ha prior to General Chun's seizure of power.

Roh Tae-Woo. General. Commander of the Korean army Ninth Infantry Division on December 12, 1979. Named defense security commander after the December 12 coup. Elected president of the Republic of Korea by popular election in 1987.

Rosencrans, Evan W. Lieutenant general. Deputy commander, U.S. Forces, Korea, and United Nations Command in 1979–80.

Scott-Stokes, Henry. Correspondent for the *New York Times* covering Korea in 1979–80.

Shin Hyon Hwack. Veteran official and businessman. Prime minister under President Choi Kyu Ha until May 17, 1980, political crackdown.

Singlaub, John. Major General. Chief of staff to commander, U.S. Forces, Korea. Reprimanded and transferred in 1979 by order of President Carter because of public criticism directed at Carter's troop withdrawal policy.

Sneider, Richard. Career foreign service officer. U.S. ambassador to Korea, 1974–78.

Sohn Jang Nae. Brigadier general. Head of J5 (intelligence) in Combined Forces Command in 1979. Subsequently posted by Chun Doo Hwan to Washington as station chief of the Korean Central Intelligence Agency.

Special Warfare Forces. Highly mobile and tough forces trained to counter North Korean attack and threats to internal security. In conditions of normal defense alert, these forces were not under the operational control of the U.S. Combined Forces Command commander. The brutal behavior of these forces in Kwangju triggered a massive urban uprising in May 1980.

Stern, Thomas. Deputy chief of mission, U.S. embassy, Seoul, 1975–79.

Sunobe, Ryozo. Career Japanese diplomat. Ambassador of Japan to Korea.

Vance, Cyrus R. Secretary of state under President Carter, 1977–80.

Vessey, John W. Jr. General. Commander in chief, U.S. Forces, Korea, 1976–79.

Wickham, John A. Jr. General. Commander in chief, U.S. Forces, Korea, 1979–82.

Wolf, Lester. U.S. representative and chairman of the East Asia Subcommittee of the House International Affairs Committee.

Yun, Archbishop. Roman Catholic leader in Kwangju during the crisis. Key member of the Kwangju citizens committee negotiating with the government authorities.

Yun Sang Won. Antigovernment activist among hard-line Kwangju rebels who requested a *New York Times* correspondent to ask Washington to instruct Ambassador Gleysteen to mediate a truce between Korean authorities and Kwangju insurrectionists.

Yushin **Constitution.** A harsh and highly authoritarian constitution that President Park Chung Hee imposed on the Korean people under conditions of martial law in October 1972. It provided for indirect election of the president by a body beholden to Park, and it allowed Park to appoint sufficient numbers of parliamentarians so that together with the elected members they could control the National Assembly.

Zablocki, Clement. U.S. representative. Chairman of the House International Relations Committee.

Suggested Reading

ALTHOUGH THERE HAS been a great deal of public commentary in Korea as well as in this country about the Carter administration's policy and actions regarding Korea, relatively little has been written or published on the basis of full access to official documentation and systematic interviews with the Americans directly involved. The most authoritative U.S. account has been the white paper issued by the State Department in 1989. Through freedom of information procedures, Mr. Tim Shorrock obtained thousands of government documents that he used as the basis for the article mentioned below. Mr. Don Oberdorfer wrote his recent book on the basis of similar documentation plus extensive interviews and personal observation. Most other published materials have been fragmentary. Perhaps my account of this controversial period, together with General Wickham's book being published this year by the National Defense University, will help to open the way to a more comprehensive historical assessment based on both Korean and American sources.

The following writings deal with U.S. policy and behavior in or toward Korea during the Carter years.

Allen, Richard V. "On the Korean Tightrope, 1980." *New York Times*, January 21, 1998.

Armacost, Michael, and Richard Holbrooke. "A Future Leader's Moment of Truth." *New York Times*, December 24, 1997.

Fowler, James. "The United States and South Korean Democratization." *Political Science Quarterly*, vol. 114, no. 2 (Summer 1999).

Gleysteen, William H. Jr. "Korea: A Special Target of Concern." In *The Diplomacy of Human Rights*, edited by David D. Newsom. University Press of America, 1986.

Lee Jae-eui. *Kwangju Diary: Beyond Death, Beyond the Darkness of the Age*, translated by Kap Su Seol and Nick Mamatas. Includes essays by Bruce Cummings and Tim Shorrock. University of California, Los Angeles, 1999.

Macdonald, Donald Stone. *The Koreans: Contemporary Politics and Society.* Boulder, Colo.: Westview Press, 1988.

Oberdorfer, Don. *The Two Koreas: A Contemporary History.* Addison-Wesley, 1997.

Peterson, Mark. "Americans and the Kwangju Incident: Problems in the Writing of History." In *The Kwangju Uprising: Shadows over the Regime in South Korea,* edited by Donald N. Clark. Boulder, Colo.: Westview Press, 1988.

Rich, Robert G., Jr. *U.S. Ground Force Withdrawal from Korea: A Case Study in National Security Decision Making.* Washington, D.C.: U.S. Department of State, Foreign Service Institute, 1982 (June).

Shorrock, Tim. "Ex-Leaders Go on Trial in Seoul; U.S. Knew of South Korea Crackdown." *Journal of Commerce,* February 27, 1996.

Stueck, William. "Democratization in Korea; the United States Role, 1980 and 1987." *International Journal of Korean Studies,* vol. 2 (Fall/Winter 1998).

U.S. Department of State. "United States Government Statement on the Events in Kwangju, Republic of Korea, in May 1980." White Paper. Washington, D.C., June 19, 1989.

Vance, Cyrus. *Hard Choices: Critical Years in America's Foreign Policy.* Simon and Schuster, 1983.

Weber, Amalie M. *Kwangju in the Eyes of the World.* Seoul: Pulbit Publishing, 1997.

Wickham, John A. Jr. *Korea on the Brink: From the 12/12 Incident to the Kwangju Uprising.* Washington, D.C.: National Defense University, forthcoming.

Wood, Joseph R. *President Carter's Troop Withdrawal from Korea.* Unpublished report prepared for Harvard University and the Council on Foreign Relations, 1990.

Index

Carter administration: human rights
issues, 30–31, 33, 34; intervention
in Korean domestic affairs, 195;
Iranian hostage crisis, 63; Kim Dae
Jung, 39–40, 177, 186–87; Koreagate,
20; Kwangju uprising, 134; North
Korea, 41–42; withdrawal of U.S.
military, 23, 26
Central Intelligence Agency, U.S. (CIA),
58. See also Korean Central Intelligence
Agency
Cha Chi Chol, 44–45, 52, 55, 56
Chang Myon, 10
China: Ford administration, 14; human
rights issues, 32; Kwangju uprising,
137; Nixon, 12; Park Chung Hee, 61;
U.S. relationships with, 2, 93, 197, 199
Choi Kwang Soo: Choi Kyu Ha, 81–82,
98, 121; Chun Doo Hwan, 108, 154,
164; Kwangju uprising, 130, 132, 137,
138, 139; political reforms, 144;
student protests, 118, 119
Choi Kyu Ha: attempted counter-coup
against Chun Doo Hwan, 96; conservatism of, 5, 125, 195; erosion of
power, 83, 122–23, 145–46, 160–64;
inaugural address, 99; as interim
constitutional leader, 54–55, 65, 68–73,
75–76, 102; Kim Dae Jung, 172; Korean
CIA, 108, 110; Kwangju uprising, 131,
139; political protests, 116, 122–23,
124; as prime minister, 48; reforms, 85,
86, 88, 90, 93, 99–100, 101, 107, 115,
117, 120, 146; seizure of power by
Chun Doo Hwan, 65, 78, 80, 82–83, 98,
110; Special Committee for National
Security Affairs, 144–45; U.S. support,
65, 67–68, 93, 147, 161, 190
Cholla people, 127, 138
Chong Seung Hua: assassination of Park
Chung Hee, 54, 55, 56, 57; charges
against, 59, 60–61; seizure of power by
Chun Doo Hwan, 59, 79, 80, 94
Chonnam University, 128
Choo Young Bock, 99, 110, 111, 160
Chosun University, 128

Christopher, Warren: Chun Doo Hwan
and, 184–85; Holbrooke and, 74;
human rights policy, 32; Kim Dae Jung
issue, 171, 143–74; misinformation, 164
Chun Doo Hwan: accusations of U.S
interventions, 60, 98; attempted
counter-coup against, 93–97; Carter
administration, 185; Choi Kyu Ha and,
85, 160–61; contacts with U.S., 183; as
director of Korean CIA, 107, 108–09,
144; election as president, 161–64;
inauguration, 164; invitation to
Washington, 182–83, 187–88, 190; Kim
Dae Jung, 155, 156, 172–75, 179, 183–
84, 185–89, 191; Kwangju uprising,
132, 154; letters from Carter, 164, 165–
67, 186; meeting with Brown, 186–87;
meetings with Gleysteen, 84–85, 87,
111, 115–17, 152–58, 164–66, 174–75;
misinformation, 66, 141, 154; nature of
regime, 169–70, 195; political policies,
153–54, 155–56, 196; political protests,
106, 107, 116, 125; Reagan administration, 185–86, 187; relationship with
Gleysteen, 91–92, 97, 98, 142, 169; response to U.S. policy statements, 156,
157, 167–68; rise to presidency, 144–
70; seizure of power, 4, 5, 59, 64, 65–66,
77, 78–82, 84–90, 94; slush funds, 193;
Special Committee for National
Security Affairs, 144–45; successor to,
191, 196; Wickham and, 161–63, 166
Chun Doo Hwan, U.S. response to:
acceptance of regime, 92, 190; criticism
of regime, 64, 65, 83, 84–85; policy
recommendations, 103–04; quality of
relationship, 97–98, 191; removal of,
95, 196; as president, 146–52, 161,
168–69
Chung Ho Yung, 130, 187
CIA. See Central Intelligence Agency, U.S
Clark, William Jr.: Carter-Park summit
meeting, 49–50; media presentations,
88; meetings with Choi Kyu Ha, 55, 83;
as political counselor, 27, 53, 74;
student protests, 120, 121–22, 123

and evolution, 102, 191–94; policy
toward Japan, 179; policy toward
North Korea, 3, 10, 12, 103–05;
sanctions, 34–35, 36, 64, 77, 91–92,
109–11, 151, 172, 174, 175, 176–77,
190, 194, 195, 196; scandals, 193; view
of the U.S., 4, 5; U.S.elections of 1980,
181; U.S. guidelines for activities, 62–
63, 88; U.S.-Korean relations before
Carter, 9–16; U.S. view, 1, 20, 155, 165,
197
Republic of Korea, human rights issues:
assassination of Park Chung Hee, 61,
72; and Carter-Park summit meeting,
35–36, 39–40; and U.S. troop withdrawal, 21, 33; missionaries, 31; regime
of Chun Doo Hwan, 151; U.S. view, 3,
15, 30–31, 32–33, 34. *See also* Carter,
Jimmy; Summit meeting of Carter and
Park
Republic of Korea, military forces:
counter-coup against Chun Doo
Hwan, 93–97, 104; crackdown on
protests, 122–26; Kim Dae Jung, 181;
Kwangju uprising, 128–31, 134, 137–
38; modernization, 20–21; political
issues, 121, 122, 145, 154; response of
officers to U.S. military, 97–98; seizure
of power by Chun Doo Hwan, 64, 65,
77–78, 80, 86, 88, 90, 94; Special
Warfare Forces, 129, 130, 131, 132, 133,
154; U.S. response to Chun Doo
Hwan, 110–11
Republic of Korea, U.S. troop withdrawal
from: assassination of Park Chung
Hee, 61, 64; background, 20–22;
Congress and, 21–22; and Carter-Park
summit meeting, 40–41; effects, 6, 7;
Ford administration, 22; Korean view,
2–3; National Security Council, 17–18;
under Nixon, 12; numbers of U.S.
military, 3, 21, 24, 25, 27, 197;
opposition, 6; reporting requirements,
22, 28; role of U.S. military, 21; U.S.
view, 17–18. *See also* Carter, Jimmy;
Summit meeting of Carter and Park

Rhee, Syngman, 9–10, 20, 124
Richardson, Spence, 140
Rich, Robert G. Jr., 29, 42, 48, 74, 115,
176, 188
Roh Jae Kyun, 78, 79, 80, 82
Roh Tae-Woo, 172, 175–76, 183–84, 191,
192, 193
Rosencrans, Evan W., 53, 118, 122, 123

Sanctions. *See* Republic of Korea
Scandinavia, 178
Schorr, Daniel, 148–49
Scott-Stokes, Henry, 140, 162
Senate Armed Services Committee, 28
Seoul: martial law, 132; military force in,
144; political repression, 31; protests,
112, 113, 120–21, 122; role of Korean
military, 132; "Seoul spring," 99–105;
vulnerability, 3. *See also* Republic of
Korea
Seoul National University, 107
Shin Hyon Hwack, 85–86, 99, 101, 102–
03, 107, 112
Singlaub, John, 23
Sneider, Richard, 23, 34, 58
Special Committee for National Security
Affairs, 144, 153
Special Warfare Forces. *See* Republic of
Korea, military forces
Sohn Jang Nae, 111
South Korea. *See* Republic of Korea
Soviet Union, 63
State Department, U.S.: Carter-Park
summit meeting, 36; human rights
issues, 31–32, 34; Kim Dae Jung, 175,
181; Kwangju uprising, 136–37;
student protests, 123
Stern, Thomas, 27, 74
Students and dissidents: arrests, 122;
economic issues, 51; following
assassination of Park Chung Hee,
71–72; hard-line radicals, 130–31;
imprisonment, 31; North Korea, 10,
106, 116; opening and closing of
schools, 70, 99–100, 101, 106–07, 122,
123, 125; participation of politicians,

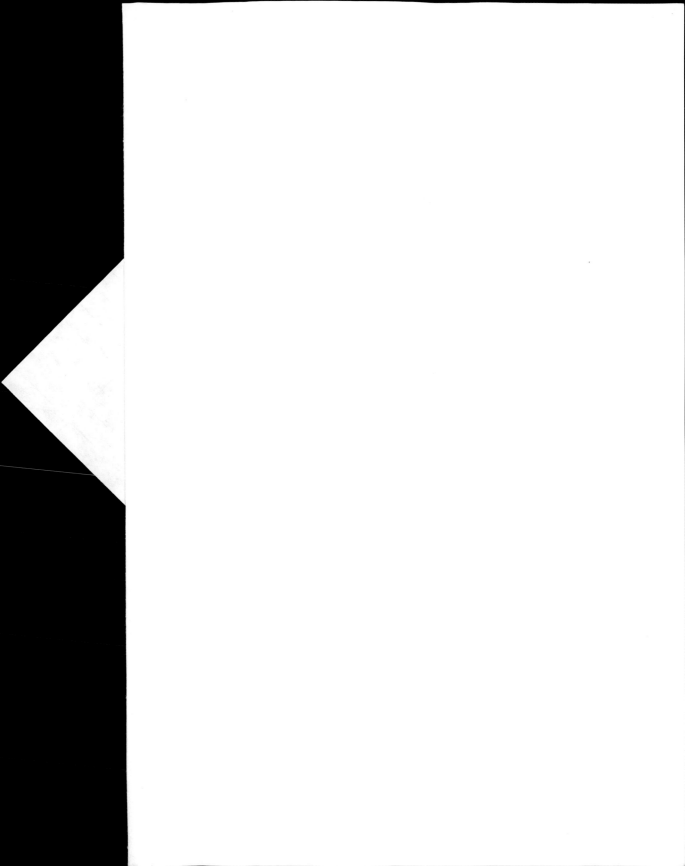

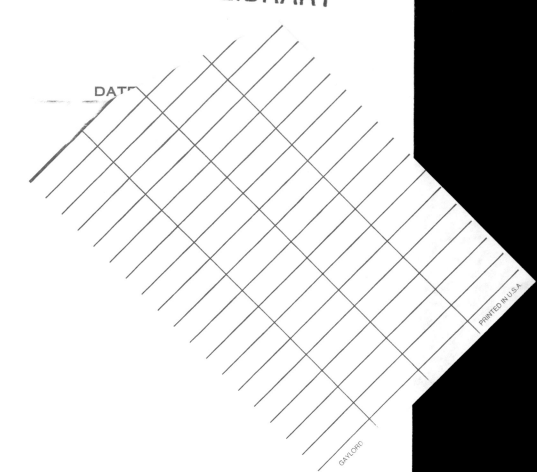